Treating Sexual Offenders

Practical Clinical Guidebooks Series

Treating Sexual Offenders

An Integrated Approach

William L. Marshall • Liam E. Marshall
Geris A. Serran • Yolanda M. Fernandez

Routledge
Taylor & Francis Group
New York   London

Published in 2006 by
Routledge
Taylor & Francis Group
270 Madison Avenue
New York, NY 10016

Published in Great Britain by
Routledge
Taylor & Francis Group
27 Church Road
Hove, East Sussex BN3 2FA

Printed in the United States of America on acid-free paper
10 9 8 7 6 5 4 3 2

International Standard Book Number-10: 0-415-94935-1 (Hardcover) 0-415-94936-X (Softcover)
International Standard Book Number-13: 978-0-415-94935-4 (Hardcover) 978-0-415-94936-1 (Softcover)
Library of Congress Card Number 2005020804

Library of Congress Cataloging-in-Publication Data

Treating sexual offenders : an integrated approach / William L. Marshall ... [et al.].
    p. cm.
Includes bibliographical references.
ISBN 0-415-94935-1 (hardbound) -- ISBN 0-415-94936-X (pbk.)
    1. Sex offenders--Rehabilitation. 2. Sex offenders--Psychology. 3. Sex offenders--Physiology. 4.
Sex offenders--Mental Health. I. Marshall, William L.

RC560.S47T74 2006
616.85'83--dc22

2005020804

Taylor & Francis Group
is the Academic Division of T&F Informa plc.

Visit the Taylor & Francis Web site at
http://www.taylorandfrancis.com

and the Routledge Web site at
http://www.routledge-ny.com

Contents

Preface

This book describes the treatment program for sexual offenders that we have developed over the past 36 years. Our research and clinical activities are seamless endeavors with each informing the other. The questions we have asked in research have always arisen in our clinical work, and our clinical work has then incorporated what others and we have empirically discerned.

For the purposes of this book, we will restrict our focus to the consideration of adult males who sexually offend, and within these offenders we will describe the issues surrounding men who rape adult females, men who molest children, and men who expose their genitals to unwilling adult females. Within these categories we will also discuss sexual sadists. There are, of course, many other types of sexual offenders (e.g., voyeurs, frotteurs, obscene phone-callers, necrophiles, and those who have sex with nonhuman animals); and there are young males (Barbaree, Marshall, & Hudson, 1993; Ryan & Lane, 1997) and women (Hunter & Mathews, 1997; Schwartz & Cellini, 1995) who also sexually offend. Data emerging over the past 15 years, in particular, are rapidly expanding our knowledge of juvenile (and even child) sexual offenders (Johnson, 1998; Task Force on Juvenile Sexual Offenders and Their Victims, 1996), and these data seem to indicate sufficiently different issues with these young offenders in that they require their own specialized approach to treatment (Miranda & Davis, 2002; Worling, 1998). At present, the small number of women who are identified as sexual offenders has limited our capacity to formulate soundly based treatment and assessment programs with these offenders. Whether anything we know about the characteristics of adult male sexual offenders, or their treatment, is transferable to juveniles or women who sexually offend remains open, but we are confident that continued research will reveal numerous unique features of female and juvenile sexual offenders.

The development of our approach occurred in the context of both a prison-based program as well as a community-based program. While our work in recent years has been exclusively in Canadian federal prisons, we operated the local community program from 1969 until the workload in prisons became too much, so our colleague Dr. Tony Eccles took over the community operation in 1992. We have also worked in earlier days in a psychiatric inpatient and outpatient setting where we ran a sexual offenders program. What we describe in this book is, in our experience, equally applicable to a prison setting, a psychiatric setting, or an outpatient community-based clinic. In an outpatient clinic, far more exhibitionists will be seen than in prison, and there will likely be more frotteurs. However, our experience suggests that the program described in this book is equally applicable to these offenders and, indeed, we consider frotteurs to be essentially the same as rapists.

In our prison settings there are numerous other programs available that compliment our sexual offenders program. For example, Correctional Service of Canada provides programs such as Reasoning and Rehabilitation, Substance Abuse, Anger Management, and Parenting Skills. Reasoning and Rehabilitation aims at modifying antisocial attitudes, developing impulse-control, and enhancing effective coping skills. Were these programs not available, we would have to provide them for many of our clients. Interested readers are referred to the following appropriate resources: Reasoning and Rehabilitation (Ross, 1995), Anger Management (Hughes, 1993), Substance Abuse (Lightfoot, 1993), Parenting Skills (Carpentier, 1995).

We have made three evaluations of the long-term effectiveness of our programs, and these are described in chapter 3 under the section "Evidence of Effectiveness." At this point we simply want to note that each of these evaluations (two for our outpatient program and one for our prison program) demonstrated a clear benefit for treatment.

The scope of this book covers what we believe to be the essential features of effective treatment for sexual offenders wherever such treatment is conducted. Our intention is to illustrate to clinicians the therapeutic style, procedural aspects, and treatment targets that are necessary to effectively change these often difficult clients. Because various aspects of our program differ from the established cognitive behavioral/relapse prevention approach, we also hope this book will provide an incentive for others to try some aspects of our approach or to conduct research that will confirm or deny the value of other features of our program.

Acknowledgments

First, we wish to acknowledge the efforts of two special people. Allana Lukacz did a wonderful and careful job of searching through our files and the official records to generate our outcome data. Allana was naïve about sexual offenders and thus had no expectations of what the data might mean. She applied herself to the task with diligence and objectivity. Jean Webber's tireless and patient work typing this manuscript and proofreading for grammatical errors represented a profoundly appreciated effort. The number of hours Jean spent re-reading the manuscript and making seemingly endless changes without ever complaining or tiring reflects her remarkable character. We are deeply indebted to these two wonderful women.

Next, we want to acknowledge the contributions to our thinking by many colleagues; in particular, we would like to mention Gene Abel, Howard Barbaree, and Tony Ward whose influences on the entire field have been outstanding. Also, the past members of our staff and the many students who have worked with us have shaped our approach to working with these difficult clients.

Our publisher, Taylor & Francis, and the series editor, Michel Hersen, are due thanks for inviting us to write this book and for supporting and encouraging us throughout. In particular, contacts with Dana Bliss of Routledge/Taylor & Francis provided excellent guidance when it was needed.

Finally, we owe a debt to our many clients over the years whose courage in facing and overcoming their problems continues to earn our admiration. We learn much about ourselves by doing this work, so we thank our clients for helping us become more self-aware and hopefully better citizens.

CHAPTER 1

Description of Disorder

INTRODUCTION

With the emergence of sexual offending into the domain of public discourse, in the 1980s in particular, many people asked why these offenses were suddenly occurring at such an apparently rapidly accelerating rate. Some members of the public and the media questioned whether this was a real phenomenon or just the result of some overly zealous investigators prompted into action by the growing women's movement. Others suggested that perhaps sexual offending had increased in parallel with the social changes initiated in the late 1960s and 1970s around all issues of sexuality. Perhaps, some suggested, it was the result of relaxed rules governing the availability of pornography or the increasing explicitness of sex in films, television, and advertising. Numerous accounts of human sexuality, however, have pointed to the occurrence of rape and child molestation throughout recorded time (Forsyth, 1993; Foucault, 1978; Licht, 1932; Taylor, 1954). Greek mythology describes how the god Zeus raped many maidens often by disguising himself in some way (Servi, 1997). Disguised as a swan Zeus seduced the beautiful Leda and sired Helen, Castor, and Pollux. The infamous Marquis de Sade described, in his 18th century novels, practices that are clearly sadistic, and he was imprisoned for several years for administering cantharides (a supposed aphrodisiac) to unwitting prostitutes so that he could engage in various sexual acts with them. Baron Gilles de Rais, who fought valiantly beside Jeanne d'Arc in the 15th century, is said to have sexually molested and even murdered countless children. He was eventually hanged and burned after confessing to his crimes. By the late 19th century several authors had described an array of sexual practices, some of which are today seen as offenses (Krafft-Ebing, 1886; Moll, 1893).

Among the reports of sexual assaults made from the 1970s on, as well as in many social surveys, victims were speaking of offenses that occurred many years earlier. When these victims were asked why they waited so long to report the assaults, they identified various reasons, such as their assumption they would not be believed, their view that the investigative and prosecutorial process would involve attacks on them and their behaviors, as well as their belief that family, friends, and even lovers would hold them responsible and reject them. Russell (1984) reported that of the cases identified in her random sample of San Francisco residents, only 2% of incest victims and 6% of the child victims of nonfamilial offenders had reported the offense to the authorities. Even more recent data reveal that sexual offending remains remarkably underreported. For example, Henry and McMahon (2000) found that 91% of cases of child sexual abuse had gone unreported, and Kilpatrick (1996) showed that 56% of women who were sexually assaulted as adults failed to report the crime. Whatever reasons silenced these victims at the time of the abuse, their reports, once confirmed, indicated two things very clearly: Sexual abuse is not a recent phenomenon, and the contemporaneous social climate serves to facilitate or inhibit reports of sexual abuse. It is now accepted that sexual abuse, in all its forms, has been an ongoing problem in all societies for all time. Changes to laws, and to the processes of investigation and prosecution of sexual abuse, appear to have made it more likely that nowadays these offenses will be reported and dealt with more effectively, although additional improvements in these processes are needed to make victims feel supported and not feel blamed when they bring forward an accusation.

FREQUENCY OF SEXUAL OFFENSES

Despite the above noted changes, it is difficult to estimate the frequency of sexual assaults, and it is all but impossible to estimate the number of offenders within any given society at any particular time. Epidemiological studies, like those done with most Axis 1 and Axis 2 disorders, are very unlikely to elicit reports from offenders that they are abusing. What such studies can do is elicit reports from victims about their abuse, although even here there are problems. It is no doubt difficult, given the continuing stigma attached to having mental illness, for people to report in surveys that they are suffering from depression, schizophrenia, or anxiety disorders. It is, however, likely to be far more difficult for most victims of sexual offending to indicate this within the context of an objective scientific survey. In fact, most published surveys of the incidence of sexual victimization have been less elegant than is demanded in an appropriate epidemiological study. Most such surveys have not attempted to obtain a demographically representative sample, and even where they have, there are no doubt many victims who would not divulge the facts of their abuse in such a survey; many other victims might refuse to participate at all; and perhaps other individuals might, in an attention-seeking ploy, falsely report being abused.

Indeed, the issue of possible false accusations presents an unresolved problem to investigators, prosecutors, and researchers. For example, nearly half of all reported cases of child sexual abuse in the United Kingdom have been deemed "unsubstantiated" by the investigative process (Westat, 1987), but this does not mean that an offense did not take place; it simply means the investigators could not formulate a case that they believed could be pursued to prosecution. While it is difficult to believe that half of all reported cases of child sexual abuse represent false accusations, there seems to be no doubt that some, but hopefully few, reports are untrue. One aspect of the truth or falsity of accusations of sexual abuse concerns the so-called "recovered memories" of abuse. This issue has been quite divisive with those (e.g., Fredrickson, 1992; Terr, 1994) who believe that certain therapeutic processes can uncover memories of abuse that have long been forgotten, pitted against those (e.g., Kaminer, 1992; Loftus & Ketchum, 1994) who point to evidence from memory research that belies the basis of these putative recovered memories. Both sides of this debate appear intractable and tend in our view to overstate their case (see comprehensive reviews in Lynn & McConkey, 1998). Aside from the problem of "recovered memories," there is at present no way to tell which accusations are true or false other than by the gathering of credible evidence, its presentation in court, and the rendering of a judicial decision. Not surprisingly, this process can be fallible, as we have seen from recent cases where convictions were subsequently overturned. However, our view is that by far the majority of reports of sexual abuse, particularly those where the accuser is willing to endure the investigation and trial, are true reports.

Peters, Wyatt, and Finkelhor (1986) reviewed research on the prevalence of child sexual abuse and reported that between 6% and 62% of females and between 3% and 31% of males had been sexually abused as a child. These reported ranges are so broad as to be all but meaningless, although the reviewers suggest that the discrepancies are likely due to methodological features of the studies (e.g., different definitions of abuse, differing samples, questioning format). In considering the 1986 Peters et al. report, Conte (1991) rather surprisingly says that "even if one takes only the lowest estimates, it is clear that sexual abuse of children is a common experience of childhood" (p. 17). It is a bit hard to see how 6% or 3% can be construed as reflecting "a common experience." Canadian national surveys, funded by a government commission, revealed that up to one-third of males and more that 50% of females reported being sexually abused as a child, with most of these assaults occurring before the victim had reached age 12 (Bagley, 1991).

In their examination of female college students in the United States, Koss, Gidycz, and Wisniewski (1987) found that 15% of these women said they had been raped and a further 12% said that they had thwarted an attempted rape. Russell (1984) interviewed a representative sample of Californian women and found that 44% reported having been raped. An international survey, reported by van Dijk and Mayhew (1992), revealed somewhat variable data, but across all countries (European, Asian, and North and South Pacific nations) the rates of rape were worrisomely high. In reviewing reports of the incidence of the sexual assault of adult females, Koss (1992) estimated that the true rate of rape was 6 to 10 times higher than the official records would indicate. Her estimate is consistent with the remarks of other researchers (Russell, 1984) and is based on the observation that very few women who indicate in surveys that they were raped, ever reported the offense. Marshall and Barrett (1990) extracted the number of rapes from the official records in Canada during the full year 1988. Taking a conservative stance, they then multiplied this rate by four, which produced an estimate of 75,000 adult female victims of rape for that year. This estimate, if even close to the true rate, reveals a frequency of rape that is startling: It indicates that a rape occurs in Canada every 7 minutes.

Very little has been reported about the rates of exhibitionism, but Rooth (1973) observed that this was by far the most commonly reported sexual crime. In addition, DiVasto, Kaufman, Jackson et al. (1984) noted that 30% of adult women reported that a male had illegally exposed his genitalia to them. Using an anonymous survey, Person, Terestman, Myers et al. (1989) reported that 4% of male university students said they had exposed themselves to an unwilling observer.

Person et al.'s (1989) report indicates another source of information on the rates of sexual crimes; that is, anonymous surveys asking whether the respondents themselves had committed such offenses. Employing a representative sample of U.S. citizens, Laumann, Gagnon, Michael, and Michaels (1994) found that 2.8% of adult males and 1.5% of adult females indicated that they had forced someone to have sex. Similarly in Ageton's (1983) U.S. sample of male adolescents, 10% of these young males said they had forced a female into having genital contact with them. Herman (1990) reported that between 4% and 17% of adult males indicated they had molested a child, and other researchers have found that approximately 15% of males reveal some likelihood of having sex with a child (Malamuth, 1989; McConaghy, Zamir, & Manicavasagar, 1993).

Clinicians working with sexual offenders have also provided evidence on the extent of sexual abuse. Abel, Becker, Mittelman et al. (1987)

obtained a certificate of confidentiality from U.S. law enforcement officials that guaranteed the reports of Abel's clinical subjects would not be subject to seizure by authorities. Under these conditions, many of Abel et al.'s sexual offending clients reported having committed numerous offenses additional to those for which they had been charged. The 232 offenders against children admitted to 55,250 attempts at child molestation, of which 38,727 were successfully completed; the 126 rapists reported having 882 victims; and 142 exhibitionists had exposed on 71,696 occasions. Studies using polygraphy (which, it must be said, has dubious scientific status) have similarly reported rates of offending that are far in excess of those recorded in the official records (Ahlmeyer, Heil, McKee, & English, 2000; Heil, Ahlmeyer, & Simons, 2003).

EFFECTS ON VICTIMS

The effects of sexual abuse on victims can be extensive, long lasting, and profoundly damaging to various aspects of the person's life. It is clear, however, that not all victims of sexual abuse suffer such major consequences; some experience numerous and seriously damaging sequelae, others experience some but not such severe consequences, and some victims appear to suffer few, if any, deleterious effects. In considering the evidence reviewed here, it is well to keep in mind that the nature of the sexual assault (e.g., the degree of force used, the intrusiveness of the sexual acts, the humiliating features of the abuse) and the prior or expected relationship of trust between the offender and victim are likely to be factors that modulate the victim's response. In terms of immediate outcomes, Finkelhor (1988) proposed four elements that he believed accounted for the magnitude of effects on child victims of sexual abuse. Traumatic sexualization results, so Finkelhor suggested, from premature and inaccurate learning about sex that took place during the abuse. Betrayal is greatest when the offender is someone the child previously trusted. Stigmatization follows from the child's fear of being blamed. Finally, powerlessness results from the offender's use of force and threats.

Burgess and Holstrom (1974) identified what they called the "rape trauma syndrome," which has features similar to post-traumatic stress disorder. They describe fear as the primary immediate post-assault response, which in some cases develops into full-blown phobias, panic disorders, or generalized anxiety. Flashbacks occur as do obsessional ruminations about the abuse. Various other signs of elevated emotional responding may also be evident, such as mood swings, irritability, loss of appetite, and sleep disturbances. Disturbances in sexual functioning, reduced feelings of attractiveness, withdrawal, deteriorating work or school performance, substance use problems, and rejection of prior friends can also result from being sexually victimized (West, 1991). In particular, Burgess and Holstrom (1979) note that fewer than 40% of rape victims had sufficiently recovered within several months of the attack. Conte and Schuerman (1987) examined the responses of 369 children who had been sexually abused. They found that 27% displayed immediate consequences involving at least four problematic symptoms. Among the total group, the unfortunate immediate sequelae included loss of self-worth, emotional distress, nightmares or other sleep disturbances, aggression, and problems concentrating. These observations match other reports (Browne & Finkelhor, 1986). Longer-term effects that have been reported for child sexual abuse include eating disorders (Root & Fallon, 1988), loss of sexual responsiveness (Lindberg & Distad, 1985), problematic sexual behaviors (MacVicar, 1979; McMullen, 1987; Silbert & Pines, 1991), personality disorders (Herman & van der Kolk, 1987), and problems in emotional development (Gomes-Schwartz, Horowitz, & Sauzier, 1985).

The evidence, then, indicates that sexual offenses are likely to produce negative consequences for the victims, which in many cases will be severe and long lasting. When we combine these negative effects with the evident high occurrence of sexual offending and the countless victims involved, we can confidently declare that this is a serious social problem that requires our urgent and devoted attention. Although sexual offending has emerged from its former cloak of secrecy and denial, we still have a long way to go before we give it the attention it deserves. In our view, it is difficult to avoid the conclusion that were the victims of sexual abuse characteristically from among the privileged males of our societies, our governments would have vigorously addressed this problem long ago. Perhaps as women's voices become more powerful, and as children's rights become fully addressed, more systematic and effective processes for dealing with this blot on our societies will be established. There are many things that need to be done. Assisting, supporting, and comforting complainants through the investigation and prosecution of alleged offenses would help victims come forward, as would providing free physical and psychological support and counseling to the victims. These would seem necessary but are all too often not available.

Devoting substantially more research money to the topic, both for the victim and offender sides of the issue, is also vital if further progress is to be made. In a particularly revealing report, Goode (1994) gave details of funding provided by the U.S. National Institute of Mental Health for various problem areas. The funding sources for studies of depression in 1993 amounted to $125.3 million, while for sexual offending only $1.2 million was made available. Certainly depression causes considerable damage to many people but so does sexual offending. A particularly ironic aspect of this imbalance in funding is that depression and various other Axis 1 and Axis 2 disorders have, as part of their etiology, the experience of being sexually victimized (Firestone & Marshall, 2003). Finally, funding treatment programs for offenders in prisons or in community programs could help reduce the incidence of future assaults by identified sexual offenders. No doubt treatment programs need to be improved but even at this time there is, as we will see, evidence that treatment of sexual offenders can have the effect of reducing the future victimization of innocent people. Such reductions in reoffense rates not only reduce harm, but they also save a considerable amount of taxpayers' dollars (Prentky & Burgess, 1990).

THE CLINICAL PICTURE

There have been essentially two ways in which sexual offenders and their problems have been described: by applying diagnoses or by simply describing the problematic features associated with the offenders. We will consider the merits of both approaches, although the present chapter will deal only with paraphilic diagnoses. Additional, or comorbid, diagnoses among sexual offenders will be discussed in chapter 5, while the problematic features of these offenders will be outlined in chapter 3.

Diagnoses

The Diagnostic and Statistical Manual of Mental Disorders (DSM) of the American Psychiatric Association (APA) in its various incarnations has described a category of the sexual disorders called paraphilias that include some disorders relevant to sexual offending: pedophilia, sexual sadism, exhibitionism, frotteurism, voyeurism, and a catchall category labeled "paraphilias not otherwise specified [NOS]." In the latter category there is mention of some sexual crimes such as telephone scatalogia, necrophilia, and zoophilia, but no guidance is given about the criteria necessary to apply these diagnoses. Unfortunately, the DSM has not served the sexual offender field at all well and has excluded many offenders (e.g., rapists and many child molesters) who have clear problems in need of treatment. Indeed, there is no evidence available indicating that those sexual offenders who meet diagnostic criteria for a paraphilia have any more problems than those who do meet such criteria, nor does there appear to be different etiological pathways between those who do or do not have a paraphilia. Most importantly, there is no evidence of a differential treatment response between those sexual offenders who do or do not fit into the DSM diagnostic categories. Finally, Wilson, Abracen, Picheca et al. (2003) report that a DSM-IV (APA, 1994) diagnosis of pedophilia is unrelated to subsequent recidivism.

Detailed criticisms of the relevant DSM categories of paraphilia have pointed to many problems (Marshall, 1997a, 1999, 2005a; O'Donohue, Regev, & Hagstrom, 2000), not the least of which concerns the failure of the DSM authors to demonstrate satisfactory cross-diagnostician reliability for any of the paraphilias. In fact, studies of the reliability of all DSM diagnoses have been limited, and several authors have complained about this unacceptable state of affairs (Kirk & Kutchins, 1994; Meyer, 2002; Reid, Wise, & Sutton, 1992). The only field trials of the reliability of the paraphilias conducted under the auspices of the DSM committee appeared in reference to DSM-III (APA, 1980) criteria (O'Donohue et al., 2000). Despite the fact that the criteria have changed in important ways over the subsequent revisions of the DSM, the authors of the latest versions claimed there was no need to repeat field trials because the DSM-III studies had shown the paraphilias to be reliable (see APA, 1996). This claim does not match what the early trials showed. As O'Donohue et al. (2000) note, all sexual disorders (paraphilias and dysfunctions) were collapsed in the DSM-III field trials, and although the initial kappa coefficient (the index of reliability) was sufficiently high (kappa = 0.92), the second part of the trial generated a kappa of just 0.75. There were only seven cases in the first part of the trials and only five in the second part. For decisions having important consequences, and surely deciding that someone has pedophilia or sexual sadism has very important consequences, the acceptable kappa must be at least 0.90 (Hair, Anderson, Tatham, & Black, 1998; Murphy & Davidshofer, 1995). The DSM data on the reliability of the paraphilias are clearly not acceptable.

In a particularly telling study, Levenson (2004) evaluated the reliability of various diagnoses made by two independent experienced clinicians in the preparation of their reports to courts examining whether identified sexual offenders met criteria for sexual violent predator (SVP) status. Since these diagnoses are among the required criteria for civil commitment, the diagnostic decisions are extremely important, both for the protection of the offender and the public. The diagnosis of pedophilia did best but still failed to meet satisfactory standards (kappa = 0.65). For exhibitionism the kappa was 0.36. Paraphilia NOS, it should be noted, was used in these reports to the court to identify rapists, as is common in most SVP cases (Doren, 2002), although this was definitely not the intention of the authors of the DSM. In fact, the reliability of simply diagnosing a client with any paraphilia was, in Levenson's study, just 0.47.

In two studies of the diagnosis of sexual sadism, Marshall and his colleagues (Marshall, Kennedy, & Yates, 2002; Marshall, Kennedy, Yates, & Serran, 2002) reported unacceptable levels of reliability. In the first study (Marshall, Kennedy, & Yates, 2002), they found that forensic psychiatrists in their daily practice applied the diagnosis to sexual offenders who, in fact, did not have the features specified in DSM for sexual sadists. These same psychiatrists failed to apply the diagnosis to sexual offenders whose offenses were characterized by torture, brutality, and seemingly humiliating acts. In the second study, Marshall, Kennedy, Yates, and Serran (2002) had 15 internationally renowned forensic psychiatrists indicate from detailed information (each offender's life history and offense history, the specific details of his worst offense, psychological and phallometric assessments, and the client's self-reported sexual interests) whether each of 12 offenders met criteria for sexual sadism. The resultant kappa was absurdly low (kappa = 0.14). It appears that the diagnosis of sexual sadism is not being (or perhaps cannot be) applied reliably.

Despite these and a host of other problems identified by O'Donohue et al. (2000) and by Marshall (1997a, 2005a, 2005b), the current edition of the DSM (DSM-IV-TR; APA, 2000) does employ criteria that provide a glimpse into the sort of problems some sexual offenders display. We will provide details of the criteria of each relevant disorder, and in chapter 3, we will provide a description of what research has revealed about these men.

All of the paraphilias are said to involve "recurrent, intense sexually arousing fantasies, sexual urges, or behaviors" (APA, 2000, p. 566) concerning the particular focus of the client's desire. Pedophilia is said to involve sexual fantasies, urges, and behaviors involving prepubescent children. It is not made clear why those adults who engage in sex with prepubescent children are said to be pedophiles, but those who molest post-pubescent children are not to be considered pedophiles. In fact, identifying the age of an offender's victim is not always straightforward. Is it the victim's age at the onset of abuse or when it is reported? In addition, offenders may not tell the truth about the victim's age and objective information may not be available. Clinicians working with sexual offenders do not make this distinction between these two groups when deciding who does or does not need treatment, and both groups appear to have a similar range of problems. Furthermore, clinicians rarely apply the diagnosis of pedophilia to incest offenders and yet many men who molest their own children begin abusing them when the child is quite young and continue to do so over many years. This certainly appears to provide evidence of "recurrent" fantasies, urges, and behaviors involving sex with a child.

DSM-IV added "behaviors" to the previous criteria that simply listed urges and fantasies about children. These additional criteria have not yet produced evident changes in diagnostic practices. If this addition of "behaviors" was taken seriously then almost all child molesters would meet criteria for pedophilia because they all engage in sexual behaviors with children. If that was the intention of the DSM authors, then diagnostic practices would have become more in line with treatment decisions, but they have not as yet. Given that diagnosticians still seem to feel that inferences must be made concerning enduring fantasies and urges about children in order to decide whether a child molester is a pedophile, current applications of the diagnosis can be expected to be unreliable. As we have seen, they do appear to be unreliable. If an inference is to be made about enduring sexual fantasies or urges about children, then we need information independent of the client's self-report, which we might suspect will not always be truthful. Phallometric evaluations or viewing time measures (see the section on "Sexual Interests" in chapter 3) have been relied on by some clinicians and researchers to identify persistent sexual fantasies or urges about children. Indeed, Freund and Blanchard (1989) see phallometry as the appropriate diagnostic test for pedophilia. We doubt that this is a satisfactory resolution.

Because rapists have not been identified in the main body of any edition of the DSM as belonging to any diagnostic category, most clinicians (when they are required to make a diagnosis) categorize rapists as having paraphilia NOS (Doren, 2002; Levenson, 2004). This is not a good solution because there are no criteria specified under that label that would describe rapists. In fact, the only diagnosis that might be appropriate would be "sexual sadism," but then only for those rapists who have sexual fantasies, urges, or behaviors that indicate sexual excitement elicited by physically or psychologically harming someone. Sexual sadism is, as we have seen, a particularly problematic diagnosis because it relies on the clinician's ability to infer such desires from evidence other than the offender's self-report, which is likely to be seen as untruthful unless he admits to sadistic desires.

For exhibitionists the diagnosis may be less problematic. These offenders typically expose themselves to numerous victims often over many years. In such cases inferring recurrent sexual fantasies, urges, and behaviors involving exposure seems straightforward, and most clinicians do not hesitate to apply the paraphilic diagnosis of exhibitionism to these clients. However, these inferences may not be as straightforward as they seem. In one study (Marshall, Payne, Barbaree, & Eccles, 1991), exhibitionists were asked about the content of their sexual fantasies. These questions were asked because very few of the exhibitionists in this study displayed sexual arousal to images of exposing despite having many victims. The exhibitionists rather sheepishly indicated that they were aroused by fantasies of one or another of their victims requesting and engaging in sexual intercourse with them. Perhaps, despite what DSM has to say, exhibitionists are not characteristically aroused by exposing, which, of course, leaves open the question of their motivation to expose. Perhaps exhibitionistic behavior is, as Freund (1990) once claimed, a clumsy attempt at courting.

There are other problems associated with the diagnoses of the various paraphilias (see Marshall 1997a, 2005a; O'Donohue et al., 2000, for details). The basic problem with these diagnoses, as they apply to sexual offenders, is that a complete understanding of the problems these offenders have is not adequately described by the criteria outlined in the various editions of DSM.

In summary, DSM criteria have not been very helpful in work with sexual offenders. Apart from the unreliability of the paraphilic diagnoses, DSM diagnoses have little relevance for the etiology, assessment, treatment, or likely prognosis of sexual offenders. Not surprisingly, many researchers, theorists, clinicians, and assessors working with sexual offenders have ignored the DSM.

The broader clinical picture will be revealed in detail in chapter 3. For the present purposes it is sufficient to note that sexual offenders have a complex range of problems that are not apparent in DSM criteria. They have a range of distorted attitudes, beliefs, and perceptions, which have their basis in underlying maladaptive schemas. Sexual offenders also lack empathy; they have low self-esteem, poor coping styles and skills, emotional and behavioral regulation problems, dysfunctional attachment styles that result in low levels of intimacy and the experience of emotional loneliness; and they commonly have sexual interests that match their overt deviant behaviors. It is only this latter feature that is related to, although not directly expressed in, DSM criteria for the paraphilias. In addition, many sexual offenders have associated anger management issues and substance abuse problems.

Such a broad range of problems reveals the magnitude of the difficulties faced by clinicians who hope to provide treatment for these offenders. The development of treatment programs for sexual offenders, in conformity with the principles of good science, began with simpleminded concepts of the basis of sexual offending. As research revealed an ever-expanding list of the difficulties that led these men to commit sexual offenses, treatment programs expanded (see Laws & Marshall, 2003, and Marshall & Laws, 2003, for a history of their developments). As we will see in chapter 2, the targets of treatment are currently quite extensive and they are based on research that has revealed the full extent of the difficulties in effective prosocial functioning that these clients have.

Etiology

There is no one accepted model of the development of a disposition to sexually offend, but most researchers and clinicians agree on a general set of factors that seem to be etiologically significant. The main models cited in the literature have been outlined by Finkelhor (1984), Marshall and Barbaree (1990), Hall and Hirschman (1991), and Ward and Siegert (2002). More recently, Smallbone (in press) has offered another model that we believe has important implications for understanding sexual offenders. It is generally agreed that single-factor explanations of the etiology of sexual offending are incomplete (Marshall, 1996; Ward & Hudson, 1998) and that a more comprehensive, multifactorial model is required (Ward & Sorbello, 2003). The above models all meet this standard to a greater or lesser degree.

Finkelhor (1984) explains the proximal factors that trigger child molestation. He proposes that four preconditions must be met before an adult will attempt to have sex with a child. These four preconditions, however, can only be met if certain factors are true. First, sexual activities with a child must be experienced or anticipated by the offender as emotionally satisfying. Finkelhor refers to this as emotional congruence and in its broader sense this fits with Howells' (1979) finding that child molesters feel more comfortable with, and less threatened by, children than adults. This notion of emotional congruence is also consistent with the idea that child molesters seek emotional comfort and intimacy with children (Marshall, 1989a). Second, Finkelhor says children must elicit sexual arousal in offenders. Fortunately, not all adult males are sexually aroused by children. Research using measures of sexual arousal demonstrate that while some nonoffender males respond sexually to images of children, very few do, whereas a substantial number of child molesters do (Marshall & Fernandez, 2003). Third, Finkelhor claims that men who seek sex with children are blocked in their attempts to meet their sexual needs with adults. Evidence on the poverty of intimacy and adult attachment skills among sexual offenders offers support for this claim (Marshall, 1993). Finally, in order to offend, so Finkelhor claims, child molesters must overcome their inhibitions against committing such crimes. They may achieve this by cognitive strategies (e.g., rationalizing and justifying offending) or as a result of altered internal states (e.g., an angry state, a strong sense of entitlement, or intoxication).

These four factors are grouped by Finkelhor into the four preconditions he says must be met before molestation can occur. The first precondition requires that the offender must be motivated to offend; that is, molesting a child must be associated with sexual arousal, blockage, and emotional congruence. Second, disinhibition must occur; that is, the offender must overcome inhibitions about offending. Third, conditions that allow the offender access to a victim must occur. For this to happen the offender must be alone with the child and the child must be vulnerable in some way; for example, the child may need affection or closeness, or in some other way be needy. Finally, the offender must, if necessary, be able to overcome any resistance by the child. He may use coercive tactics (e.g., he may bribe, coerce, threaten, or be forceful), or he must desensitize the child by grooming him/her over time.

There is evidence that these features of child molestation do occur (see Marshall, Serran, & Marshall, in press). However, theories of etiology also need to explain how it is that these proximal factors arise. Thus, an additional theory needs to identify more distal factors. In addition, Finkelhor's model has not been applied to other sexual offenders, although there seems no obvious reason to suppose that it would not be capable of accommodating the necessary adjustments to do so.

Hall and Hirschman's (1991) account is meant to include all sexual offenders. They propose somewhat similar factors to Finkelhor but add more distal, or at least more enduring, personality problems. They claim that for sexual offending to occur the following conditions must be met: the offender must be sexually aroused by his target (or rather by the class of his targets, i.e., children or adult females); he must hold attitudes and beliefs as well as have distorted perceptions about his victim or his class of victim; he must experience emotional dysregulation; and he must have personality deficits. These latter deficits are said to be activated under certain conditions, which then generate each of the other three factors. This aspect of Hall and Hirschman's account has important implications. As we will see in chapter 3, there is evidence that sexual responsivity to deviant acts is likely to be greater when men are intoxicated, angry, emotionally upset, or have had problematic experiences with which they are unable to cope. However, emotional dyscontrol may just as likely trigger what Hall and Hirschman call personality deficits as the other way round. Hall and Hirschman describe the particular combination of these factors that trigger specific kinds of sexual offenses. Again, however, their model is more concerned with the factors that more immediately result in offending; they do not satisfactorily explain how the personality deficits arise or why some men with similar problems, or in similar states, do not offend.

Ward's recent theorizing has encompassed a failure to self-regulate (Ward & Hudson, 2000), an inability to achieve the goals of a good life (Ward & Marshall, 2004), and a pathways-to-offending model (Ward & Siegert, 2002; Ward & Sorbello, 2003). Self-regulation governs the way in which people order their lives so that they can successfully achieve the goals they are seeking. Much of the research in the broader psychology literature on general self-regulation points to the crucial role of control over (i.e., regulation of) emotions (Baumeister & Vohs, 2004). Affective dysregulation leads to an inability to focus on plans and their execution. Emotional lability diverts people from focusing on the long-term effects of their behavior and produces a narrowing of attention onto immediate satisfactions. As such, emotional problems produce behaviors that are not properly aimed at (i.e., regulated toward) the achievement of personal goals. Sexual offenders, so Ward claims, manifest poor behavioral regulation in that their offending behavior is concerned only with the relatively momentary satisfaction of short-term desires and fails to produce longer-term satisfaction.

Of course, these offenders also characteristically fail to articulate a comprehensive set of goals that would lead to enhanced life satisfaction and they often seem without direction in their life. People who derive maximum satisfaction in life have reasonably well-articulated goals that cover a diverse range of issues (Deci & Ryan, 2000; Emmons, 1999; Schmuck & Sheldon, 2001). It is from these notions that Ward has derived his description of the good lives model (Ward, 2002; Ward & Marshall, 2004; Ward & Stewart, 2003a). He suggests that sexual offenders fail to achieve the goals necessary to have a satisfactorily fulfilled life and that in order to compensate for this they seek more immediate satisfactions without regard for the long-term consequences of these behaviors. Thus deficits in self-regulation are at the basis of a failure to achieve a good life, such that Ward's two models (self-regulatory failure and the good lives approach) essentially point to different aspects of the same problem.

Ward's (Ward & Siegert, 2002; Ward & Sorbello, 2003) pathways model describes the steps sexual offenders take to offend that reveal their problems in self-regulation and their lack of concern for long-term goals. He suggests that sexual offending results from the combination of four issues: intimacy deficits, distorted sexual scripts, problems in emotional regulation, and cognitive distortions. The particular interplay of these four factors in any one sexual offender leads to his adoption of one of five etiological pathways (the reader is referred to Ward & Sorbello, 2003, for details of each of these pathways).

Although Ward has not yet clearly integrated these three models (i.e., self-regulation, good lives, and pathways), it is clear that this is the direction of his thought. The real advantage of the integration of Ward's models is that it involves both distal and proximal factors and attempts to account for the diverse ways in which sexual offenders pursue and enact their abusive behaviors. The origins of behavioral dysregulation, as well as the origins of poorly articulated life goals, are said to derive from disrupted childhood experiences as well as problematic experiences in teenage and adult years, particularly with regard to relationships and sexual experiences.

Our current view of the development of sexual offending represents an integration of much of what Ward outlines into our own etiological account. We developed our theory over many years by identifying the influence of a variety of specific factors, such as problematic parent–child bonds (Marshall, Hudson, & Hodkinson, 1993; Marshall & Marshall, 2000; Starzyk & Marshall, 2003), childhood sexual abuse (Dhawan & Marshall, 1996), social and cultural influences (Marshall, 1984, 1985), the role of exposure to pornography (Marshall, 1989b), conditioned sexual interests (Barbaree & Marshall, 1991; Laws & Marshall, 1990), adult attachment style and the capacity for intimacy (Marshall, 1989a, 1993, 1998), poor coping skills (Cortoni & Marshall, 2001; Marshall, Serran, & Cortoni, 2000), mood fluctuations (Marshall, Marshall, & Moulden, 2000; Marshall, Moulden, & Marshall, 2001), sexual compulsivity (Marshall & Marshall, 2001), and the failure to achieve the general goals of a satisfying life (Ward & Marshall, 2004).

At the base of our model are the problematic childhood experiences of males who become sexual offenders. These early experiences involve poor child–parent attachments; childhood physical, sexual, and emotional abuse; neglect; inconsistent discipline; and early exposure to pornography. Some combination of these experiences leads the emerging sexual offender to acquire: a low sense of self-worth; a failure to internalize the confidence, attitudes, and skills necessary to meet his needs prosocially; and a self-interested disposition or a sense of entitlement. Finally, these developmental experiences and their associated problems prompt the developing sexual offender to seek comfort in immediate rewards (e.g., sex as manifest in early and frequent masturbatory practices), rather than work toward goals that have delayed rewards. Unable to effectively consolidate relationships with peers during adolescence, which is a time when sexual interests are rapidly and fully awakened and when the shift from parental bonds to peer bonds occurs, the teenaged offender-to-be turns to the avid pursuit of self-interested goals and immediately secured satisfactions. Because sex is immediately and powerfully rewarding, such a young male is likely to seek sex with whomever and by whatever means are available. Because coerced sex (either with an adult, a peer, or a younger child) requires none of the skills the young male has failed to acquire, it represents an easy route to self-satisfaction and to the comfort of rewards that he is not able to obtain otherwise.

As he moves into adulthood bereft of the range of skills, confidence, and attitudes needed to achieve well-rounded satisfaction from his life, the young man emerging from the above background will be relatively unable to cope with life's problems. He will also be likely, by dint of his inadequacies, to create problems for himself, and he will not have the skills necessary to deal with these difficulties. He will likely respond to these problems by either giving up efforts to cope and submitting to the consequences of this (i.e., being miserable or angry) or by avoiding the issues (e.g., using intoxicants to avoid thinking about his problems). Finally, when either placed in a situation where access to victims is readily available (e.g., as a parent, or in his job or leisure activities) or by actively seeking out a victim, he may commit a sexual offense and begin a process of becoming a chronic offender.

One apparent deficit in our model concerns the fact that some seemingly well-flunctioning individuals (e.g., professionals, academics) commit sexual offenses. However, apparent high functioning in some areas is not always matched by effectiveness in other areas, and, in any case, no theory can be expected to allow for all instances of any specific behavior. Indeed the apparent success of Freud's psychoanalytic theory to explain all behavior was seen as a clear flaw to its true explanatory power (Popper, 1963).

Smallbone (2005) has recently proposed a model that suggests it is the interaction (or mutual facilitation) of three basic systems that are evolutionarily entrenched: the caregiving (or nurturing) system, the attachment (or bonding) system, and the sexual system. Smallbone's model is particularly helpful in describing the immediate factors that produce sexual behaviors between an adult and a child when they are in close proximity over time (e.g., incest, or the offenses of a teacher, priest, or scout leader). Smallbone points to the physical proximity of the neurobiological mechanisms that underpin these three systems and suggests that the activation of one may facilitate the activation of the other two. For example, a father whose wife is intimately and sexually remote, may, by devoting his nurturing efforts to his child, come to develop such a strong bond with the child that he/she becomes his main source of satisfying his attachment needs. The activation of his attachment system in conjunction with the simultaneous activation of the nurturing system may over time produce a relationship with the child where the adult begins to treat the child as if he/she were an adult intimate partner. This state of affairs is likely (along with the facilitation provided by the ongoing activation of the nurturing and attachment systems) to lead to the activation of the sexual system, particularly as the physical comforting aspects of the behaviors become more pronounced. Like Ward's model, and ours, Smallbone's theory sees the origin of the failure to properly distinguish these three systems as lying in the childhood, teenage, and adult experiences of sexual offenders.

Smallbone's model is readily incorporated into ours, and chapter 3 provides evidence on the features of sexual offenders that emerge from their problematic childhood, youth, and adult experiences. The various references cited above that outline each of the factors in our overall etiological model detail the evidence in support of the origin of these factors. More specifically, the formal statements of our theory (Marshall, 2001a; Marshall & Barbaree, 1990; Marshall & Marshall, 2000) provide details of the supporting evidence.

Course and Prognosis

Very little is known about the course of sexual offending. No longitudinal studies have been conducted as yet and the few cross-generational studies have so far provided limited information that might address this question. Unfortunately, the majority of information we have on sexual offenders is either on teenagers (a more recently developing field) or on adults between ages 20 and 50 years.

The recent evidence on elderly sexual offenders (Marshall, Malcolm, Marshall, & Butler, in press) suggests that they might have features quite different from younger offenders. Similarly, the evidence on juvenile sexual offenders (Barbaree & Marshall, in press; Barbaree, Marshall, & Hudson, 1993) indicates that far from all of them go on to become adult sexual offenders. Thus, the course of sexual offending may run the lifespan in only a few of these males, but who these few are we cannot as yet predict.

Official records of arrests and convictions reveal only part of the history of sexual offending, and in those jurisdictions where there are statutes of limitation on prosecution, these records tell us even less. It appears, however, from all sources of information (clinical, official, and victim reports) that some offenders commit only one or two sexual crimes while others become repetitive offenders. Among the repetitive offenders, some offend for only a limited time while others appear to have a lifetime problem. Why these differences emerge is not presently understood, but in some cases the cessation of offending might simply reflect reductions in opportunities. For example, the children of an incestuous father may grow up and leave home, or they may be removed if the abuse becomes known. However, even the later access to grandchildren does not always trigger a return to offending in these men.

The onset of sexual offending ranges in age across almost the entire lifespan, with some beginning their abusive behaviors prior to pubescing (Johnson, 1998), others starting as teenagers (Barbaree, Marshall, & Hudson, 1993), and some begin to offend as adults (Marshall, Barbaree, & Eccles, 1991). Even among the latter, there are sexual offenders who commit their first offense in their 60s, 70s, or 80s (Marshall, Malcolm, Marshall, & Butler, in press). In the early days of modern approaches to dealing with sexual offenders, it was often assumed that most, if not all, men who sexually abused others commenced their offending during their teenage years. This led to proposals to treat juvenile offenders so that the later number of adult offenders would be significantly reduced. It is now known that the majority of juvenile sexual offenders do not develop into adult sexual offenders even in the absence of treatment (Barbaree & Marshall, in press).

What does appear to be clear is that an initial sexual offense creates, or enhances, an appetite for offending in many of these men, no doubt through conditioning and other processes (Laws & Marshall, 1990). Sexual offending, by its nature, evokes sexual excitement which is a very pleasing state that is likely to serve as a reinforcer for the deviant acts. However, sexual offending is also associated with a variety of other sources of arousal/excitement that are also likely to function as part of a reinforcement complex. Sexual offending involves power and control and is a risk-taking behavior. These elements generate satisfaction and excitement. Sexual offending also often involves some degree of aggression (in some cases quite significant aggression), and aggression has been shown to function as a secondary reinforcer (Leon, 1969; Storr, 1972), which increases the rates of any behaviors associated with aggression, such as sexual abuse. Darke (1990) has shown that some rapists enjoy humiliating and degrading their victims. The antisocial elements of sexual offending might also generate excitement (similar to the childhood enjoyment of "naughtiness") that could function as a reinforcer. Indeed, the complex and many-featured array of sources of excitement (and, therefore, reinforcement) generated by sexual offending make it a wonder that any offender is ever able to voluntarily stop offending, particularly since the elements of the offense are typically subsequently rehearsed in deviant fantasies while the man is masturbating (Laws & Marshall, 1991; Wright & Schneider, 1997). Despite all the obvious sources of excitement associated with sexual offending, sexual excitement is the only source of arousal that has been subjected to any amount of empirical scrutiny. This neglect of other aspects of arousal needs to be addressed if we are to expand our understanding of sexual offending.

Our guess is that most men who commit a sexual offense will continue offending unless something outside of themselves interrupts the process. Unless they are identified as an offender or prosecuted or removed from access to victims, it seems likely that a man who has committed a sexual offense will repeat the offensive acts over many years.

Outside intervention, however, even simply in the form of prosecution and imprisonment, appears to result in low rates of reoffending. For example, in Hanson's studies of recidivism (Hanson & Bussière, 1998; Hanson, Gordon, Harris et al., 2002), the reoffense rate for untreated sexual offenders, collapsed across all actuarial risk levels, was less than 20%. These data suggest that incarcerating sexual offenders may reduce the propensity to offend in some of these men. For child molesters there does not appear to be an aging process that naturally ends offending. Most rapists, however, seem to burn out somewhere after age 40 years and very few exhibitionists are identified after age 50 years. What natural processes produce this cessation of offending in rapists and exhibitionists is not known, but it appears to reflect the similar "burn-out" phenomena apparent in most nonsexual offenders (Hirschi & Gottfredson, 1983).

This brief review of evidence that might be relevant to understanding the course of sexual offending is also relevant to considering the prognosis once the problem has been identified. However, there are also other valuable sources of information. The work of several researchers who have developed risk assessment instruments has produced data telling us how likely offenders with certain characteristics will be to continue offending. Hanson's excellent work (Hanson, 1998a; Hanson & Bussière, 1998; Hanson & Thornton, 2000), in particular, has provided a basis for distinguishing those sexual offenders who are at greatest risk to reoffend after they have been identified. We noted above that the overall rate of reoffending was quite low. However, these rates of reoffending vary according to the offender's established risk level. Based on the records of several thousand sexual offenders, it has been possible to distinguish the levels of risk among sexual offenders. These factors include: sexual interest in children (as measured by phallometry), number of prior sexual offenses, stranger victims, male victims, young age of offender, unmarried status, diverse sex crimes, diverse nonsexual crimes, and features of an antisocial personality. In excess of 50% of high-risk offenders will reoffend, whereas less than 10% of those who are low on the actuarial indices are likely to reoffend. In an interesting recent development, both Hanson (2002) and Barbaree, Langton, and Peacock (in press) have reported a significant decline in risk to reoffend as sexual offenders age. This age-related decline in risk is evident across all risk categories identified by actuarial instruments. So perhaps, after all, sexual offenders generally do turn out to cease offending as they age. However, there are some who appear to begin their sexual offending quite late in life (Marshall, Malcolm, Marshall, & Butler, in press).

Our view is that treatment of sexual offenders, particularly treatment that conforms to the more recent cognitive behavioral models, can significantly alter the course and prognosis of sexual offending, although others disagree with this view (e.g., Rice & Harris, 2003). As we will see more clearly in chapter 3, our treatment program has been shown to reduce the number of sexual offenders who go on to continue abusing. To date, however, research has not revealed ways to identify which changes induced by treatment result in this reduction in recidivism. Similarly, no researchers to date have examined what changes in sexual offenders' overall functioning (e.g., features of quality of life) result from effective treatment. While the primary goal of sexual offender treatment is the reduction of recidivism, we also want our treated clients to become more effective and useful members of society. We do not want them to remain damaged individuals who are burdens on society but who no longer sexually offend. As it turns out, effective sexual offender treatment not only reduces the likelihood of subsequent repeat sexual offending, but it also reduces the more general disposition to offend in a nonsexual way (Hanson et al., 2002). There are, therefore, some good grounds to hope that treatment of sexual offenders changes the course of their offending and markedly improves their prognosis.

CHAPTER 2

Overall Description of Treatment Strategy

INTRODUCTION

Behavioral programs for sexual offenders developed in the 1960s and early 1970s (Abel, Levis, & Clancy, 1970; Bancroft & Marks, 1968; Evans, 1968; Fookes, 1969; Marshall, 1971, 1973), but these programs quickly expanded to involve a more comprehensive range of treatment targets by employing the emerging cognitive behavioral approach (Abel, Blanchard, & Becker, 1978; Marshall & Williams, 1975). In the early 1980s, Marquis and Pithers (Marques, 1982; Pithers, Marques, Gibat, & Marlatt, 1983) described the integration of cognitive behavioral therapy (CBT) with the relapse prevention (RP) approach being developed by Marlatt (1982). This CBT/RP combination proved irresistible to clinicians because it made sound logical sense and it gave them a way to increase the likelihood that their sexual offender clients would maintain treatment gains after the termination of therapy. In fact, the enthusiasm for this combination was so strong that no one called the approach into question until the 1990s when Ward and his colleagues challenged the theoretical bases (Ward & Hudson, 1996; Ward, Hudson, & Marshall, 1994; Ward, Hudson, & Siegert, 1995), and Marques and her colleagues generated rather disappointing evaluations of California's CBT/RP program (Marques, Day, Nelson, & West, 1994; Marques, Nelson, Alarcon, & Day, 2000). However, these events did not lead to the abandonment of RP but rather they produced some significant revisions to its application (see Laws, Hudson, & Ward, 2000, for some of these revisions).

Throughout the period from 1970 to the end of the 20th century, new treatment targets were added and procedures were developed to achieve all of the goals, old and new, to which CBT with sexual offenders was aimed. These innovations, however, did not see the light of day in all CBT/RP programs. Some programs included a very broad range of targets while others had more restricted aims. This makes it impossible to describe a "typical" CBT/RP program for sexual offenders. To make things even more difficult, treatment for sexual offenders is constantly evolving as a result of empirical research and clinical intuitions. What we will do in this book is describe the current form and the theoretical and empirical bases of our own treatment program. Since we have played some role in the evolution of sexual offender programs, we hope this does not seem to our readers to be too arrogant; it is simply a convenience.

Our program's structure, content, and procedures are the result of a long and continuing process of development (Hudson, Marshall, Johnston, Ward, & Jones, 1995; Marshall, 1971, 1973, 1995, 2001b, 2004a,b; Marshall, Anderson, & Fernandez, 1999; Marshall & Barbaree, 1988; Marshall, Earls, Segal, & Darke, 1983; Marshall & Eccles, 1991; Marshall & Fernandez, 1998; Marshall & McKnight, 1975; Marshall & Redondo, 2002; Marshall & Serran, 2004a; Marshall & Williams, 1975) and each aspect is based on the available research literature. Our own clinical hunches have often played an initiating role in the development of our treatment targets and processes, which we then subject to research and clinical trials. The program adopts a cognitive behavioral approach to treatment (Marshall, Anderson, & Fernandez, 1999, 2001; Marshall & Fernandez, 1998) modified by the inclusion of an effort to facilitate emotional expression and regulation (Kennedy-Moore & Watson, 1999; Ward & Hudson, 2000). The program is implemented in a way that emphasizes the role of the therapist (Marshall, 2005c; Marshall, Fernandez, Serran et al., 2003; Marshall & Serran, 2004b; Marshall, Serran, Fernandez et al., 2003; Marshall, Serran, Moulden et al., 2002; Serran, Fernandez, Marshall, & Mann, 2003), and it derives from our formulations of the etiology and maintenance of sexual offending (Marshall, 2001b; Marshall & Barbaree, 1984, 1990; Marshall & Marshall, 2000) which are variants on a social learning model (Akers, 1977; Bandura, 1969).

TREATMENT INTENSITY

The range of risk levels of the clients in our prison-based program spans the spectrum from high to low risk. Given this disparity among our clients, the duration of time spent in treatment varies. Our program operates on a rolling basis (i.e., open-ended), which is to say clients progress at their own pace and remain in treatment until they either meet all treatment goals or until it is decided that further efforts are unlikely to produce any further benefits. This means that some clients, including most of the high risk or moderate/high risk offenders, stay in treatment for longer than do the moderate or lower risk offenders. However, the average time in treatment has been slightly more than 4 months and no one exits treatment before completing at least 3 months. Some of the most difficult and problem-ridden clients remain in treatment for 6 months but this is rare and no one has yet continued beyond six months.

Because of initial budgetary limitations we were only able to provide two 2.5-hour group sessions per week, accompanied by limited individual counseling over the 4-month period. With experience we have come to the conclusion that this provision of treatment is sufficient considering we can extend or reduce the duration of treatment to meet each client's rate and style of learning and the range of his problems. Based on our understanding of human learning research (Baker, 2001; Domjan, 1998; O'Donohue, 1998), particularly as it applies to spaced or massed practice, we believe that two sessions per week allows time for our clients to consolidate what they are learning and permits time for them to implement and practice their between-sessions assignments. Under these conditions the enthusiasm clients have for treatment is maintained and fatigue is not a factor for either clients or therapists. The advantage of our rolling program approach is that each client's deficits receive intense focus, but where they are already somewhat skilled (e.g., perhaps in social functioning), the focus is reduced proportional to the degree of their skill. In addition, since each client's problems (e.g., cognitive distortions, empathy, relationship issues) are focused on throughout treatment, and all clients are required to fully participate in all aspects of treatment even when they are not the focus, each group member repeatedly receives both direct and vicarious exposure to every target of treatment. Thus, the amount of time spent on the actual deficiencies of each client is approximately the same as, or more than, they would receive under a closed program that ran for far longer. This flexibility of delivery and the repeated exposure to problematic issues allows us to meet the responsivity factor (both general and specific) that is critical to effective offender treatment (Andrews & Bonta, 1998).

SELECTION OF PARTICIPANTS

Once it has been established that an inmate in our institution has committed a sexual offense (either an offense that resulted in his current incarceration or that appears on his past record), he is referred to our program for a determination of his suitability for treatment. Our policy is to accommodate all incoming sexual offenders into one of our programs unless they adamantly refuse treatment. In the latter cases we do our best at interviews to convince them that it is in their long-term interest to enter treatment. For these purposes we adopt a motivational interviewing approach from Miller and Rollnick's (1991) original version. These tactics have apparently been successful, since over 95% of those sexual offenders who are offered treatment agree to enter our program.

We accept low-functioning offenders but structure our treatment for them in a way that effectively engages them. We rely heavily on Haaven's excellent approach (Haaven & Coleman, 2000; Haaven, Little & Petre-Miller, 1990) to assist these low functioning clients (e.g., using visual aids, being concrete, being repetitive), and in collaboration with the client we appoint another group member, whom they trust, to assist them, particularly with written homework. Similarly, for clients who are illiterate we also provide a scribe (again a fellow group member whom they trust) to assist them with written homework. Scribes, in both cases, are instructed to write only what the client tells them; they are not to reformulate what the client says nor are the scribes to provide clients with advice and assistance on what to say. For the most part, with monitoring, this seems to be effective.

Among the 622 clients we have treated over the past 15 years in our present program (not including the deniers), 5.6% were identified at entry to our program as high risk, 13.2% were at moderate/high risk, 36.7% were at moderate risk, 27.0% were at low/moderate risk, and 17.5% were deemed to be low risk to reoffend.

OVERALL DESCRIPTION OF THE PROGRAM

Our prison program operates in a context where various features relevant to treating sexual offenders are provided by other programs (e.g., anger management, substance abuse), so readers need to keep in mind that a fully comprehensive approach to these offenders must include procedures to modify these additional problematic features. Our program is continually evolving, although the rate of change has slowed over the past 5 or 6 years. Its content, procedures, and style of delivery, are all based on the large body of research now available. Its continued development will similarly be research-based, although many of the hypotheses that our research examines derive from clinical experience. We make changes to the program only when research is clear or when decisions must be made in the absence of research (e.g., our treatment adjustments for psychopathic clients). The program follows the recommendations of Andrews and Bonta (1998) in extending treatment depending on risk level, focusing on responsivity issues, and targeting criminogenic factors. Its delivery involves a semi-structured, cognitive behavioral approach that integrates emotional expression and regulation and operates in a rolling format.

We choose a rolling program approach for several reasons: it provides the flexibility necessary to allow the admission of urgent cases; it allows clients who have made progress to assist others and model-appropriate responding; it encourages the use of the therapist skills we have shown to maximize treatment changes; it promotes the therapist flexibility necessary to address responsivity issues; it provides for repeated vicarious learning of each of the targets of treatment; it facilitates rapid attainment of group cohesion and ensures it is maintained; it appears to facilitate a speedier attainment of treatment goals; and it reduces the likelihood of boredom by both clients and therapists. In a closed group approach, if there is flexibility in the time spent on each component of treatment, then the group will continue until the slowest participant in each component meets the treatment goals. This will necessarily involve overtreatment for some clients, which is not at all desirable since there are suggestions that overtreating clients may destroy whatever benefits treatment might otherwise confer (Marshall & Yates, 2005). If, as is usually the case, a closed group format spends a specific, nonflexible amount of time on each component, then some clients will not be able to reach all treatment goals. This is also seen by us as a disadvantage of closed formats. A rolling program lends itself rather better than a closed group approach to keeping clients in treatment until they are functioning satisfactorily on all treatment targets.

New clients enter the group when a space becomes available as a result of another client completing the requirements to the best of his ability, or when, as rarely happens, a client is removed from the program. Thus, the program operates continuously throughout the year. When staff members are at conferences or on holidays, another therapist temporarily fills their place. The rolling aspect of the program allows the therapist to spend more time on those treatment targets in which each client is most deficient, and the therapist also can return to earlier issues quite readily if this is necessary. A rolling program approach also maximally facilitates attention to responsivity factors, such as the client's learning style and general abilities (general responsivity) as well as day-to-day fluctuations in mood or cooperativeness (specific responsivity). We have already noted that we accept into treatment low functioning clients and clients who are to some degree psychopathic. For the low functioning men, we earlier noted how we make our discussions with them more concrete, explicit, and repetitive. For the more psychopathic clients, we attempt to identify personally designed strategies that will motivate them (e.g., more immediate, self-interested rewards) and that fit with their learning styles. Of course we try to develop personally designed approaches for all our clients, but the psychopathic clients are, so everyone agrees, a particularly difficult client group. Whether our strategies are optimal or not, we cannot at this time empirically affirm, but they are based on developments in process by colleagues elsewhere (Ralph Serin, personal communication; David Thornton, personal communication).

Although the program is structured in the sense that there are specified topics or targets covered in an order (albeit a somewhat flexible order), the manner of delivery of treatment is significantly closer to a psychotherapeutic process than it is to modularized psychoeducation. One of the main features of the program is an emphasis on the role of the therapist. We (Marshall, Fernandez, Serran et al., 2003) have reviewed the extensive body of the general clinical literature on the influence of process variables (i.e., role of the therapist, optimal features of the therapist, client's perceptions of the therapist's features, the therapeutic alliance, and the group climate). Although much of this literature derives from studies of traditional psychotherapy, there is a growing body of research within the behavioral, cognitive, and cognitive behavioral literature that essentially identifies the same variables (see Schaap, Bennun, Schindler, & Hoogduin, 1993, for a summary of this literature).

On the basis of our review, and in cooperation with H.M. Prison Service's Offender Behaviour Programmes Unit in the United Kingdom, we have conducted studies examining the influence of therapist features in sexual offender treatment. We were able to demonstrate an influence for numerous therapist behaviors on the changes induced by sexual offender treatment (Marshall, Serran, Fernandez et al., 2003; Marshall, Serran, Moulden et al., 2002). One therapist behavior that consistently produced either no benefits, or more typically had a negative effect, was an aggressively confrontational style of challenging the clients. This observation was subsequently confirmed independently by Beech and Hamilton-Giachritis (2005). The features of the therapists that maximally produced benefits in these studies were: empathy, warmth, directiveness, and rewardingness. In addition, therapists who are flexible and who challenge clients in a firm but supportive manner, generate the greatest changes across all targets of treatment. Together these features accounted for between 40% and 60% of the variance in a set of indices of treatment benefits.

These findings are particularly interesting because they resulted from an examination of H.M. Prison Service's institutional sexual offender programs, which are highly structured and in which the therapists must rigorously follow a detailed treatment manual. Programs with greater flexibility might reveal a more profound influence for the therapist. Our findings on the influence of the therapist in sexual offender treatment are consistent with the general body of literature addressing the role of the therapist in the treatment of various disorders (see Marshall, Fernandez, Serran et al., 2003, for a review). Therapists who display these positive features also gain the compliance and commitment to treatment of sexual offenders

(Drapeau, 2005) and facilitate the creation of a productive group climate (Beech & Fordham, 1997; Beech & Hamilton-Giachritsis, 2005). Ensuring that sexual offender therapists function as empathic, warm, flexible, rewarding, and directive also creates a more optimistic view of the likely benefits of treatment in both the therapists and clients (Drapeau, 2005). As a result of these findings, therapists in our program are specifically trained in and enact the features that the research has revealed to be influential.

Consistent with cognitive behavioral approaches to the treatment of any kind of disorder, but especially those disorders where clients may express some reluctance to change (e.g., addictive and offending behaviors), we emphasize a motivational approach. A style derived from Miller and Rollnick's (1991, 2002) motivational interviewing is adopted throughout the processes of pretreatment interviews and treatment itself. In addition, we articulate, as a major aspect of the goals of treatment, our intention to assist each client to acquire the skills, attitudes, and self-confidence necessary to achieve higher levels of life satisfaction. This is consistent with our emphasis, in the later aspects of treatment, on the development of self-management plans that focus on approach rather than avoidance goals (Mann, Webster, Schofield, & Marshall, 2004) and that are modeled on the "good lives" approach outlined by Ward (2002). We suggest to our clients that in pursuit of their deviant acts they were attempting to meet the same broad range of needs that other people seek in more prosocial ways. Thus, we tell clients that the needs they were pursuing are normative; it is the direction in which they attempted to satisfy these needs that is problematic. For a more detailed description of the positive approach to treatment that we explicitly adopt, the reader is referred to Marshall, Ward, Mann et al. (2005).

Clinical meetings are held each week for a 3- to 4-hour period during which time all ongoing cases are discussed in as much detail as is necessary. In these clinical meetings all staff contribute to the discussion of all cases. We believe these weekly clinical meetings are not only essential to maintaining the integrity of our program, as well as ensuring that standards of treatment delivery remain high, they also serve to avoid burnout of staff and to maintain their enthusiasm for the work. Regular individual meetings between the director (W. L. Marshall) and treatment staff are scheduled to provide additional confidence that quality standards are maintained. In addition, onsite supervision is provided on an intermittent but consistent basis (i.e., at least once every 3 months), except when it is a new staff member when onsite supervision and individual consultations are more frequent. All staff are actively involved in various research projects and each is the lead researcher on at least one project. This ensures that our staff stay up to date with the literature, and it also maintains their enthusiasm for their clinical work. We operate in as nonhierarchical way as possible so as to encourage the free and confident expression of ideas.

Reports are structured according to the goals of treatment and provide a post-treatment risk assessment and recommendations for further treatment if necessary, as well as suggestions for release processes, and postrelease supervision. In order to facilitate report writing we have developed an end-of-treatment therapist rating scale (see Appendix). This scale rates clients on 17 targets of treatment and distinguishes between their observed intellectual understanding of each target and the degree to which they have either demonstrated the behavior or appear to have emotionally integrated the issue. In cooperation with our colleagues in H.M. Prison Service, we have demonstrated satisfactory interrater reliability for all items on the therapist rating scale, but as yet we have not been using it long enough to see how the ratings predict outcome. However, recent evidence from Barbaree and his colleagues (Barbaree, in press; Barbaree, Langton, & Peacock, 2005; Langton, 2003) indicates that, contrary to their earlier report (Seto & Barbaree, 1999), ratings of treatment participation and progress do predict recidivism in treated sexual offenders. Primarily our ratings, which are more detailed than those employed by Barbaree and his colleagues, serve to indicate when a client has reached treatment goals as well as being a guide to writing reports.

Targeted Skills

Our program employs a skills-oriented approach to intervention based on cognitive, behavioral, emotional, and social learning approaches. The skills-oriented methods and techniques have been chosen based on both the empirical literature and clinical experience. All of our program targets involve a complex array of behavioral, cognitive, and emotional skills. To illustrate, let us take the example of empathy enhancement. First, we help clients recognize their own emotional states as well as the emotional states of others, and in doing so we facilitate and encourage the regulated expression of emotions. Next, we assist clients in modifying their cognitions by having them identify (i.e., incorporate within their conceptual framework) the negative consequences to their victims as well as having them modify their perceptions of the victims' behaviors at the time of the offense. We expect these changes to, over time, alter the schemas our clients have about other people, particularly those who belong to the class of potential victims. We then expect clients to behaviorally display empathy both by their actions (e.g., comforting other distressed group members) and by their verbal behavior (e.g., expressing remorse about the harm they have caused).

Similarly with self-esteem we encourage and facilitate the expression of behaviors such as engaging in social and pleasurable activities, as well as verbal (or subvocal) behaviors such as complementing themselves when they do things that deserve rewards and repeating positive self-statements throughout each day. These activities are aimed at enhancing their perception of themselves which should, eventually, change their self-schemas. Enhancements of self-schemas have the effect of generating greater emotional self-regulation (Leary & Downs, 1995).

In attempting to move our clients to adopt a more secure attachment style, in order to thereby meet their intimacy needs, we target relevant behaviors, cognitions, and emotions. Effective attachment involves a deep emotional bond with a loved person, a behavioral commitment to another person, and a recognition both of the client's own self-worth and of the other person's rights and needs. Adequate (i.e., secure) attachments to parents provide the basis for the acquisition of emotional self-regulation (Sroufe, 1996; Thompson, 1994), and secure adult attachments also appear to be related to greater self-regulation in general (Hirschi, 2004; Vohs & Ciarocco, 2004). Developing a secure attachment style requires a shift in schemas about the self (i.e., to an acceptance of "I am a lovable person") as well as schemas about others (i.e., others are capable of giving love) (Bartholomew & Perlman, 1994).

The modification of deviant sexual fantasies also involves this complex of processes. Clients employ one or another explicit behavioral procedure (e.g., masturbatory reconditioning, satiation, olfactory or ammonia aversion) as well as a covert procedure (i.e., covert association), each of which is aimed at attenuating or enhancing the sexual interest (which has decidedly emotional components) in either or both deviant and appropriate sexual activities.

The recognition of a prototypical offense pathway quite obviously, and explicitly, involves identifying the behavioral steps, the distorted cognitions necessary to proceed to offending, and the emotional arousal associated with both the pathway and the terminal act. Also the formulation of a self-management plan involves identifying risk-promoting and risk-reducing behaviors, emotional states that similarly raise or lower risk, and ways of thinking that allow or curtail progress along the offense pathway.

Thus, all aspects of our treatment program rely on the development of behavioral skills as well as the self-regulation of behavior, adaptive emotional expression, the generation of prosocial schemas, and the enhancement of positive self-schemas. All these aspects of skills training fuse in the processes involved in addressing each target of our program.

Behavioral Skills

Our approach to the enhancement of behavioral skills, as well as the therapist's enactment of various pro-therapeutic behavioral skills (see

Fernandez, Shingler, & Marshall, 2005), rest on the comprehensive knowledge of effective behavior-change procedures derived from studies of animal and human learning (O'Donohue, 1998). The literature on classical conditioning (Ayres, 1998; Boutin & Nelson, 1998; Falls, 1998; Kehoe & Macrae, 1998), operant conditioning (Allan, 1998; Dinsmoor, 1998; Donahoe, 1998), observational learning (Mineka & Hamida, 1998), and memory retrieval (Morgan & Riccio, 1998) are particularly relevant.

A number of techniques are used to correct the behavioral deficiencies our clients display and to enhance their abilities to function appropriately. These techniques include role plays, written work, skill-building exercises, behavioral practice between treatment sessions, as well as behavior modification techniques to change sexual arousal patterns.

Specific skills training is used to address known criminogenic factors associated with sexual offending. While sexual offenders present with a variety of criminogenic needs that are treatment targets, they also have generic skill deficits that influence not only their sexual offending but their functioning in general. For example, sexual offenders have been found to be deficient in the way in which they cope with problems in their lives (Cortoni & Marshall, 2001; Marshall, Cripps, Anderson, & Cortoni, 1999; Marshall, Serran, & Cortoni, 2000; Neidigh & Tomiko, 1991). Child molesters tend to use emotion-focused problem-solving strategies as a general response to difficulties. As a result, rather than attempting to generate problem-focused solutions, these offenders tend to concentrate on their inadequacies and to experience depression, anxiety, or anger. Similarly, rapists tend to use an avoidance-focused, rather than a task-oriented, problem-solving strategy (Cortoni, 1998). We have developed specific procedures aimed at training our clients in problem-focused coping and increasing their use of effective strategies for dealing with specific difficulties they may face. These procedures have been shown to be effective (Serran, Firestone, Marshall, & Moulden, 2004). Thus, our program is designed not only to teach specific skills to address known criminogenic needs (e.g., modifying deviant sexual arousal, avoiding and dealing with specific risk situations), but also to impart generalized skills that will help clients avoid future problems that might increase their risk.

Cognitive Skills

Our understanding and modification of cognitive processes rests on general cognitive science (Nelson, 1995; Oakhill & Garnham, 1996) as well as research in social cognition (Augoustinos & Walker, 1995; Forgas, Williams, & von Hippel, 2003; Kunda, 1999), and, particularly, on the application of cognitive processing models to clinical phenomena

(Abramson, 1988; Ingram, 1986). More specifically our approach derives from cognitive theories and research that identifies the important role of schema in guiding perception and in generating attitudes, beliefs, and behaviors (Neisser, 1982; Thorndyke & Hayes-Roth, 1979), and on the application of research and theories about the role of schemas in psychological problems by various authors (Beck, 1999; Huesmann, 1988; Mann & Beech, 2003; Young, 1999).

Information processing models distinguish structures, propositions, operations, and products. Cognitive structures refer to the architecture of stored knowledge (i.e., memory). Repeated experiences, stored as memories, lead to the construction of scripts and schemas which are said to be cognitive propositions (Ingram & Kendall, 1986). Scripts are either acquired behavioral sequences (Abelson, 1981) or learned emotional sequences (Fehr & Russell, 1984) that guide the individual's own behavior as well as his expectations about the behavior of others. Schemas are similarly generated by repeated experiences stored in memory. A schema represents a prototypical abstraction or stereotype of a given concept (e.g., a particular category of people) and consists of related knowledge and assumptions about the concept (Thorndyke & Hayes-Roth, 1979). In terms of function, schemas, like scripts, influence attention, perception, emotional responding, and behavior (Bem, 1981; Fiske & Taylor, 1991; Segal, 1988), particularly in situations where there is less than optimal information (Hollon & Garber, 1988). Schemas function as heuristics and include stereotypical views of others.

The processes by which information is perceived and interpreted is referred to as cognitive operations. These operations mediate between the external environment and the individual's schemas and scripts, and generate cognitive products. Cognitive products are generated by the individual by referencing his/her perceptions to his/her stored schemas or scripts. These products are what has generally been referred to in the sexual offender literature as "cognitive distortions" (Abel, Gore, Holland et al., 1989; Bumby, 1996; Neidigh & Kropp, 1992). The possibility of cognitive products being "distorted" (i.e., not a match for what is consensually agreed to be a normative view) is maximized by four factors: (1) the nature of the relevant schema, (2) current needs or desires, (3) current emotional and cognitive states, and (4) diminished available evidence.

Unsatisfactory experiences are likely to generate distorted schema; for example, repeated failures in relationships with women may entrench negative schema about women, about relationships, and about the self. Current needs or desires, such as strong, unsatisfied, sexual desires, may interact with prior schemas about women or children to allow sexual abuse to occur. Similarly, emotional distress is likely to trigger negative schema about women and children, and a transitory loss of self-esteem is likely to do the same. The cognitive products in these cases may suggest that women deserve to be raped, that the man is entitled to have sex if he wants to, or that children (or this particular child) wish to have sex with adults.

When sexual offending is taking place, the offender is typically in an aroused state (a combined product of sexual arousal, general excitement, some degree of fear or anxiety, and possibly generalized anger or feelings of power), which has the effect of diminishing or restricting the range of available information (Cosmides & Tooby, 2000; Izard & Ackerman, 2000). Tversky and Kahneman (1974) showed that under conditions of uncertainty people adopt shortcuts to process information and make judgments; that is, they ignore some features of the environment and focus only on limited aspects that serve their current needs. Ward, Hudson, and Marshall (1995), relying on Baumeister's (1991) concept of "cognitive deconstruction," suggested that sexual offenders during the offense process typically shut down concerns about abstract issues (e.g., right and wrong, a concern for others, long-term consequences) and focus only on the procedural steps necessary to meet their current desires. Alerting sexual offenders to the early steps in their offense pathway before a cognitively deconstructed state is engaged and reminding them of the possible negative consequences to themselves (as per our "covert association" procedure) will hopefully serve to abort the pathway.

Challenging every instance of a manifestation of the client's underlying schemas (i.e., his cognitive products), offering alternative more prosocial views, and having the client repeatedly rehearse in group these alternative views (i.e., attitudes and perceptions) should eventually change the schemas. In addition, helping clients understand the likely origins of their schemas (derived from their autobiography and further elaborated in discussions of their relationship history) can help them see why they hold such views and how these views and perceptions work to their personal disadvantage. As Young, Klosko, and Weishaar (2003) pointed out, dysfunctional coping styles generate the negative emotions that provide the need to maintain maladaptive schemas; enhancing coping skills and entrenching an effective coping style should therefore contribute to the modification of maladaptive schemas. Our approach to modifying cognitive distortions is a match for Young et al.'s (2003) schema therapy.

Emotional Skills

The third aspect of our program concerns the development of emotional (and thereby more general) self-regulation. There is now a considerable body of literature on self-regulation (Baumeister & Vohs, 2004) and also on emotions (Lewis & Haviland-Jones, 2000) and emotional expression (Kennedy-Moore & Watson, 1999). Research on emotions has demonstrated a clear relationship between mood control and social judgment (Forgas & Vargas, 2000), general well-being (Diener & Lucas, 2000), as well as physical health (Booth & Pennebaker, 2000; Leventhal & Patrick-Miller, 2000) and mental health (Keenan, 2000). Similarly the degree of self-regulation, including the regulation of emotions, is significantly related to crime (Hirschi, 2004), the expression of sexual behavior (Wiederman, 2004), the abuse of alcohol and other substances (Hull & Slone, 2004; Sayette, 2004), and the formation of effective attachment relationships (Calkins, 2004). Therapists of various orientations claim that encouraging clients to express their emotions during treatment is essential to effective therapy (Bohart & Tolman, 1998; Goldfried, 1982; Greenberg & Pavio, 1997; Safran & Segal, 1990) and leads to enhanced self-understanding and greater self-acceptance (Roemer & Borkovec, 1994). Therapists need to move clients beyond the easy route of rational and emotionally disengaged analyses of feelings to more active emotional analyses. However, therapists have to make a judgment about when to raise the client's awareness of his feelings and when to encourage reflection.

These observations suggest that developing adequate self-regulatory processes and control over the expression of emotions should diminish the tendency to sexually offend. In addition, in an excellent study of the interplay of emotions and rational thinking during the treatment of sexual offenders, Pfäfflin (in press) has demonstrated that maximal treatment change occurs when a rational understanding of an issue is accompanied by emotional expression. Thus, appropriate emotional expression during treatment facilitates the achievement of within-treatment goals (e.g., reduced distortions, enhanced empathy).

Consistent with this orientation, our program takes a self-management approach to dealing with potential postrelease risks. Most importantly, our self-management component emphasizes the development of a healthy lifestyle within which it should be possible to achieve the client's individually designed good life plans. Evidence indicates that the achievement of such personal goals is significantly related to emotional regulation (Baumeister & Vohs, 2004). It has been shown, for example, that goals are readily achieved when a person maintains a positive emotional state, whereas negative emotional states are associated with the failure to achieve personal goals (Carver & Scheier, 1990).

It is important to note that regulatory control over the appropriate expression of emotions is dependent on the accuracy with which a person is able to recognize his own emotions and those of others (Harris, 2000).

The ability to recognize emotions in themselves and in others is related to the frequency with which people feel confident to discuss emotions (Harris, 2000), which typically has its beginning in the free discussion of emotions occurring in the person's family of origin (Dunn, Brown, & Beardsall, 1991). Inhibited emotional expression (i.e., the "bottling-up" of emotions) produces damaging psychophysiological consequences (Pennebaker, 1997), whereas uncontrolled emotional expression is destructive of interpersonal relationships (Anderson & Guerrero, 1998), impairs active coping (Carver, Scheier & Weintraub, 1989), and intensifies distress (Laird, 1974). Emotional insight (i.e., the ability to recognize one's own emotions and the emotions of others) is necessary to direct thoughts and actions (Mayer & Salovey, 1997) and is essential to the regulation of emotions (Mayer & Gaschke, 1988). The first step in our empathy component which trains each client in recognizing emotions in themselves and in others, and our encouragement of emotional expression accompanied by feedback throughout treatment, is aimed at increasing effective emotional regulation. Understanding and regulating emotions allows people to develop and maintain intimacy in relationships (Buck, 1991) and to experience and express empathy toward others (Watson & Greenberg, 1996).

Both Greenberg's emotionally focused therapy (Greenberg & Pavio, 1997) and Kennedy-Moore and Watson's (1999) approach to enhancing emotional expressiveness in therapy, offer treatment approaches aimed at developing emotional self-regulation. To these approaches we have added components derived from the above review of the literature on emotions (Lewis & Haviland-Jones, 2000) and self-regulatory processes (Baumeister & Vohs, 2004).

This, then, ends our summary of the literature on which we rely for the skill training aspects of our treatment approaches to modifying the problematic behavioral, cognitive, and emotional aspects of our clients. We have attempted to show how each target of our program involves each of these three aspects and how our overall program integrates each treatment target within this behavioral, cognitive, and emotional framework.

HOW SKILLS ARE TAUGHT

Treatment involves a combination of didactic instruction (quite limited), role plays, modeling, group discussion, written exercises, shaping, over-learning, rehearsal, self-monitoring, and a high level of interpersonal interaction with treatment providers and other group members. The use of verbal encouragement serves as the primary method of reinforcing desired behaviors, but we also occasionally use access to enjoyable activities (e.g., discussion of the prior day's sports matches or a particular movie) at the end of a treatment session when that seems useful. The use of a wide array and variety of methods is a basic principle of adult learning. Therapists model both appropriate interpersonal skills and problem-solving techniques as well as prosocial attitudes, and they are appropriately attentive to issues of responsivity. It is also recognized that the emotional tone of the treatment environment is important.

Sequence and Time Allotted to Skills Building

The program begins with an initial orientation and an introduction to treatment, which functions as the starting point for the therapeutic collaboration.

In this initial orientation, confidentiality issues are outlined and both a confidentiality agreement and a consent to treatment form are signed by both the clients and therapist. The goals of treatment are identified, and each target (e.g., autobiography, disclosure, empathy) and its content are described as well as listed on a series of posters hung in sequence around the walls of the group room. Essentially, the content of these posters is a match for what is described in this chapter under each of the targets of treatment. It is emphasized to all group members that they must contribute to the discussions of all topics and that passive observation is not acceptable. Full active participation not only increases the likelihood that all clients will absorb the materials, but it also provides evidence of how well they have assimilated each of the issues.

Because we operate as a rolling program, the sequence of addressing treatment targets unfolds for each client rather than across a set block of time for all clients. While each client deals with each issue in much the same sequence (i.e., self-esteem, life history, acceptance of responsibility, pathways to offending, victim empathy/harm, social skills, coping and mood management, deviant sexual arousal, and self-management plans), in any one session different issues will be focused on for different clients. Furthermore, since all clients are required to participate in every discussion, and to challenge each other, each client is repeatedly exposed to each issue. The therapist models appropriate challenging, which involves supportively encouraging each client to question his current perspective and to consider alternative ways of construing the issue in question. When challenging someone else, each client typically draws on his own experience, and as a consequence, further enhances his own understanding and skills. This approach to treatment facilitates the achievement of a cohesive group climate, and since the program runs continuously throughout the year without breaks, the group climate tends to be maintained. Since group cohesiveness is vital to producing beneficial effects with sexual offenders (Beech & Fordham, 1997; Beech & Hamilton-Giachritsis, 2005), we make every effort to ensure that it is achieved and maintained.

As all aspects of the program involve the acquisition of behavioral, cognitive, and emotional skills, the time devoted to skill acquisition is equal to the total treatment hours plus practice time between sessions. It is, therefore, difficult to estimate the total time clients spend in acquiring skills but it is in excess of 130 hours for the offense-specific program (including between-sessions practice and homework). Readers need to keep in mind that our clients also participate in offense-related programs such as anger management, substance abuse, reasoning rehabilitation, and parenting. Extensive treatment activities are designed to be practiced by clients between treatment sessions (see Homework at the end of each of the component descriptions under Specific Targets in this chapter) either in the context of the prison or in visits (conjugal and others).

TREATMENT METHODS

General Features

As mentioned earlier, our approach employs a rolling (or open-ended) program with clients remaining in treatment until they either reach acceptable levels of functioning on the targets of treatment or until we feel we cannot make any further gains. These determinations are based on the primary therapist completing our therapist rating scale and then presenting the case and the justifications for the ratings at our weekly clinical meeting.

Retaining clients until the therapist ratings indicate they have reached satisfactory levels of functioning is quite important, since Marques, Wiederanders, Day et al. (2005) have recently shown that those sexual offenders who met the goals of treatment (or "got it" as they described it) had markedly lower recidivism rates than did those who failed to achieve the goals of treatment.

Clients are told that to the degree to which they effectively participate in treatment they will have a greater chance of achieving happier and more fulfilled lives in the future than they did in the past. We indicate to clients that to the degree to which they succeed in becoming more fulfilled and happy in their day-to-day living, these changes will reduce the risk that they will reoffend in the future. While this accurately depicts what we aim for in treatment, it is presented at the beginning of the program to enhance motivation. During this discussion all other group members, who of course have already experienced this opening segment, are required to give the newcomer encouragement and to express their feelings about the value of the program. Of course, in pursuing these goals we do not ignore the need to identify potential future risks and to develop strategies to deal with these risks. It is just that our emphasis is on helping clients find better, more personally satisfying ways to live.

We then point out that in order to determine what knowledge, skills, attitudes, and self-beliefs they need to acquire to build toward the attainment of a fulfilling life, we must first examine in detail what they did prior to and during their offense, what their life history has been to this point, and how they view their victim and his/her suffering. We then briefly describe each of the targets of treatment that will be addressed in the program. In addition, these targets, and some of the steps involved in each, are posted on the walls of the treatment room to indicate to newcomers, and to remind continuing participants, of the issues that will be covered. This is also meant to show them that the whole program is integrated and to discourage them from thinking that the components or targets are independent of one another.

In pursuit of these attempts to motivate our clients we also assist them in generating a cost-benefit analysis of both continuing to offend or living an offense-free lifestyle. Although sexual offenders can usually identify quite readily the costs of offending in terms of being caught and punished, they typically have not considered the stress offending has generated in their lives and the work involved in keeping their offending secret. Having to lie much of the time about where they were and what they were doing, as well as having to manipulate others and the victim in order to set up situations to offend, not only requires effort, careful attention to detail, and a good memory, it is frequently unsuccessful and always tiring. Making explicit the personal benefits of successful treatment and the costs associated with continued offending, we believe enhances the motivation of our clients to change. We have evidence from one of our other programs that such tactics effectively move clients from the early stages of Prochaska and DiClemente's (1994) motivational model to the later, more treatment-engaging stages, and that it raises their hope for the future as well as their sense of self-efficacy (see Marshall & Moulden, 2005, for a detailed description of that program).

We also explain to clients the boundaries of confidentiality. They are told that they must not disclose to anyone what is said in the group or who is a member of the group. We also apprise them of the limits to our confidentiality; that is, we must report all salient issues to authorities, including any revelations of undetected offending they make, but only if the information is sufficiently detailed to allow an investigation to proceed.

Throughout the whole program all group members are required to participate in all discussions even if the topics concern issues they have already addressed, or even if they have not yet gotten to that point in treatment themselves. Sometimes lack of participation is due to shyness, anxiety, or lack of skills. For such clients we may develop a specific additional program that teaches them relaxation exercises and possibly involves desensitization (see Marshall & Segal, 1988). In cases of timidity we still insist the clients participate, although our expectations for them may initially be lower than for others. We might initially reward these clients for lesser degrees of participation than would be our standard for others. If the client is disruptive in any way, or is either generally hostile or hostile toward another group member, or is argumentative or oppositional, then we will address the issues openly. If these attempts to deal with problems do not resolve them and the client continues to be disruptive, then he will be suspended for 2 weeks to reflect on his behavior. When he reenters treatment, if he is still problematic his participation will be terminated. Suspensions are rare and, over the past 14 years only eight clients have been terminated. Of those eight, four sought reentry within a year and participated appropriately when readmitted.

It should be noted that all our clients participate in other programs that address additional identified aspects of their difficulties, such as substance abuse, family violence, anger management, and the Reasoning and Rehabilitation Program (formerly known as Cognitive Skills). We refer to these as "offense-related" treatment targets while the issues addressed in the sexual offenders' program are described as "offense-specific" targets (Marshall, Anderson & Fernandez, 1999). Table 2.1 describes both these sets of targets, although the list of offense-related targets does not exhaust all the possible relevant targets since some clients have quite idiosyncratic problems that are at least tangentially related to their offending.

It is important to point out that while we consider the offense-specific targets to be critical, the group discussions of these issues often reveal additional problems or a broader scope to each aspect of their targeted problem than was previously realized. Clients also often bring outside issues to treatment sessions. For example, they may be having difficulties in a divorce process or they may complain about an argument they had with prison staff. We see the discussions of these external issues as opportunities to illuminate the dysfunctional ways our clients respond to problems in their lives and therefore as opportunities for them to learn more adaptive ways to behave and think. Some clinicians respond to clients raising so-called "nontherapy issues" as if they are not relevant to the treatment process and they inform the clients that these issues are not part of the group program. Clients are told to deal with such problems themselves or with the

TABLE 2.1   Targets of Treatment

OFFENSE-SPECIFIC TARGETS	OFFENSE-RELATED TARGETS
1. Autobiography	1. Substance use/abuse
2. Self-esteem	2. Anger management
3. Acceptance of responsibility	3. Parenting skills
- Denial/minimizations	4. Cognitive skills (now called
- Schema (cognitive distortions)	"Reasoning and
- Victim harm	rehabilitation")
- Empathy	5. Spiritual issues
4. Offense pathways	6. Other psychological problems
5. Coping styles/skills	
6. Social skills	
- Anger	
- Anxiety	
- Assertiveness	
- Intimacy/loneliness	
- Attachments	
7. Sexual interests	
8. Self-management plans	
- Avoidance strategies	
- Good life plans	
- Warning signs (self and others)	
- Support groups (professional and personal)	
- Release plans (work, accommodation, leisure activities)	

help of someone else. We believe this is an inappropriate response and results in the therapist missing an opportunity to learn more about a client's thinking and behavior, as well as causing the client to miss an opportunity to learn.

The following section describes the offense-specific targets.

SPECIFIC TARGETS

Self-Esteem

Our first target is the enhancement of self-esteem, although this target is addressed and revisited throughout the program. We target self-esteem in the early stages of treatment primarily to facilitate active participation and to enhance the clients' belief in their capacity to change as well as increasing their commitment to change. Evidence from the more general literature indicates that people low in self-esteem underestimate their capacity to change, that they are afraid of change, are unlikely to practice tasks set for them, and that they readily give up in the face of minor obstacles (Baumeister, 1993). Also Miller (1983) demonstrated that enhancing the self-esteem of problem drinkers was a necessary prerequisite for behavior change to occur and, particularly, to be maintained. Similarly, Cliska (1990) and Heatherton and Polivy (1991), found that increasing the self-esteem of dieters markedly reduced relapse rates. Of course, the evidence on Bandura's (1977) notion of the related concept of self-efficacy indicates that enhancement of the belief in a capacity to change is essential to achieving the goals of treatment with a wide range of problems. We have found that increases in the self-efficacy of sexual offenders results in an increased motivation to change and in enhanced hope for the future (Moulden, Marshall, & Marshall, 2005).

As a result of our findings (noted in chapter 3) that an acute negative mood could readily be induced in sexual offenders who were very low in self-esteem, we believe that raising self-esteem might provide a protection to these otherwise vulnerable clients.

Enacting the appropriate therapist behaviors (outlined above) and creating a productive group climate, has been shown, by itself, to increase the self-esteem of both sexual offenders (Beech & Fordham, 1997) and nonoffenders (Marshall, Fernandez, Serran et al., 2003; Schaap et al., 1993) involved in group therapy. We insist that our clients do not describe themselves as sexual offenders (or any of the more derogatory colloquial descriptors) but rather as someone who has committed a sexual offense. Distinguishing people from their specific behaviors has a long history in behavior therapy (Thorpe & Olson, 1997). Employing negative self-descriptors increases shame (i.e., "I am a bad person"), whereas describing oneself as a person who has committed an offense increases guilt (i.e., "I have done a bad thing"). Shame is an obstacle to change whereas guilt facilitates efforts to change (Bumby, Marshall, & Langton, 1999; Proeve, 2003; Proeve & Howells, 2005). Prior to treatment, sexual offenders characteristically display shame rather than guilt about their offenses and their feelings of shame are significantly correlated with their levels of self-esteem (Sparks, Bailey, Marshall, & Marshall, 2003).

In addition to ensuring that therapists enact the appropriate therapeutic styles and create the appropriate climate, we also employ several specific procedures that we have previously shown to be effective in enhancing self-esteem in a group of nonoffending community subjects who described themselves as seriously lacking a sense of self-worth (Marshall & Christie, 1982; Marshall, Christie, Lanthier, & Cruchley, 1982). These procedures require the clients to (a) become sensitized to everyday moderately pleasurable activities and then increase the frequency with which they engage in these activities; (b) increase the range and frequency of their social activities; and (c) identify 8 to 10 positive statements about themselves, write them on a pocket-sized card to carry with them, and then repeat each of these statements three times on three different occasions each day in the context of engaging in a pleasurable or social activity. Other group members are required to assist in identifying the target client's positive qualities for this exercise, and they and the therapist compliment the client on these qualities. Most people low in self-esteem find it difficult to accept compliments (Baumeister, 1993), so we ensure that their positive qualities are pointed out to them in group and we instruct them to respond appropriately to these compliments. Checks are made at each session to ensure the client is following the requirements and again input from other participants is helpful.

Homework: The required between-sessions homework for this target of treatment involves (1) identifying pleasurable activities and increasing the frequency with which they engage in these pleasurable activities on a regular basis; (2) increasing the range and frequency of social activities; and (3) identifying and rehearsing daily each of their positive self-statements. At each treatment session, a check is made to ensure the client is following these requirements. Feedback from other group members and nontreatment staff can confirm or deny that the client is, indeed, practicing the required behaviors.

Acceptance of Responsibility

Some sexual offenders categorically deny they committed the offense(s) for which they have been convicted. Others minimize various aspects of the offense in a way that presents them as less culpable. Of course, it is possible that some of the categorical deniers are telling the truth, since wrongful convictions have been identified. However, clear cases of wrongful convictions are statistically rare. Similarly, to describe some aspects of a sexual offender's report of his offense as "minimizations" relies on an unquestioning acceptance of the veridicality of the victim's statement or the police officer's report. Despite these caveats, clinicians working with sexual offenders quite properly assume that their clients will likely distort their presentation of the offense in a self-serving way. It is best to keep in mind, however, that some aspects of the discrepancy between the offender's report and that of the victim may reflect errors on both their parts. Attempts to essentially bully clients into producing precisely the same description of events as the victim may not only be misplaced but are likely to force the offender into saying what he thinks the assessor or therapist wishes to hear.

For clients who deny having committed an offense and who refuse to enter treatment aimed at overcoming their denial, we have developed an alternative Deniers' program (Marshall, Thornton, Marshall et al., 2001). This Deniers' program is mentioned here, but not fully described, so that readers will understand that we attempt to engage in treatment all sexual offenders who are referred to us. If an offender appears to be equivocating about his guilt, we take him into our regular program but modify our strategies somewhat. If an offender indicates he did (or probably did) commit the offense(s) but has suffered a loss of memory for the events, we accept him into treatment. Once the client is in treatment, we employ the specific strategy we have developed (described in chapter 5) to enhance recall.

Initially, any move (however small) in the direction of an acceptance of responsibility by our clients is rewarded. As the client makes progress, larger steps are required before he is complimented. There are, of course, many aspects to the full acceptance of responsibility but issues of denial and minimization are critical.

Aspects of denial and minimizations are focused on early in treatment but continue to be addressed as they arise throughout treatment. The same is true of the so-called "cognitive distortions" (i.e., attitudes, beliefs, and perceptions). We construe cognitive distortions as the products of underlying schemas elicited by current internal (e.g., mood states, intoxication) and external (e.g., who they are with) circumstances. Similarly, we see denial and attempts to minimize their offenses or responsibilities as reflecting currently activated schemas about the self (e.g., schemas of shame). Such attempts to reduce responsibility are attempts to defend their image of themselves. In some cases, offenders have a need to be seen by others, and perhaps also by themselves, as "perfect" and as having no flaws. Such a self-schema is almost always personally damaging.

In attempting to modify schemas (including schemas of the self) we attempt, by repeatedly challenging the overt distortions and by asking the client if he can recognize how his specific distortions are connected, to have him recognize the interrelatedness of these distorted thoughts, attitudes, and perceptions (see Langton & Marshall, 2000; Mann & Shingler, 2005). A discussion with each client, meant to identify the possible origins of his maladaptive schemas and how their expression is related to transitory emotional states and to increases in sexual desire, is helpful. This latter aspect is clarified by a collaborative discourse between the client, the therapists, and the rest of the group. As in all discussions, all group members are specifically prompted, if need be, to participate.

Our goal here, and for all treatment targets, is to have each client develop a generic disposition toward the issues. We do not want a client, for example, to simply work at eliminating his view that women are sexually manipulative. We want him to recognize that this and other negative attitudes toward women are all related and stem from an underlying negative schema about women. Moreover, we want the client to see a relationship between a host of negative maladaptive ways of viewing his world and to recognize the costs to himself and others of these negative schemas.

The initial focus on the acceptance of responsibility occurs in the context of the client giving a disclosure of his offense(s). In the case of multiple victims or offenses, we select at most two offenses that seem prototypical. Some sexual offender therapists and researchers appear to believe it is necessary to know about every offense the client has committed, including those not reported in the official records, and to know the total number of victims each offender has had (Ahlmeyer, Heil, McKee, & English, 2000; Heil, Ahlmeyer, & Simons, 2003). Although it is not made clear why this information is vital, presumably it is so that each offender can be made to take responsibility for his complete offense history. There is, however, no evidence to indicate that requiring clients to admit to every detail of every offense reduces subsequent reoffending. Hanson and Bussière (1998), for example, found no relationship between any aspect of denial and later reoffending. It seems likely to us that requiring an exhaustive account of every aspect of every offense would be seen by the offender as a continuation of the legal and punitive process. We doubt such a process would enhance the client–therapist relationship or that it would be productive in terms of treatment.

As each client discloses his offense, the therapist asks questions aimed at probing for details. Our experience is that most clients have told and retold (or rehearsed in imagination) their account of their offense in rather broad terms, not in the details dear to the heart of a behaviorist. It is for these highly specific details that we probe. This tactic characteristically catches the client unprepared and it frequently leads to him divulging information about the offense that was not previously known or to revealing greater responsibility than he had previously admitted. When asking probing questions the therapist adopts a stance of supportive and collaborative inquiry and encourages all other group members to similarly ask for details. Because our program operates as a rolling format, most members of the group will have sufficient experience in the program to know they are expected to actively participate and to supportively challenge one another, but encouragement from the therapist is occasionally required, particularly for new entrants.

Once the client's initial disclosure is complete, he is given approval for his efforts. Even if his disclosure has been less than adequate, he is still encouraged for his effort. The therapist indicates to the client that giving a disclosure is difficult and requires a certain amount of courage. However, the client is also told that this is just the first disclosure and that more discussions and disclosures will be required. At the next disclosure, the official information from police and victim statements (and court records if necessary) is shared with the client. The police reports and victim statements are all available to us and are nowadays quite detailed, providing information rarely described by the offender's first disclosure. Discrepancies between his disclosure and the official information are then discussed. This discussion is posed to the client in the form of collaborative inquiry and as necessary for the therapist to be clear so that he/she can best assist the client to deal with his problems. At all challenges, which are done in a firm but supportive manner, it is made clear to the client that such challenges are done with one goal in mind, as is everything we do in the group: that is, to help him learn to live a personally more satisfying and fulfilling future life that is also offense free. Most clients fail to provide a satisfactory disclosure at their first attempt so they are required to repeat it, hopefully modified by feedback, at subsequent sessions until it is satisfactorily close to the official version, or as close as this particular offender is likely to get at this stage. In fact, issues related to full disclosure and the acceptance of responsibility recur throughout treatment so the initial disclosures are really only first steps. For example, when discussing harm to the victim during the later empathy segment, issues are inevitably raised that refer to full disclosure and acceptance of responsibility, and this is true for the discussion of all issues.

If a client has difficulty accepting the victim's account of the offense, he is asked to participate in role-play exercises in which he plays the victim and the therapist portrays the offender in a discussion of what took place in the lead up to and during the offense. We do not role-play actual enactments of the offense because there have been suggestions that such enactments can result in problems (Pithers, 1997) and because we have shown that they do not add to the benefits derived from treatment (Webster, Bowers, Mann, & Marshall, 2005). In addition, we focus on the victim's verbal and nonverbal behaviors in order to infer the victim's perceptions and emotional responses, rather than concerning ourselves with the sexual details of the offense. These latter features are not ignored but are rather de-emphasized to diminish the likelihood that group members might be aroused by them.

During subsequent repetitions of the client's disclosure, he typically expresses distorted perceptions, offense-supportive attitudes, and other distorted thoughts. These distortions (perceptions, attitudes, thoughts) are challenged in a supportive but firm manner. As noted, evidence of distortions and a failure to take responsibility appear throughout treatment and they are not only consistently challenged, they are reframed in prosocial terms. Evidence of distortions also comes from accounts of interactions with other inmates or staff in the institution. When a client either acts inappropriately toward staff or expresses anger or distress when a staff member will not accede to the client's wishes, the therapist uses this to illustrate the underlying schema or the generic behavioral script that is guiding the client's overt response. Indeed, no opportunity is missed to assist the client in recognizing his maladaptive schema or his generic problematic scripts, and he is helped to see the connections between these more general responses and his offenses.

In attempting to modify dysfunctional schema, we have adapted our approach from descriptions provided by Sperry (1999) and Young et al. (2003) in their work with personality disordered clients, which to some extent parallels the program developed by Buschman and van Beek (2003) for personality disordered sexual offenders. The first step requires the therapist to allow the client to become sufficiently emotional for the dysfunctional views to become evident. In the more commonly employed cognitive behavioral approach with sexual offenders, the level of analysis tends to emphasize rationality at the expense of emotional expression. Not only does this miss opportunities for the client to develop emotional self-regulation, but it also ensures that offense-related schema will remain unexpressed. We encourage emotional expression throughout treatment and we attempt to challenge our clients' thinking in a way that produces some degree of emotional arousal, but not so much arousal as to overwhelm the client or to produce problematic levels of anger. This is a balance that can be achieved by communicating support while at the same time being firmly challenging. Once emotional states are engaged the client's offense-related cognitions emerge.

When the client expresses these problematic cognitions (attitudes, beliefs, and perceptions), the therapist employs the following strategies. First, the client is assisted in clearly identifying these cognitions and in understanding that they emerge only when he is distressed in some way. In this way he can see that these cognitions are state dependent and do not describe his normal functioning. This helps the client distinguish himself as he usually is (i.e., as a prosocial person) from his state when he offends.

Next, the therapist helps the client recognize the schemas that link together all of the dysfunctional (or distorted) cognitions he has expressed. Once agreement is achieved on the nature of the schema, the therapist works with the client to identify the likely origins of these schemas. For example, negative attitudes toward women may result from the client's experiences with his parents; he may have perceived his mother as judgmental or unloving or he may have seen her as failing to protect him from his cruel or condemnatory father. These negative attitudes may have resulted from bad experiences in adolescent or adult relationships with females. Whatever the assumed origins, the client is encouraged to view these past experiences in a way that does not determine his present and future life.

The validity of these schemas is then challenged. The client's tendency to overgeneralize from limited instances is questioned. For example, his mother may, from his perspective, have presented an unfortunate model, and he may have viewed his problematic relationships with women as their fault; but no matter how extensive he claims his negative experiences with women to have been, there are many women (surely many he has met) who have not treated him badly. We also attempt to get the client to recognize that his own behavior (and his perceptions) played a role in his past problems, and we encourage him to attempt to take the perspective of the women in his life who he says caused him problems. Finally, we ask the client to write an essay on (or if he is not sufficiently literate, to describe in group) challenges to his dysfunctional schemas. He is to articulate an argument that contradicts each of his dysfunctional schemas.

While this process occurs in the above way early in treatment (i.e., typically during his offense disclosure), dysfunctional schema frequently continue to emerge throughout treatment. Indeed, if they do not it is usually because the client is not being sufficiently challenged to call forth the emotions that trigger dysfunctional schema. For example, if a client becomes upset (distressed or angry), the therapist should continue to question him rather than stop to comfort him unless, of course, the client is incapable of continuing or becomes physically threatening. This can be done in a supportive and caring way even though the client remains upset. Similarly, creating a climate where emotional expression is viewed as normal and acceptable facilitates the likelihood that clients will enter a state where problematic schemas will emerge. Finally, supportive and firm challenges that push clients typically evoke emotional responses. All emotional expressions in treatment should be countenanced and encouraged while at the same time discouraging inappropriate behavioral reactions to these emotions. Whenever dysfunctional schemas emerge the procedures outlined above are reinstated.

Homework: Clients are required to consider, between sessions, the feedback they have received regarding both their disclosures and their expressions of offense-supportive beliefs, attitudes, and perceptions. For those clients who have trouble accepting that their victim's perspective of the offense is legitimate, we ask them to write a description of the offense as though they were the victim; this is meant to complement within-session role-plays. The task is presented to the offender as requiring him to essentially take a devil's advocate position. This essay is read aloud to the group by the therapist and feedback is elicited from all group members with additional comments being provided by the therapist. The client is then required to rewrite the victim's view and it is re-presented to the group. This process is repeated until the essay is deemed to be satisfactory or until it is clear that further progress is unlikely. In addition, clients are required to consider, between sessions, the possible relationships between their various attitudes and perceptions, in order that they can identify and then modify the underlying schemas.

Elaboration of Life History

Sometime within the first two sessions each client is asked to begin the process of producing a written autobiography. This autobiography is to cover important events from his childhood, adolescence, and adult life including: relationships (parental, other family, peers, romantic, sexual), sexual experiences, health, education, work, leisure, and any other issues the client considers to be important. Clients are asked to write (or type) this so that it can be read by the therapist. If the client is illiterate he is asked to identify a person he trusts, and who understands what is required, to act as a scribe. This scribe is carefully instructed to do no more than write, in the client's own words, what the client tells him. For clients who are intellectually disabled, we use a more concrete format by providing the client with a model "life line" that has segments for childhood, adolescence, early adulthood, and later life experiences. A scribe is also identified for these clients.

When a first draft of the autobiography is completed, the therapist reads it to the group (or a synopsis if it is too lengthy) and the content is taken up for discussion and clarification. This discussion provides feedback to the client who then may be asked to revise the autobiography accordingly.

The aim of this exercise is to assist the therapist in better understanding the client, to provide a basis for identifying areas to emphasize in treatment, to generate hypotheses about the client's underlying schema and his need to offend, and to identify potential background factors that will help in building the offender's offense pathways.

Homework: The client is required to produce a written autobiography, which may require revisions as a result of within-session feedback.

Pathways to Offending

What we call "pathways to offending" has traditionally been labeled "offense chain" or "offense cycle." All too often in the literature the discussion under these labels has excessively, and in some cases exclusively, focused on the steps (cognitive, emotional, and behavioral) involved in accessing a victim. We address these steps to offending but we also place emphasis on what we call "background factors." These background factors create a temporary vulnerability, or offense-prone disposition, in the client and set the stage for him to either seek a victim (i.e., begin the steps to offending) or take advantage of an unanticipated opportunity to offend. These background factors are essentially the same as those identified by Hanson and Harris (2000) as stable and acute dynamic risk factors. Since humans are, above all, flexible in seeking to attain their goals we pay somewhat less attention to the details of a putative offense chain (since this is very likely to change from offense to offense) and give rather more attention to both the generic features of the steps to offending (e.g., seeking any opportunities to be alone with children, always ready to recognize a potential adult victim) and the generic characteristics of the background factors. In the latter case, we not only look for general tendencies (e.g., relationship difficulties, repetitive mood swings) but also for the persistent features that trigger the background factors (e.g., what prompts a client to get angry or to set off on a drinking bout).

Relevant background factors typically continue to emerge throughout the treatment process but they particularly arise from the client's offense disclosure and autobiography. The types of background factors we attempt to help the offender identify are those that put him in an emotional state or a state of mind where he disregards the considerations (e.g., the possibility of getting caught or of harming a victim) that might otherwise constrain his deviant behavior. We have likened this to a state of "cognitive deconstruction" (Ward, Hudson, & Marshall, 1995), wherein people focus only on the steps necessary to the attainment of an immediately desired goal (typically one they would customarily eschew) and set aside consideration of other issues that might prevent them from pursuing the goal.

Background factors that place the client in a state where concern about the immediate satisfaction of his desires is paramount characteristically involve the same factors that have been shown to trigger deviant sexual fantasies. These include any combination of the following: relationship conflict, other relationship stressors, rejection, financial or work-related stress, various mood states (both negative and positive), low sense of self-worth, boredom, emotional loneliness, and feeling humiliated or oppressed. In addition to these somewhat distal factors, more immediate factors likely to trigger the steps to offending include anger or other transitory mood states, as well as intoxication (alcohol or other drugs) and engaging in deviant sexual thoughts, all of which often occur as an immediate response to the more distal background factors. All of these background factors are modifiable and are addressed in subsequent treatment, either in our program or as a result of referral to another specialized program (e.g., anger management, substance abuse).

The first step in outlining a client's pathway to offending is to assist him in identifying his relevant background factors. Many of these factors will be apparent from a careful read of the client's autobiography or gleaned from the to-and-fro of the discussion around his self-esteem and disclosure. However, in working on modifying the factors that have already been identified, new ones may emerge so the pathway may be changed at any time throughout treatment. Next, we help clients develop alternative ways of construing these background factors (attributions that point to ways they can change rather than seeing these factors as beyond their control). We also get them to generate ways to reduce the likelihood that these problems will arise in the future and to deal more effectively with them when they do arise. In the rest of our program we attempt to provide the skills and attitudes necessary for our clients to reduce the frequency of, and deal effectively with, these background factors.

Examining the client's offense disclosure and his autobiography also serves as a basis for building, along with the client, the range of steps and strategies he has typically used to access a victim. In Pithers' (1990) statement on relapse prevention he outlined a single pathway that he believed represented the prototypical route to offending by all sexual offenders. Since this seemed to contradict clinical experience, Ward and his colleagues (Ward & Siegert, 2002; Ward & Sorbello, 2003) outlined a model proposing that sexual offenders follow one of five pathways to offending. While each of the proposed pathways is familiar to clinicians dealing with sexual offenders, Ward's discussion seems to imply that each offender will consistently follow one particular pathway. This appears to contradict everyday observations of human behavior, which clearly suggests that people who are successful at whatever endeavor they pursue (in this case, unfortunately, it is the sexual abuse of others) employ a flexible approach. There may be a first choice plan but the successful person has both backup plans and the adaptability to act on whatever opportunities are available. Presumably the influence of various background factors, which may differ from offense to offense, produces a similar versatility of responses. It would be easier if each sexual offender did follow the same single pathway, as was suggested in the original version of the relapse prevention model (Pithers, 1990), or if they followed only one of five possible pathways, as suggested by Ward and his colleagues. This however, seems remarkably unlikely.

Since it seems certain that sexual offenders do not function so inflexibly, we consider it necessary to have each client develop a generic attitude to the description of the possible paths he might follow in order to offend. As mentioned earlier, we assume that while each offender has developed a characteristic set of ways to be alone with a victim, he can also be expected to adopt ad hoc strategies as the situation demands. Thus, when we are having the client generate his "pathways to offending" we consistently remind him that such an outline will simply illustrate his typical approach. If necessary, we illustrate this by asking the client what other response he might have made to each step along the way of accessing his victim. We do this here (and, as will be seen later, we also do this when constructing self-management plans) so that the client does not conclude that if he simply avoids these specific steps in the future, he will not reoffend. Our goal is to get each client to see that he has in the past been flexible in seeking a victim by adjusting to unpredictable circumstances. We want him to recognize that this means there may be situations arising in the future that he has not yet experienced and they may place him at risk.

Identifying the offender's typical pathways to offending at this stage allows the remainder of treatment to be more appropriately focused on enhancing the skills, attitudes, perceptions, and feelings that are necessary for each individual to achieve an offense-free life. Of course, throughout treatment other aspects relevant to the offense pathways emerge and as a result the pathways and treatment focus must be adjusted. This is particularly true of attitudes and perceptions and their associated emotions. Homework: Between sessions each client is required to give thought to and generate a list of his relevant background factors, his state at the time of the offense, and the steps he took to gain access to his victim(s).

Victim Empathy/Harm

Our approach to the understanding and treatment of empathy is based on our model of empathic processes first outlined by Marshall, Hudson, Jones, and Fernandez (1995) (Figure 2.1) and elaborated on by Marshall (2002) (Figure 2.2).

This latter model suggests that some people fail to display empathy because the sight of another person in distress upsets them so much they give full focus to reducing their own distress. This might be expected to characterize the client's responses when issues of victim harm are raised. These individuals clearly have emotional dysregulation problems, extreme emotional vulnerability, and possibly a narcissistic response to the world. Still others fail to respond empathically because they either dislike or are hostile toward the distressed person (or who the distressed person represents to them), or they disregard the other person's distress in order to achieve their own ends. Among these individuals are those who are either psychopathic or are experiencing anger directed toward, or displaced toward, the distressed person. Sadistic individuals would also fit into this category, although they are not hostile to their victims but rather derive pleasure from the suffering of others. The majority of sexual offenders, however, are neither psychopathic, sadistic, nor hostile toward their victim. Either they respond with distress or defensiveness

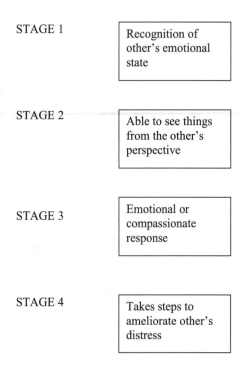

FIGURE 2.1   Earliest stage model of empathy.

when victim harm is raised, or their own needs override the possibility of them feeling any concern toward their victims. This allows sexual offenders to suspend empathy toward their victims, at least while they are abusing them. Thus, the majority of sexual offenders appear to fit into either the top or the middle row of our empathy model depicted in Figure 2.2. It is only those individuals who follow the lower pathway in Figure 2.2 who display empathy. Few, but some, sexual offenders express a fully empathic response to their victims during assessment and treatment, although even these clients apparently suspended these concerns while they were offending.

Some of the sexual offenders who fit into the middle pathway of our empathy model (i.e., the psychopaths, the sadists, and the hostile offenders) present difficulties in treatment since sensitizing them to the suffering of victims might add to the pleasure they derive from offending. Surprisingly, we have had no more problems in dealing with empathy among the psychopathic offenders than we have had with nonpsychopathic offenders. Psychopathic offenders appear to respond to our approach in much the same way as the others. For the hostile offenders, we first examine the reasons why they are hostile to potential victims. We

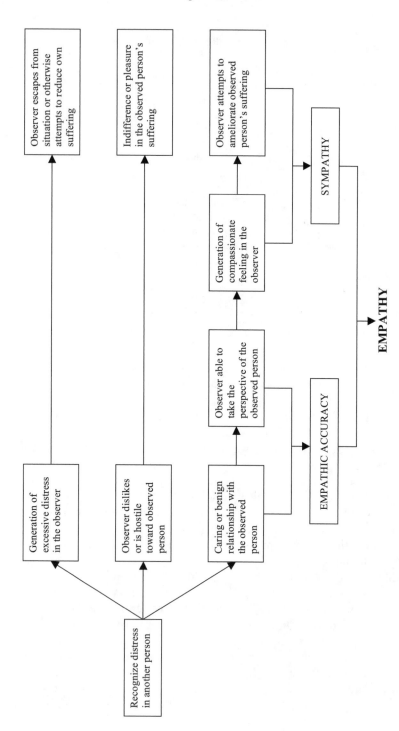

FIGURE 2.2   Expanded model of empathy. From Marshall (2002).

consider the underlying schemas and their origins, and through discussions and feedback, we attempt to extinguish this hostility. In our discussions we attempt to elicit some limited degree of the hostility so that we can more readily understand its meaning and use this opportunity to help the client begin the process of learning to modulate his emotions. Of course, participation in other programs aimed at addressing anger or violent tendencies also facilitates the achievement of our immediate goal with these clients. Once hostility is reduced, we follow the path of addressing empathy deficits outlined below.

Sadistic offenders present the greatest difficulties. Genuine sexual sadists (if such individuals can be reliably identified) gain pleasure (supposedly sexual in nature) from the suffering of their victims, so that alerting them to the extent of victim suffering would be problematic without first modifying this disposition. Accordingly, we engage these clients (thankfully, they are very few in number) in a process that aims to reduce this tendency by highly personalizing the victims of sexual abuse. We ask them to consider someone for whom they have strong affectionate feelings being a victim of sexual abuse. We then make the point that all victims of sexual abuse have people in their lives who love them. This aspect of our approach rests on a remarkable single-case analysis of a sadist by Barbaree (1990). Barbaree measured this man's sexual arousal to descriptions of consenting sex, rape, and nonsexual physical abuse of three different women: his ex-wife; a female friend who still offered him support but also supported his ex-wife; and, finally, his current female partner. He expressed very strong hostility toward his ex-wife, some, but markedly less, hostility toward his female friend, and very warm affectionate feelings toward his current partner. When his current partner was the subject in the sexual scenarios, this man showed strong sexual responses to consenting sex with her but no arousal to raping her. When the woman in the scenarios was his friend, he showed somewhat diminished overall arousal that was equal to both consenting and rape scenes. When his ex-wife was the target person he showed no arousal to consenting sex, significant arousal to rape, and full erections to the scene where she was being nonsexually assaulted. Even sadists, it appears, constrain their sexual sadism to women they love.

As part of this individual treatment, we have the sadistic client implement the behavioral procedures that are described later under the heading Deviant Sexual Interests/Arousal. All sexual sadists are also referred to the institutional psychiatrist for consideration of their suitability for the use of antiandrogens. The psychiatrist's administration of medications proceeds in step with the sadistic offender's involvement in group treatment and is integrated with that work. Whether or not we are successful with sexual sadists remains unknown, as we have not had sufficient numbers of these offenders complete our program and be released into the community; we simply do the best we can given the current state of understanding, limited though that is.

Our model describing an ideal empathic response is a four-stage unfolding process (Marshall, Hudson, Jones, & Fernandez, 1995). The first stage involves the recognition of distress in another person. As we have seen, our research has shown that sexual offenders are deficient at recognizing emotions in others (Hudson, Marshall, Wales et al., 1993), and our clinical experience suggests that sexual offenders are not good at recognizing their own emotions. Accordingly, the first step in enhancing empathy is to increase the ability of our clients to recognize emotions in themselves and in others.

We begin this process by having each client describe a distressing experience from his past, other than being identified, prosecuted, and imprisoned for his offense. The target offender is encouraged to describe this experience in detail and as emotively as possible. Once he finishes his description, each other group member, in turn, is required to identify the emotions displayed by the target person as he retold his unpleasant experience. Each participant is encouraged to identify an emotion that others have not yet reported. Once this is completed, each group member is then required to describe an emotion he experienced while listening to the target client. Both of these processes (i.e., identifying emotions in the target person and in themselves) are meant to increase their awareness of their own and others' emotions as well as legitimize the expression of emotions within the group. The latter is viewed as important both because research (Beech & Hamilton-Giachritsis, 2005; Pfäfflin, 2005) has shown that the expression of emotions in treatment by sexual offenders facilitates the achievement of treatment goals and because the exercise assists offenders in gaining control (or regulation) of their emotions.

We target both general and specific empathy, but our primary focus is on developing victim empathy through an exploration of the harm that befalls (or may befall) victims of sexual abuse. Our research has encouraged us to believe that the primary empathy deficit in sexual offenders is toward their own victims (Fernandez & Marshall, 2003; Fernandez, Marshall, Lightbody, & O'Sullivan, 1999), although some also have difficulty feeling empathy toward the victims of other, unknown offenders. We construe these findings to indicate that most sexual offenders are not so much devoid of empathy but rather withhold empathy from their victims (i.e., they follow the middle pathway in Figure 2.2). This allows them to continue offending without experiencing as much shame as they otherwise would. Thus, for most of our clients, the apparent empathy deficits are seen as yet another manifestation of their widespread and self-serving cognitive distortions. In overcoming these specific cognitive distortions, the earlier and continuing focus on such issues facilitates the clients' understanding and prepares them to be challenged and to reconsider their views.

To more directly assist them in recognizing these harm-related distortions, however, we engage a three-step exercise. First, a group discussion focuses on eliciting from the group a list of consequences (behavioral, emotional, cognitive, and health-related) that are typically experienced by victims of sexual assault both during and after (short-term and long-term) an assault. The consequences generated by this discussion are listed on a flip chart.

Second, the therapist asks each client to consider the relevance of each of the listed consequences for his own victim. He is also asked to identify any features of his behavior, or features of the victim, or their prior relationship, that may have exacerbated the consequences to the victim. In addition, the client is asked to describe any potential effects that may be experienced by both the victim's family and his own family. His responses to these questions typically lead to challenges from the therapist or the group, until a satisfactory level of responding is achieved. If a client is having difficulty, we will have him write a diary entry as if he is the victim on the morning after the offense. If he is still having difficulties, we employ a role-play where the offender plays the victim as he/she would have been the day after the offense. In this role-play, the offender is required to elaborate the consequences as the victim would if he/she had the opportunity. As noted earlier, we do not use role-play reenactments of the actual offense. For particularly stubborn clients, we ask them to consider the hypothetical situation where someone they love is the victim of sexual abuse. In this latter procedure, the offender is asked to describe how devastated his loved one would be and how this would affect himself. This attempt to personalize sexual offending appears to be effective.

Third, each client is required to write two hypothetical letters (i.e., they are not to be sent to victims): one is supposedly from the victim to the client describing the victim's distress, anger. and confusion; the other is a reply to the victim from the offender wherein he takes full responsibility, acknowledges the victim's distress and anger, indicates that although he betrayed the victim's trust other males are trustworthy, and points out that he is doing everything he can to minimize the chances of reoffending. The aim of the first letter from the victim is to get the client to develop his perspective-taking skills, which Hanson and Scott (1995) have shown is typically deficient. The goal of the second letter is to assist the client in rehearsing a sympathetic response. Both letters are read out to the group by the therapist and the target client is challenged on the adequacy of the contents of the letters. In particular, we want to see an emotional rather than an intellectual tone to these letters, and we want the distress expressed in specific rather than in general terms. For some clients it seems to be more effective to have them write a diary entry that their victim might have written the day after the offense or on the first anniversary of the offense. The expected content of this diary entry, and its purpose, is similar to that of the letters.

Homework: The primary task for between-sessions work is writing the letters from and to the victim or the diary entry. Of course, they are also required to give consideration to the issue of victim harm that has been discussed in treatment sessions and how this relates to their own victim. They may also be required to write down the consequences of a hypothetical offense against someone they love if this is deemed to be necessary.

Social Skills

If a client displays deficits in conversational skills or assertiveness, or is hostile, angry, or anxious, the therapist uses every opportunity throughout the course of treatment to challenge the client and have him practice appropriate behaviors. For example, failure to participate in group discussions is not tolerated even if it is due to anxiety or social ineptitude. Each client is required to respond to every issue and is not permitted to offer one-word responses; this repeated and prolonged exposure to the source of their anxiety (i.e., participating in group discussions) has been shown in studies of socially anxious people to attenuate distress (Marshall & Segal, 1988). Hostility and anger expressed in the group is first legitimized (i.e., the client is told it is appropriate to feel upset) and then the source of the anger or hostility is explored. Once the source is identified, the client is assisted to see that not directly addressing the issue is unhelpful and, if necessary, he is given the chance to role-play a more appropriate way of dealing with the source of the problem. If his response is disproportionate to the problem, a discussion ensues that attempts to help him come to a more realistic, and personally useful, way to respond.

If anxiety is severe, the client is referred to either the institutional psychologist or psychiatrist. If anger and hostility persist and prove disruptive, the client may be withdrawn from the program until he satisfactorily completes the institutional anger management program. Some socially deficient clients are also referred to the "Toastmasters" program in the institution, which is a program run by outside volunteers to train inmates in public speaking. This latter program has been very beneficial for many of our clients. In one of the studies in our series on the treatment of anxiety disorders, we (Hayes & Marshall, 1984) demonstrated that effectively targeting public speaking produced generalizations that

TABLE 2.2   Bartholomew's Adult Attachment Model*

ATTACHMENT STYLE	VIEW OF SELF/ OTHERS	INTERPERSONAL STYLE	INTIMACY LEVEL
Secure	- Positive self - Positive others	-Comfortable with intimacy -Seeks mutual support, reciprocity	-High
Preoccupied	- Negative self - Positive others	-Seeks constant approval of others -Meet affection and security needs through sex -Overly dependent in relationships	-Fluctuating, unfulfilling
Fearful	- Negative self - Negative others	-Desires intimacy -Mistrustful of others, fears closeness, rejection -Keeps partner at a distance to avoid rejection/hurt	-Superficial, unfulfilling
Dismissive	- Positive self - Negative others	-Sees no value in closeness -Autonomous -Minimal disclosure -Blaming, hostile	-Low, often nonexistent

*Adapted from Bartholomew & Horowitz (1991).

diminished anxiety and increased skills in other areas of social functioning. For underassertive clients, we use role-plays that provide an opportunity for the offender to practice appropriately responding to people he has identified as suppressing his assertiveness. This procedure is adopted from Gambrill's (2002) excellent program for enhancing assertiveness.

The primary focus in this part of our program is, however, on building relationship skills. Initially, the therapist outlines the features of secure and insecure attachments styles and identifies the problems associated with the latter, as well as the personal behaviors associated with each style (Table 2.2).

Next, the therapist provides a list of the benefits of achieving satisfactory intimacy (greater sexual, relationship, and life satisfaction, and better physical and mental health) and the problems that emotional loneliness brings. Clients are then assisted in identifying their prototypical attachment style (i.e., secure, anxious-ambivalent, fearful-avoidant, or dismissive-avoidant). This is explored by having the client provide written details of the interactions, problems, and positive features of his current or past relationships. With the help of the therapist and other group members, the client then identifies behaviors and remarks he made during these prior relationships that contributed to either their failure or their dysfunctional nature. This helps him recognize how his insecure attachment style affected his past relationships and how this style will continue to cause problems in the future unless he changes his style.

Of course some of our clients do not have an insecure attachment style but they may in other ways have caused problems or allowed their partners' behaviors to cause problems. On this point it is important to note that attachment styles, while reasonably consistent over time, do fluctuate under conditions of stress or due to changes in the partner's behavior (Horowitz, Rosenberg, & Bartholomew, 1993). When stressed, a person who ordinarily behaves in a secure way may become anxious and constantly seek reassurance from and proximity to his partner. If this is maintained over time, it may cause problems in the relationship. All clients are required to write out a list of their own behaviors (or lack of behaviors) that caused problems in their current or past relationships.

Once the client recognizes his past relationship problems, and how he contributed to them, he is encouraged to believe that he can change once he knows how to function better in relationships. Thus, the next step is to assist clients to better understand effective relationship skills. First, a discussion on human sexuality focuses on sexual activities and other behaviors that maximize mutual satisfaction with the emphasis being on equality, spontaneity, and affection. Because equitability is one of the best predictors of sexual satisfaction, we make sure our clients understand that sexual offenses cannot lead to maximum sexual satisfaction since such offenses are inherently inequitable. For some clients more detailed sex education is required. Many, if not most, of our clients benefit from a limited discussion of normative sexual behaviors. We attempt to diminish sexual prudishness by identifying the full range of normative sexual activities both in terms of their frequency of occurrence in the population at large, as well as in terms of the role such activities may play in maximizing sexual satisfaction. We remind clients repeatedly that equitability in relationships, along with spontaneity, and variability of activities, as well as affectionate interchanges during sex, are the best predictors of sexual satisfaction, which in turn predicts relationship satisfaction and life satisfaction. Remarks on these latter issues are meant to motivate our clients to change.

Next, a consideration of the following topics is engaged: origins of attachment styles (i.e., relationships with parents and early teenage and adult relationship experiences); effective communication; jealousy;

compatibility; and living without a partner. The observation, noted in chapter 1, that sexual offenders have typically had problematic and disruptive childhood relationships with their parents that provided a basis for their adult relationship problems, is quite relevant to treatment. Some treatment providers may assume that correcting the adult attachment style of sexual offenders and training them in intimacy skills will correct the problems these clients have with relationships. We do not believe this to be true. Certainly implementing attachment and intimacy training is necessary, but the childhood experiences of these offenders has typically left them with many unresolved emotional issues that lie at the basis of their adult attachment schemas. Under conditions of stress we can expect these dysfunctional schemas (beliefs about themselves and others and about relationships) to reemerge. To change these dysfunctional schemas it seems to us to be necessary to resolve at least the most important aspects of their unfortunate childhood experiences.

Clients are encouraged to seek out partners with whom they are compatible, rather than identifying potential partners on the basis of looks or other superficial features. They are encouraged to seek age-appropriate partners with whom they share a reasonable number of interests. We emphasize the need to do enjoyable things together with their partners, both because this will contribute to cementing the relationship and because it will produce a more fulfilling life for them. Clients are advised to progress slowly in relationships so they can determine the likely long-term value of the relationship before they fully commit to the potential partner. Suspicious (i.e., unfounded) jealousy and well-founded jealousy are distinguished and the basis for each are considered. Discussion focuses on elucidating these differences, identifying the problems caused by suspicious jealousy, examining the factors that give rise to suspicious jealousy, and on considering what they might do in response to actual infidelity by their partner. If they are in a current relationship, they are asked to write out the positive and negative aspects of this relationship. These are then discussed and suggestions for change are generated. Consideration is given to the many forms of communication that are effective in relationships, the issues that require effective communication, and the importance of equitability and respect in relationships that find expression in communication. Effective communication and patient and respectful discussions of all issues between partners create the equitable climate that ensures sexual, relationship, and life satisfaction.

We also consider with our clients the benefits they might derive from living alone if this seems a real possibility for at least a time after their return to the community. We stress the need to avoid rushing into a relationship just to avoid being alone, and we also encourage them to recognize that being without a partner offers an opportunity to explore possibilities (e.g., hobbies, travel) that may be constrained within a relationship. Clients are also encouraged to view being without a partner as an opportunity to develop self-sufficiency.

During this aspect of the program role-plays are employed to facilitate the client's understanding of the issues and as a way for him to learn more about his dysfunctional style. In this context the therapist also helps the client recognize that loneliness (particularly, emotional loneliness) can be experienced even when they are in a relationship. Loneliness is, of course, the reciprocal of intimacy and has been shown to predict aggression toward others (Check, Perlman, & Malamuth, 1985).

This aspect of our program, then, aims primarily at increasing intimacy skills and reducing loneliness and enhancing the development of a secure attachment style.

Homework: All clients with deficiencies in assertiveness or who are anxious or socially inept are required to plan and enact activities between sessions that will serve to help them overcome these problems. Hostile clients are required to attempt to resolve issues that occur between sessions by more appropriate actions. All clients complete written exercises that outline the nature of their past and present relationships and the way their behaviors either contributed to problems or enhanced their relationships. Clients are also required to practice their newfound relationship skills during their conjugal visits and report back to the group.

Coping and Mood Management

The first step in this section is to provide clients with a description of the coping styles that have been identified in the general psychology literature: problem-focused; emotion-focused; avoidance-focused (Parker & Endler, 1996). We (Marshall, Cripps, Anderson, & Cortoni, 1999; Marshall, Serran, & Cortoni, 2000) have shown that child molesters, in particular, consistently adopt an emotion-focused coping style, but we have also observed that many sexual offenders engage in avoidance-focused coping, including using sex as a coping strategy (Cortoni & Marshall, 2001). We (Serran & Marshall, 2005) have also shown a clear connection between mood and dysfunctional coping that is bi-directional.

Group discussions follow our description of the three coping styles. During these discussions the therapist assists clients in identifying the coping styles they have used in the past and any skills deficits they have in dealing with particular problems. In addition, the emotional and behavioral antecedents of poor coping and the consequences of failing to adequately cope with life's problems are identified. Each client is required to describe past situations where he believes he coped well, in addition to situations where he felt unsatisfied with his response or with the consequences of his response. Once several illustrative situations and responses have been described, a discussion ensues that identifies problematic coping or a lack of the skills and confidence necessary to adequately cope. In helping an offender identify instances of poor coping, the therapist elicits suggestions from the client and the group about how he could have better dealt with the situation. Role-plays are employed to give the client the opportunity to rehearse adequate coping and to practice the necessary skills. It is made clear to clients, at this point, that even when they cope well others may not support their response, so that in the real world effective coping may not always produce positive results. Satisfaction is to be derived, we point out, from behaving appropriately, even if others attempt to discourage or dismiss these attempts.

Clients are also asked to describe ways in which they could reduce stress in their lives. It is now well established that prolonged, or even acute, stress has damaging effects on physical health as a result of compromising the immune system (Sapolsky, 1994). These effects, however, can be ameliorated by developing effective coping styles and strategies (Sapolsky, 1994). Similarly, stress can produce a variety of psychological problems (Prkachin & Prkachin, 2003). Since much of the stress in the lives of our clients comes from dysfunctional relationships, they will have already acquired some skills in reducing stress in the component dealing with relationship issues. However, there are other sources of stress in their lives. Some offenders have characteristically worked long hours with little leisure, others have abused alcohol or drugs, some have mismanaged their finances, and some have excessively catered to the needs of others while neglecting their own needs. Many of these stressors lead the sexual offender to adopt a sense of entitlement which Hanson, Gizzarelli, and Scott (1994) have shown to be a common problem among these men that leads to offending (Harris & Hanson, 1999). Also Hanson and Harris (2000) have shown that emotional dysregulation is a risk factor for sexual offenders, and stress quite clearly generates strong and uncontrollable emotional responses (Russek & Schwartz, 1997). The therapist helps the client generate suggestions regarding what he could do when distressed about difficulties in his life; for example, seek the comfort of his support group, enter counseling, attend his family physician, or seek psychiatric help. However, the main focus in this part of treatment is on helping each client develop an appropriate coping style as well as generating strategies for self-managing their emotions.

Lazarus and Folkman (Lazarus 1991; Lazarus & Folkman, 1984) have identified an appraisal process that people initiate when faced with stress, part of which involves the degree to which a person believes he/she is able to cope. The result of this appraisal determines the quality and intensity of their emotional response, which in turn determines the adequacy of their coping response. Assisting our clients to use a task-focused coping style, and providing them with practice in enacting adequate coping skills, should increase their confidence in their ability to cope and thereby reduce the intensity of their emotional response. Repeated practice between sessions in implementing their new-found coping skills should, therefore, reduce their emotional volatility. Given that emotional dysregulation has been identified as a problem for sexual offenders (Ward & Hudson, 2000) and has been shown to lead to an increased likelihood of reoffending (Hanson & Harris, 2000), training in adequate coping styles and skills should contribute to reducing future risk of relapse among sexual offenders.

Because the majority of our clients are low in self-esteem, and low self-esteem is strongly correlated with emotional dysregulation (Baumeister, 1993), we might expect the earlier component of treatment aimed at enhancing self-esteem to reduce the tendency among sexual offenders to respond to distress in an emotionally dysfunctional way. Also, since self-esteem and coping are positively correlated among sexual offenders (Marshall, Cripps, Anderson, & Cortoni, 1999), we might expect an increase in self-esteem to facilitate the acquisition of effective coping. We have also taken steps to directly modify emotional responsivity within the empathy training component. Thus, it is not just this component that affects coping and mood management but rather the program as a whole. This, of course, is true of all other targets of treatment.

Homework: Initially in this section, our clients are required between sessions to identify past situations where they failed to cope so that this can serve as a topic for within-session discussions. Once this has been discussed they are expected to consider between sessions the emotional effects of these failures and to examine possible ways they could cope better. Finally, once they have had experience of role-playing appropriate coping responses, they are required to put these into practice on every possible occasion in their nontherapy time. They then report back to the treatment group on the effectiveness of or problems associated with the enactment of their attempts at better coping with problems.

Deviant Sexual Interests/Arousal

Table 2.3 lists the criteria we have developed to identify clients who need either behavior modification techniques directed at deviant sexual arousal profiles, or medications to address excessive sexual desire (also

TABLE 2.3   Criteria for Implementing Behavioral Procedures
to Modify Sexual Arousal Patterns

1. Sexual history reveals high rates of deviant acts that are persistent over time.

2. Phallometric evaluations reveal either: (a) equal or greater arousal to deviant than to normative sexual acts; or (b) arousal to deviant acts ≥30% full erection (i.e., approximately 9–10 mm of increase in penile circumference).

3. Client self-reports persistent deviant sexual fantasies, or rapid unwanted arousal to staff or persons depicted in media.

4. Client's institutional behavior reveals he is collecting inappropriate images from magazines and newspapers, or that he is persistently watching television shows depicting his preferred class of victims.

5. Client's institutional records show he has attempted to sexually assault staff or other inmates.

called "sexual compulsivity," "hypersexuality," "sexual preoccupation," or "sexual addiction").

Phallometric assessments are completed on all our sexual offenders who are willing to be assessed, so we will clarify here our criteria for defining a sexual arousal profile as in need of treatment. It is important to note that we do not rely alone on phallometric responses to decide whether or not to employ procedures to modify deviant sexual interests, at least in part because phallometry does not always reveal deviance in clients for whom we might otherwise suspect deviance (Marshall & Fernandez, 2003). Table 2.3 describes the overall criteria we employ to make this decision.

The following describes our process of deciding if a phallometric profile indicates a need to intervene. To calculate degree of arousal, we first average the peak responses to each stimulus within each of the deviant or appropriate stimulus sets. As a first step we use a relative criterion that calculates the proportionate degree of deviant responding against responses to appropriate stimuli (i.e., some form of deviant index). Next, we use an absolute criterion that reflects the magnitude of arousal to deviant stimuli regardless of the degree of arousal to appropriate stimuli. These two criteria are used in combination to determine the need for treatment. For example, if a client displays arousal to deviant stimuli that is ≥80% of his arousal to appropriate stimuli, then in most cases this will serve to indicate a need for intervention. The intervention in this case would involve increasing appropriate arousal and reducing deviant arousal. The exception to this relative rule would be when overall absolute arousal is low (<15% of full erection or ~5 mm of change in the strain gauge), in which case we would intervene only if the client's offense record involved several victims over many years. As an example of our absolute criterion, if the client displayed 80% full erection (or >25 mm change) to appropriate stimuli and ≥30% full erection (>10 mm change) to deviant stimuli, we would definitely attempt to reduce arousal to the deviant stimuli but we would not have to enhance appropriate sexual interests.

Medications

Generally, behavior modification procedures are implemented as the first choice but if they fail to modify arousal patterns, or if the client displays excessive sexual preoccupation or has sadistic features, then we refer him to a psychiatrist who is sophisticated in the use of selective serotonin reuptake inhibitors (SSRIs) and antiandrogens. The administration of one or another of these drugs is meant to complement psychological treatment; cooperation between the psychiatrist and our team is excellent.

Typically the aim of antiandrogenic medications is to reduce circulating testosterone levels to the low end of, or just below, normative levels. This is meant to allow the client to still function sexually while able to control his sexual urges. In some cases (e.g., sexual sadists) the aim may be adjusted to lower testosterone levels even further. Bradford (2000; Bradford & Fedoroff, in press) has generated a system for deciding when to use medications which takes into account the possible need to eliminate sex drive in some cases. He advocates the use of medications for all "hands on" sexual offenders, whereas we tend to be more conservative in our use of medications. We rarely employ antiandrogens and then only for two classes of offenders. Those clients for whom behavioral procedures appear to be ineffective in controlling high levels of deviant arousal may be referred to psychiatry for hormonal assays. If the results indicate high levels of circulating testosterone, our psychiatrist will administer antiandrogens to lower testosterone to the low end of normative levels. Sadists and other very dangerous offenders (dangerousness here is defined in terms of a combination of risk to recidivate and risk to harm) are typically required to remain on antiandrogens postrelease for an indefinite period dependent on how they function.

The SSRIs are used with clients at the lower end of dangerousness who do not have deviant arousal patterns, but do manifest a high frequency of sexual outlets (i.e., 11 or more per week; see Kafka, 1997). We have found the SSRIs to be effective with clients who manifest compulsive-like sexual behaviors (Pearson, Marshall, Barbaree, & Southmayd, 1992).

Clients taking antiandrogens or one of the SSRIs are required to keep daily diaries of the frequency and intensity of sexual fantasies (appropriate and deviant) as well as their frequency of masturbation.

Behavioral Techniques

The specific behavioral techniques we employ include: foul odor aversion (rarely used), ammonia aversion (uncommonly used), covert association (our modification of what was previously called "covert sensitization"), masturbatory reconditioning (we reserve the use of this term to describe procedures involving masturbating to appropriate fantasies, sometimes called "thematic shift" or "directed masturbation"), and verbal satiation. Typically we implement the combination of masturbatory reconditioning and satiation as our first choice followed by, or sometimes coincident with, covert association. Ammonia aversion is reserved for those offenders whose deviant thoughts are triggered by a variety of stimuli throughout each day (typical of exhibitionists), while olfactory aversion is rarely used. We prefer to use behavioral procedures that are likely to have a minimal negative impact on the client–therapist relationship, so that is why aversive procedures (i.e., foul odor aversion and ammonia aversion) tend to be our last choice. All behavioral techniques are described in individual sessions with the client. Clients' reports of practice with the procedures are also done one-on-one at the end of each group session.

Foul odor aversion: This involves associating relevant deviant images/thoughts with the presentation of a foul odor which the client inhales. In the past we have used valeric acid, mercapto-ethanol, or rancid meat as the foul odor (Marshall, Keltner, & Griffiths, 1974). The foul odor is inhaled by the client contingent on the presentation of a depiction of his deviant sexual interests.

Foul odor aversion, while typically rapidly effective and apparently enduringly effective, tends not to cement good client–therapist relationships and presents some practical problems. For instance, foul odor molecules adhere to clothing and linger in the therapy room. More importantly, the olfactory system habituates rapidly and it is difficult to clear the system after presentation of the odor. These factors mean that very few pairings of the odor and the deviant images can occur within each session, thereby slowing down the presumed conditioning process. For these reasons we use foul odor aversion as a last resort and we spend considerable time preparing the client for the procedure.

Ammonia aversion: When clients report a high frequency of deviant thoughts that are viewed by the client as intrusive and task-interfering, we may implement ammonia aversion. This procedure involves having the client carry, at all times, a small vial of smelling salts (salts of ammonia). Whenever an unwanted sexual thought occurs, the client is instructed to open the vial, hold it close to his nasal openings, and take a rapid inhalation. Since the effects of ammonia aversion are mediated by the pain system (rather than the olfactory system), this inhalation immediately removes any thoughts the client is having, thereby giving him the opportunity to replace these thoughts by some nonsexual thoughts. In our program, the client reports his use of this procedure on an individual basis at the end of each group session.

Covert association: We changed the descriptor for this procedure from its original title of "covert sensitization" for two reasons: (1) we wanted to distinguish it from the original way it was implemented by Cautela (1967) and the way it is often currently applied in the sexual offender field (Dougher, 1995; Maletzky, 1991); and (2) we believe the effective element of this procedure is simply the association between imagining the sequence of the deviant chain of behaviors/thoughts and imagining possible actual consequences, rather than any aversive effects arising from this pairing. In terms of the latter, some practitioners have complained to us that the negative consequences they have their clients rehearse in covert sensitization appear to rapidly lose their aversive qualities with repetition. This is precisely what we would expect based on basic learning research with the use of low-intensity punishers (Azrin, 1960; Azrin & Holz, 1966).

We frame our conceptualization of the basis of this procedure on both contiguity theory (Guthrie, 1935) and contingency theory (Colwill & Rescorla, 1986), which together can be seen as representing a modern version of associationism (see Hall, 1991, and Wasserman & Miller, 1977, for descriptions of associative learning). This explanation of learning simply claims that by repeatedly pairing two stimuli, or a stimulus and a response, the first stimulus will come to automatically elicit the second stimulus or the response. In this view the consequences need not be aversive. What we want to happen as a result of our revised version (i.e., covert association) is that with repeated practice, the early steps in the offense sequence will elicit automatic thoughts of the consequences, thus aborting the offense sequence at an early stage.

Clients are assisted in constructing several offense sequences, some of which replicate the behavioral/emotional/thought chains of their prior offenses while others are reconstructions of their fantasies. We aim for at least five sequences (although some may later be replaced by other sequences if the client considers that to be useful), which are then broken up into six to eight steps. The client is then helped to construct realistic, if unlikely, negative consequences to offending; for example, being caught in the act by a victim's father or brother or by the police; being denigrated by his family, friends, and workmates; having his name appear in the media as a sexual offender; losing his job, family, friends, and home; and being sent to prison. The offense sequences are written on one side of pocket-sized cards with the consequences being written on the other side. The client is instructed to read each sequence and its consequences on at least three occasions each day between treatment sessions. He is to continue this practice for several weeks with checks being made on an individual basis at the end of each group session to ensure he is maintaining the practice.

In the early stages of applying this procedure, the client is told to read each sequence through to the terminal behavior before reading the consequences. Over the weeks of practice he is to move the interruption of the sequence and the reading of the consequences to progressively earlier steps in the sequence until by the end of the practice (after 4–6 weeks) he is reading the consequences at the point when he is contemplating initiating the offense or fantasy sequence.

Masturbatory reconditioning: This term refers to procedures associated with masturbation that are meant to increase sexual responsiveness to appropriate stimuli and decrease sexual responsivity to deviant acts. To achieve the former goal, we use what Laws and Marshall (1991) called "thematic shift" procedures.

In thematic shift, clients are first assisted in developing appropriate sexual fantasies and in identifying a person with whom they might have consenting sex. Our aim is to identify (real or imagined) peer-aged adults (male or female depending on the client's preference) who are likely to be compatible with the client and with whom he might have a sexual relationship. We avoid use of pornographic images, or images of celebrities, unless the man is so devoid of attraction to more appropriate images that there seems no other option. In these latter cases, we allow the use of less appropriate (but still normative) images as a first step in the process of shaping attraction to compatible peers. Although we might allow use of visual images initially, we encourage the elaboration of fantasy material involving appropriate partners. Throughout this process we check to ensure that the images are appropriate in terms of the person and the behaviors.

The client is instructed to use the following procedure whenever he normally masturbates. He is told to initiate masturbation by whatever images (e.g., deviant thoughts) are necessary to generate arousal at which point he is to switch to the appropriate images. If he experiences a loss of arousal, he is to switch back to deviant fantasies until re-aroused at which point he returns to fantasizing an appropriate partner and behavior. It is sometimes necessary for some clients to switch consistently back and forth between the deviant and appropriate fantasies during masturbation for at least the first several sessions. The client is told that this practice is unlikely to enhance the attractiveness of deviant fantasies, since they are near asymptotic in sexual valence, but that the pairing of sexual arousal with the appropriate images (even briefly) will, if repeated often enough, eventually endow these images with strong sexual evocativeness. It is emphasized to the client that he must practice this procedure every time he masturbates.

Some, but few, clients express a disinclination to masturbate. When that happens we either recruit a minister from the client's religion, who we already know will reassure the client that in his circumstances masturbating is acceptable, or we engage a procedure we developed to reduce feelings of guilt associated with masturbating (Marshall, 1975). At the end of each group session, a check is made to ensure the client is maintaining the practice.

In order to reduce responsiveness to deviant images we employ verbal satiation. This is a variation developed by Laws (see Laws & Marshall, 1991) on Marshall's (Marshall, 1979; Marshall & Barbaree, 1978; Marshall & Lippens, 1977) original masturbatory satiation. The basic underlying principle of satiation is that the repeated evocation of a currently attractive behavior (or in this case a fantasy) will lead to a loss of its positive valence. Procedures based on this idea were originally described by Knight Dunlap (1932). However, not only does satiation involve the repeated evocation of desired sexual fantasies, these evocations are required to occur when the client is in the refractory state (i.e., when reinforcement is absent). This refractory period occurs almost immediately (within 2 minutes) after orgasm and describes a state where the man is unresponsive (relatively or in some cases absolutely) to sexual stimuli which would otherwise be provocative (Masters & Johnson, 1966). Thus, satiation involves at least two processes (i.e., repetition of desired fantasies and the association of this repetition with nonreward) that can be expected to extinguish the attractiveness of previously desirable behaviors/fantasies (Falls, 1998).

In our application of this procedure, verbal satiation is paired with masturbatory reconditioning which serves to generate the necessary refractory state, with the repetition of the deviant fantasies continuing for 10 minutes after ejaculation. The advantage of pairing satiation with masturbatory reconditioning is that the latter procedure generates the satisfaction necessary to meet the needs that the client was previously satisfying by his deviant fantasies and behaviors. There is evidence showing that the availability of an alternative source of reinforcement has the effect of increasing the suppression of a punished behavior (Herman & Azrin, 1964; Perry & Parke, 1975).

Summary of Behavioral Procedures

It is important to note that we commonly implement more than one of these various behavioral procedures. Many clients who display deviant arousal also show deficits, to some degree, in arousal to appropriate sexual activities. If one goal is to reduce deviant arousal then we characteristically employ satiation and covert association as our first choices. If appropriate arousal needs to be enhanced then masturbatory reconditioning will be employed prior to satiation. Since we want our clients to be able to meet their sexual needs in appropriate ways, we must attempt to make appropriate sexual acts attractive.

Once clients who have used one or another of the above techniques and have completed the whole treatment program, they are administered a post-treatment phallometric evaluation. If this assessment does not reveal positive results, we may initiate a referral to the institutional psychiatrist. However, this has never happened perhaps because, as we have demonstrated (Marshall, 1997b), our overall program, without employing any behavioral techniques to modify arousal, effectively normalizes sexual interest patterns manifest at phallometric evaluations even among very deviant clients.

Homework: The primary between-sessions work required in this component involves practicing the combination of masturbatory reconditioning and satiation on every occasion they masturbate and rehearsing their covert association procedure on a daily basis. Individualized checks are made at the end of each treatment session to ensure these practices are maintained. Most clients with these needs also keep daily logs of the frequency and intensity of both deviant and appropriate urges and fantasies, excluding, of course, those rehearsed in treatment procedures.

Self-Management Plans

In the context of designing with our clients what we call "self-management plans" (similar to, but not identical with, what has previously been called "relapse prevention plans"), we emphasize building alternative prosocial ways of living that are likely to produce greater life satisfaction than the clients achieved in the past. In presenting this to our clients, we suggest to them that they were attempting in their offending behavior to meet the same needs as the rest of us; it is simply that the way they attempted to meet these needs was inappropriate. Meeting these needs appropriately, we suggest to them, will lead to a more fulfilling and satisfying life that will, as a consequence, reduce their risk to reoffend.

Ward's introduction of the good lives model (Ward, 2002; Ward & Stewart, 2003a,b) has helped make our approach to this component of treatment more precise and focused. We have articulated the role of the absence of a good life in the etiology of sexual offending as well as its relevance for treatment (Ward & Marshall, 2004). In our treatment programs, we have long emphasized the need to generate behaviors and attitudes in our clients that are both exclusive of offending and experienced as satisfying to our clients (Marshall, 1971, 1989a, 1996; Marshall & Eccles, 1991; Marshall & Serran, 2000; Marshall & Williams, 2000); and Mann has pointed to the value of setting approach goals for sexual offender clients rather that simply identifying risks they should avoid (Mann, 2000; Mann, Webster, Schofield & Marshall, 2004). As a result of these considerations, we have identified ways to approach the treatment of sexual offenders that focus on building goals that are positive and rewarding for them and that provide ways to increase their optimism about the possibility of change (see Marshall, Ward, Mann et al., 2005, for a full discussion of these various tactics).

Table 2.4 provides an outline of the good lives model. Using this model we assist clients in identifying their own personalized good lives plan. Many aspects of the goals of this component have already been realized in earlier sections of treatment. For example: completing their autobiography helped identify behavioral deficits and responses that needed to be, and were, modified; modifying their cognitive distortions reduced their use of disadvantageous schemas and increased more prosocial ways of viewing their world; the social skills and self-esteem components involved enhancing skills and attitudes that facilitate the achievement of aspects of a good life; the acquisition of more effective coping styles and skills reduced emotional dysregulation and the need to use intoxicants; and changing sexual interests increased motivation to seek a more prosocial life.

The aim in the self-management segment of treatment is to integrate what has been learned and to identify additional skills that need to be enhanced to achieve a personally designed good life. Most of these additional skills can be acquired by the client after discharge from our program. For example, a significant target here concerns what the client will do with his leisure time. Many of our clients have had little in the way of constructive and satisfying leisure pursuits prior to being identified as an offender. Idle time typically leads to the experience of boredom, which appears to be a significant risk factor (Pithers, Beal, Armstrong, & Petty, 1989). Therefore, offenders are helped to identify leisure activities that will effectively fill their idle time and are consistent with their interests and capacities but do not place them in risky situations. Implementing these leisure activities typically occurs postdischarge and any skills they

TABLE 2.4 Good Lives Model

1. Human Needs

These are innate propensities that determine the conditions necessary for
psychological well-being and fulfillment. Individuals can flourish (i.e.,
achieve their potential) only when these needs are met.

2. Primary Goods

a. Life—healthy/optimal functioning, sexual satisfaction
b. Knowledge
c. Excellence in work and play—mastery
d. Excellence in agency—autonomy and self-directiveness
e. Inner peace—freedom from turmoil and stress
f. Relatedness—intimate, romantic, kinship, community
g. Spirituality—meaning and purpose in life
h. Happiness
i. Creativity

Achievement of these goods depends on possession of internal conditions
(skills and capacities) and external conditions (opportunities and supports).

When these are not met the person will have a poorly integrated self,
frustrating and unsatisfying relationships, low self-worth, failure to fulfill
potential, and a sense of hopelessness and helplessness. As a result he/she will
seek to meet these vaguely understood needs in maladaptive or non-
normative ways, and will display hostility/aggression, and emotional distress.

need (e.g., learning to play 10-pin bowling or how to fish) can similarly
be learned postdischarge.

Despite our emphasis on developing a personalized good lives approach for each client, we do not ignore the very real risks our clients might
face. There are clearly some situations they should avoid while there are
other risks that appear unpredictably. Clients must be well prepared to
deal with these potential risks. The research of Hanson and Harris (2000)
on stable and acute dynamic risk factors has proved extremely helpful in
identifying a range of potential risks. In terms of identifying these factors,
we attempt to get the client to develop a generic disposition toward risk.
The client describes the sequences he went through to access victims and
from this we help him identify a general set of situations or behaviors
from his past that might set the opportunity to reoffend. However, we
stress the importance of being alert to the possibility of novel risks arising unanticipated. We offer suggestions of such possible risks and ask the
client to generate several responses to each.

Our experience suggests that having the client provide detailed lists of the steps he went through in the past in order to offend is not helpful on its own and, indeed, may be disadvantageous. Relapse prevention advocates (e.g., Pithers, 1990) have proposed that such lists form the basis for identifying future risk situations that should, as a consequence, be avoided. Formulating future plans based solely on avoiding past risks seems to us to be unlikely to be helpful. More to the point, having clients aim only at avoiding risks seems unlikely to be effective. For example, Mann et al. (2004) have clearly shown that the general psychology literature indicates that avoidance goals are rarely maintained, whereas approach goals, if reasonable, are. Second, relapse prevention plans typically get elaborated to a degree that often overwhelms clients and certainly reduces the likelihood they will maintain the vigilance called for by RP advocates. Furthermore, these specific lists of risks cannot possibly identify all possible future risks, most of which cannot be anticipated. Finally, these lists may convince clients (particularly those prone to concrete thinking) that if they avoid these specified identified risks they will be safe from reoffending. Although it is sometimes difficult to get clients to see beyond the experiences of their past and to develop a generic disposition toward risk, that is our goal and in most cases we are successful.

As an example of what we mean by a generic disposition, let us consider the client's view of his high-risk situations. What we want each client to recognize is not only his past experiences, mood states, and circumstances that have put him at risk, but also possible future circumstances that he cannot fully anticipate, but that may present risks. If clients generate a list of high risk situations based only on past offending experiences, they may believe it is safe to remain in a situation they have not previously experienced but that may, nevertheless, be a potential risk. Throughout treatment we do our best to encourage our clients to think in these generic rather than concrete terms. Generalizability of what is learned in treatment is the goal but this only happens if it is programmed into treatment rather than left to chance (Thorpe & Olson, 1997). To that end we do not consider it useful to exhaustively list all possible future risks.

Having clients formulate future plans that serve their interests in seeking a fulfilling life (and one that involves activities exclusive of offending) instills an optimism and enthusiasm in clients that markedly increases the chances they will adhere to these plans. Nevertheless, each client is assisted in generating a set of indicators (warning signs) that indicate he may be moving toward risk: one set that would alert him and one set that would be observable to others. These lists of signs of risk are derived from both the client's past history as well as situations he may unexpectedly encounter in the future. These lists provide prompts to discuss with the client several responses he can make to each identified potential risk. He is required to generate back-up responses should his first attempt to reduce his risk fail. We include these lists of warning signs in our post-treatment report, which is eventually passed to the client's community parole officer, a community treatment provider, and members of his support group.

Having support groups can help the client ease his way back into society and assist him in times of trouble. Clients are required to develop two lists of people who will assist him once he is released. The first list includes the various professionals with whom he will have contact (e.g., community parole officer, treatment provider, other counselors or psychiatrists, ministers of religion), while the second includes family members, friends, and workmates. These social supports have been seen as essential to assist the client to adhere to his self-management (or relapse prevention) plans (McGrath, Cumming, & Burchard, 2003; Wilson & Picheca, in press), and supports are also helpful in attenuating the effects of stress in clients' lives (Prkachin & Prkachin, 2003).

Finally, each client has to generate a set of release plans: gradual steps to return to the community, if required; initial residence in a halfway house, if necessary; the town where he intends to reside; the location of his possible accommodation (not to be near access to potential victims); type of job; potential companions; and leisure activities. It is the client's responsibility, with the therapist's assistance and advice, to develop the necessary contacts and to ensure these release plans are both complete and attainable. The therapist checks that this has been done and that none of the release plans is likely to increase the client's risk to reoffend.

CHAPTER 3

Research Basis

INTRODUCTION

Since the late 1960s, research has revealed an ever-increasing range of problems associated with sexual offenders who are thought to require treatment (see Laws & O'Donohue, 1997). A corresponding range of treatment programs has also been described, and each of these programs targets some or all of the problems identified below. The following list of specific problems (i.e., treatment targets) is not exhaustive but does cover those problems that appear in most, if not all, treatment programs described to date. We will describe each of these problems separately and provide evidence regarding their relevance. We will then describe evidence on the effectiveness of treatment procedures in producing changes in these features. Finally, we will review data on the effectiveness of treatment programs in reducing reoffending.

SPECIFIC PROBLEMS

Problematic Cognitions

The descriptor "cognitive distortions," while in common use in the sexual offender field for many years, has never been satisfactorily defined in a way that has produced agreement about its meaning. It has been used to describe almost any cognitive product that is viewed as functionally related to deviant sexual acts and thought to differ from what a prosocial person would consider appropriate (or nondistorted). The facts of any social interaction (appropriate or coercive) cannot readily be accurately ascertained post hoc, given that each participant's social perceptions are colored by his history and that his accuracy of recall may be either flawed or influenced by personal needs. It seems, therefore, rather arbitrary to classify some cognitions as distorted, particularly by people (e.g., therapists) who did not observe the social exchange. Perhaps a better way to think about the so-called "cognitive distortions" of sexual offenders is to see these cognitions as understandable ways of construing or representing events, actions, or people, in a way that serves to protect the self. People low in self-esteem, for example, constantly strive to perceive things in a way that defends their fragile self-image (Baumeister, Tice, & Hutton, 1989; Wills, 1981). Keeping these concerns in mind, we think about the cognitive distortions displayed by sexual offenders as dysfunctional in the sense that they do not allow the client to deal effectively with his past in a way that will allow him to both overcome his deviant propensities and build a better future life.

Some sexual offenders deny they committed an offense, while others (perhaps most) minimize their culpability in various ways. Researchers have often confused these two separate issues. We will restrict our use of the term "denial" to the claims of those clients who say they did not commit the crime for which they were convicted. Any attempt by clients to deny aspects of the offense or to reduce their responsibility, we will describe as "minimizations." Table 3.1 outlines the way we view these two features of distortions.

These phenomena, in whatever way they are identified, are characteristic of sexual offenders. For example, Barbaree (1991) described 54% of rapists and 66% of child molesters as categorically denying having committed an offense, with 98% of all the offenders either denying or minimizing to some degree.

The last two features (i.e., denial of deviant thoughts and denial of aforethought) listed in Table 3.1 need some comments. These two

TABLE 3.1   Features of Denial and Minimization

COMPLETE DENIAL
False accusation
  • Police out to get me
  • Victim hates me
  • Victim trying to get financial compensation
  • Victim's mother wants to deny access to children
Wrong person
  • Victim mistakenly identified the client
Memory loss
  • Cannot remember but client sure he did not do it

PARTIAL DENIAL
Memory loss
  • Cannot remember but it probably happened

TABLE 3.1   Features of Denial and Minimization (continued)

Was not abuse
- Victim consented
- He/she lied about his/her age
- It was only a massage
- It was done for educational/protective purposes
- It was love

Denies having a problem or that he needs treatment
- I did it but I am not a sexual offender
- I have no sexual interest in, or fantasies about, children or rape
- I have learned my lesson so I know I will never do it again

MINIMIZATIONS
Concerning offense(s)
- Did not happen as often as victim claims
- No use of threats, coercion, or force
- Less sexually intrusive than victim claimed
- Only one victim

Concerning responsibility
- Victim was prostitute so how can it be rape
- Victim was seductive
- Victim's parents were neglectful
- I was intoxicated
- I was depressed/stressed/angry
- My partner was not sexually interested
- I have a high sex drive or I am a sex addict
- Victim said no but he/she clearly wanted it

Minimizing harm
- Friends/family tell me victim is okay
- Victim's current problems not caused by me
- I was loving/affectionate so no harm
- I was not forceful so no harm

Denies planning/fantasizing
- It was a "spur-of-the-moment" thing
- It just happened
- Victim started it
- I have never had deviant sexual thoughts
- I did not think about it before it happened

features can only be seen as denials or minimizations if it is accepted that all sexual offenders have deviant sexual fantasies and all plan their offenses in advance. Some offenders clearly have recurring deviant fantasies and no doubt all have sexual thoughts about their victims in the moments prior to the actual abuse, but there is no evidence demonstrating that all sexual offenders have recurrent deviant sexual fantasies or that they all plan their offenses in advance. No one can know what an offender is thinking except the offender himself, and, since cognitive processes occasionally work in quite mysterious ways, sometimes not even the person himself is fully aware of the content of his cognitions (Sobel, 2001).

Aside from denial and minimizations, the term cognitive distortions has been used rather loosely and has included perceptions (e.g., a child molester might perceive a particular behavior by a child as an invitation to sex), justifications (e.g., an exhibitionist might claim that since he did not touch his victims, he is not really harming them), postoffense rationalizations (e.g., a rapist might conclude that since the victim was wearing a tight blouse and a short skirt that she was "asking to be raped"), as well as endorsements of traditional or hostile attitudes toward women, a sense of personal entitlement, and various other dysfunctional attitudes and beliefs. Underpinning all these aspects of cognitive distortions, however, are schemas (Neisser, 1982; Thorndyke & Hayes-Roth, 1979). In cognitive science (Nelson, 1995; Oakhill & Garnham, 1996) and social cognition research (Augoustinos & Walker, 1995; Forgas, Williams, & von Hippel, 2003), schemas are seen as the basis for guiding perceptions and generating attitudes, beliefs, and behaviors. Schemas are stored in memory as "theories" based on the sum of personal experiences with people (individuals as well as groupings of people), events, and behaviors (where the latter schemas are often called "scripts"). Schemas allow us to make sense of our world in a way that is consistent with past experiences and current desires and goals. To date there has been little research with sexual offenders on the characteristic schemas they hold, although studies are emerging (see Hanson, 1998b; Mann & Beech, 2003; Mann & Hollin, 2001; Myers, 2000; Serran, Looman, & Dickie, 2004).

The idea of schemas derives from information processing models that distinguish structures, propositions, operations, and products (Langton & Marshall, 2000; 2001; Marshall & Langton, 2004). Cognitive structures refer to the architecture of stored knowledge. Repeated experiences, stored as memories, lead to the construction of scripts and schemas that are said to be cognitive propositions (Ingram & Kendall, 1986). Scripts are either acquired behavioral sequences (Abelson, 1981) or learned emotional sequences (Fehr & Russell, 1984) that guide the individual's own behavior as well as his expectations about the behavior of others. In terms of function, schemas, like scripts, influence attention, perception, emotional responding, and behavior (Bem, 1981; Fiske & Taylor, 1991; Segal, 1988), particularly in situations where there is less than optimal information (Hollon & Garber, 1988).

The processes by which information is perceived and interpreted is referred to as cognitive operations. These operations mediate between the external environment and the individual's schemas and scripts and generate cognitive products. These products are what have generally been referred to in the sexual offender literature as "cognitive distortions" (Abel, Gore, Holland et al., 1989; Bumby, 1996; Neidigh & Krop, 1992). The possibility of cognitive products being "distorted" (i.e., not a match for what is consensually agreed to be a normative view) is maximized by four factors: the nature of the relevant schema, current needs or desires, current emotional and cognitive states, and diminished available evidence. Unsatisfactory experiences are likely to generate distorted schema; for example, repeated failures in relationships with women may entrench negative schema about women, about relationships, and about the self. Current needs or desires, such as strong, unsatisfied, sexual desires, may interact with prior schemas about women or children to allow sexual abuse to occur. Similarly, emotional distress in sexual offenders may trigger negative schema about women and children, and a transitory loss of self-esteem might generate a schema of entitlement which may justify offending. The cognitive products in these cases may suggest that women deserve to be raped, that the man is entitled to have sex if he wants it, or that children (or this particular child) wish to have sex with adults.

Pro-offending perceptions (guided by schemas) may only be apparent when other factors elicit a desire to sexually abuse. Thus, it may be difficult to discern these problematic perceptions (from which to infer the underlying schema) in the context of pretreatment assessment, but they will almost certainly become apparent over time within the context of treatment when various feelings are aroused and when cognitions are challenged.

Abel, Becker, and Cunningham-Rathner (1984) were among the first to identify "cognitive distortions," and they developed a scale to measure these distortions. Because Abel's scale was thought to be so open to dissimulation (Langevin, 1991), other researchers have attempted to develop better scales. Bumby (1996), for example, described two such scales (the MOLEST scale and the RAPE scale) and provided evidence on their reliability and validity. Webster, Mann, Wakeling, and Marshall (2005) tested their Sex with Children Is Justifiable scale on large samples of child molesters and normal comparison subjects. They found solid evidence that the scale discriminated in the expected direction between the groups. The scale also demonstrated test-retest reliability and tracked beneficial changes with treatment.

Rapists have been shown to hold attitudes toward women that are prejudicial (Scott & Tetreault, 1987) and hostile (Koss & Dinero, 1989; Marshall & Moulden, 2001) and that justify violence toward women (Dewhurst, Moore, & Alfano, 1992). Furthermore, rapists agree with a variety of myths about rape that serve to rationalize offending (Burt, 1980; Koss, Leonard, Beezley, & Oros, 1985; Malamuth & Check, 1983; Marshall & Hambley, 1996). Because the measures used to assess these tendencies are transparent, some studies have failed to find distortions among rapists (Field, 1978; Sattem, Savells, & Murray, 1984; Segal & Stermac, 1984). More fruitful research might focus on the schemas that shape perceptions and generate the distortions and inappropriate attitudes revealed by the above research. Some, but few, studies of the schemas of sexual offenders are now available.

Hanson (1998b) has described three schemas associated with sexual offending: egocentric self-perception; over-evaluation of sex in the pursuit of happiness; and the belief that some people are legitimate victims. In her studies, Myers (2000) found that schemas of control and distrust of women typified the rapists, while child molesters had schemas of personal worthlessness and passivity (essentially they saw themselves as victims). Both rapists and child molesters displayed a schema of sexual entitlement, a disposition Hanson, Gizzarelli, and Scott (1994) had previously reported.

Mann and Hollin (2001) identified five schemas characteristic of rapists: (1) Grievance where revenge or punishment of women was seen as justifiable. (2) Self-as-victim which reflected self-pity and the belief that unjustifiably bad things happen to them. (3) Control indicating a need to be in charge or have power over others. (4) Entitlement suggesting that the offender had the right, or deserved, to do what he wanted regardless of others. (5) Disrespect for certain women, implying that particular women are not entitled to the usual standards of respectful behavior. In a second study, Mann and Hollin (2001) found that problematic schemas were much more evident in rapists than in child molesters, although both displayed aberrant schemas. In their explanations for their offenses, the child molesters' responses were characterized more by victim blame, excuses, a desire for intimacy, and deviant sexual arousal.

Serran, Looman, and Dickie (2004) used Young's Schema Questionnaire (Young & Brown, 2001) in their examination of rapists and child molesters. They found that child molesters were characterized by schemas of emotional deprivation, abandonment, mistrust, defectiveness, and self-sacrifice, while rapists held schemas of self-sacrifice, unrelenting standards, and punitiveness.

Self-Esteem

Self-esteem constitutes a schema-driven appraisal of the qualities and capacities of the self and could as readily have been included under problematiccognitions. For our purposes, it is important to note that a range of features, relevant to treatment, is generated in people who are low in self-esteem. Table 3.2 describes an array of such characteristics. All these features can be understood as obstacles to effective engagement in treatment and, as a consequence, they reduce the possibility of benefiting from treatment.

Extensive research has demonstrated that both child molesters and rapists have lower self-esteem than do other offenders and community nonoffenders (see Marshall, Anderson, & Champagne, 1997, for a review). In their thorough appraisal of available studies of recidivism in sexual offenders, Hanson and Bussière (1998) observed that general psychological problems (including low self-esteem) did not serve as predictors of recidivism. However, subsequently, Thornton, Beech, and Marshall

TABLE 3.2   Treatment-Relevant Features Characteristic of People
With Low Self-Esteem

People with low self-esteem:

1. Expect to fail at any novel task

2. Are reluctant to commit to change

3. Are hesitant to try new behaviors

4. Fail to practice when learning new skills

5. Are easily discouraged in efforts to change

6. Readily give up trying

7. Resist efforts of help

8. Engage in excessive cognitive distortions

9. Lack empathy

10. Lack social skills

11. Are consistently emotionally distressed

12. Suffer episodic negative affect

13. Are unempathic

14. Reactive to self-relevant feedback and feel threatened by challenges

15. Have a poorly defined self-concept

Note: These are derived from the various chapters in Baumeister's (1993) book.

(2004) demonstrated that pre-treatment self-esteem scores significantly predicted postrelease success or failure. In fact, the strength of this predictor was approximately equivalent to the strength of predictions based on actuarial measures of risk.

A related issue concerning mood fluctuations is relevant here. Hanson and Harris (2000) found that an acute negative mood state is very likely to precipitate a reoffense. In our (Marshall, Marshall, & Moulden, 2000; Marshall, Moulden, Marshall, 2001; Serran & Marshall, 2005) attempts to induce a negative mood in sexual offenders, we found that only those subjects low in initial self-esteem were affected by the mood induction procedure. This suggests that sexual offenders low in self-esteem will more likely respond to life's stresses and problems by generating an acute mood state, which (according to Hanson's research) will put them at risk to reoffend.

In addition, self-esteem has been shown to be correlated among sexual offenders with most of the other targets of treatment. In addition, Fernandez, Anderson, and Marshall (1997, 1999) found few cognitive distortions among child molesters who had adequate self-esteem but extensive distortions in those low in self-esteem.

Empathy

Empathy deficits have been accepted in the literature as one of the key problems of sexual offenders that must be addressed in assessment and treatment (Knopp, Freeman-Longo, & Stevenson, 1992). However, the results of studies of sexual offenders using trait measures of empathy revealed inconsistent results. Rice and her colleagues (Rice, Chaplin, Harris, & Coutts, 1990, 1994) found empathic deficits among rapists, but three other studies found no differences between sexual offenders and appropriate comparison groups (Hoppe & Singer, 1976; Langevin, Wright, & Handy, 1988; Seto, 1992).

In two of our studies we found that child molesters (Fernandez, Marshall, Lightbody, & O'Sullivan, 1999) and rapists (Fernandez & Marshall, 2003) had their most significant empathic deficits toward their own victims: They neither saw their victims as distressed nor did they feel sympathy for them. It is important to note that the variance in empathic responding among the sexual offenders in these two studies was very high in response to their own victim, indicating that some were quite empathic while others displayed next to no empathy. Other researchers have made similar observations (Beckett & Fisher, 1994; Buschman, 2003; Fisher, Beech & Browne, 1999; Hanson & Scott, 1995; McGrath, Cann, & Konopasky, 1998).

Marshall, Hamilton, and Fernandez (2001) found that empathy deficits and cognitive distortions were significantly correlated; greater victim empathy deficits were matched by more extensive cognitive distortions. Others have shown that increasing empathic feelings toward their victims has the effect of reducing the cognitive distortions displayed by sexual offenders (Bumby, 1994; Pithers, 1994; Schewe & O'Donohue, 1993). As a result of these observations, Bumby, Marshall, and Langton (1999) suggest that by distorting their perceptions of the victim's harm or distress, sexual offenders are protecting themselves from the experience of shame. Shame results from an attribution of responsibility for harm to others that places the blame on unchangeable aspects of the self ("I hurt my victim because I am a bad person"). Guilt, on the other hand, distinguishes the person from specific aspects of their behavior ("When I abused my victim that was a bad thing to do"). Guilt motivates attempts to change whereas, shame results in the person giving up (see Tangney & Fischer, 1995, for a full discussion of these issues). Shame triggers protective cognitive distortions and is associated with low self-worth, whereas guilt is not associated with either (Bumby et al., 1999). Thus, we construe empathy deficits as cognitive distortions that serve the purpose of avoiding shame and maintaining whatever self-worth the sexual offender currently has. Facilitating the recognition and acceptance of the harm each offender has done is an important early step in treatment. However, directly enhancing sexual offenders' general capacity for empathy is valuable both because some have a limited general capacity and because it allows empathy to be more readily transferred to their victims, the victim's family, and the offender's own family.

Social Skills

Deficits in a broad range of social skills have been considered to be central to the propensity to engage in sexually offensive behaviors (Barlow, 1974; Stermac, Segal, & Gillis, 1990; McFall, 1990). The basic notion underlying this belief is that deficiencies in the capacity to meet those needs (e.g., emotional, intimacy, and sexual needs) that are ordinarily met in prosocial interactions with others leads sexual offenders to turn to vulnerable targets where their lack of skills is offset by the use of coercive and deceptive tactics. Barlow (1974) suggested that sexual offenders had deficits in conversational and assertive skills, and McFall (1990) claimed that rapists were unable to accurately read social cues from women. Others have pointed to poor assertive skills (Edwards, 1972), intimacy and attachment problems (Marshall, 1989a; 1993), and sexual and emotional inadequacy with adults (Fisher, 1969; Fisher & Howell, 1970), as well as simple social inadequacy (Clark & Lewis, 1977; Laws & Serber, 1975), fear of adult relations (Howells, 1979), and generalized anxiety (Stevenson & Wolpe, 1960). There are some, but inconsistent, findings supporting these claims (Stermac et al., 1990), but it must be said that other than intimacy and attachment deficits, the evidence is not strong that sexual offenders consistently display a broad range of social problems.

In a more general sense Marshall (1971) pointed out that if child molesters were to make a change in their sexual interests from children to adults, then treatment providers would have to ensure that these offenders were equipped with the necessary skills, attitudes, and self-confidence to act on these changed interests. Consistent with this idea, a recently emerging focus of research and treatment has been the interrelated issues of intimacy, attachments, and loneliness.

Marshall (1989a) formulated a model that attempted to explain acts of sexual abuse as maladaptive strategies to achieve some degree of intimacy. He noted that sex and intimacy are often, in the minds of some men, seen as inseparable, with sex being the typical route chosen to achieve intimacy (Hatfield & Rapson, 1996). If sex were seen as the means to achieve intimacy then the pursuit of sex with partners who can be controlled would be a logical step for men deficient in the skills and confidence necessary to meet their needs with adult equal partners. Subsequent research has confirmed most aspects of Marshall's suggestions (Bumby & Hansen, 1997; Garlick, Marshall, & Thornton, 1996; Seidman, Marshall, Hudson, & Robertson, 1994; Ward, McCormack, & Hudson, 1997). Bumby and Hansen (1997) also observed that rapists and child molesters were afraid of intimacy with adults, which matches Howells' (1979) earlier finding that child molesters see adults as threatening and rejecting, whereas they see children as accepting and loving.

The capacity for intimacy is said to be formed in the earliest years of life and to depend on the quality of the child's bond (or attachment) with his/her parents (Bowlby, 1969, 1973, 1980). According to Bowlby, these early experiences between child and parent serve as templates for all future relationships. Good quality parent–child bonds lead to the entrenchment of a positive schema about relationships and the self, whereas the opposite results from poor quality attachments. Recent research has extended this notion of attachment to the way in which adults form romantic relationships (Bartholomew & Horowitz, 1991; Hazan & Shaver, 1987; Weiss, 1982). Table 2.2 in chapter 2 describes the various attachment styles and the associated views of self and others. People with insecure attachment styles experience little intimacy and are, as a consequence, emotionally lonely.

Research with sexual offenders has clearly demonstrated dysfunctional adult attachment styles (Cortoni, 1998; Hudson & Ward, 1997; Jamieson & Marshall, 2000; Smallbone & Dadds, 1998; Ward, Hudson,

& Marshall, 1996; Ward, Hudson, & McCormack, 1997). Child molesters appear to be more likely to have preoccupied styles while rapists tend to have fearful or dismissive adult attachment styles (Bumby & Hansen, 1997). As a result of considering these issues, Ward, Hudson, Marshall, and Siegert (1995) outlined a theory that attempted to explain the specific targets and behaviors involved in sexual abuse as dependent on the particular form of adult attachment style displayed by each offender.

Specifically they proposed that a preoccupied adult attachment in sexual offenders would lead them to seek out a victim who would be easy to control (i.e., a child). Such offenders, it was suggested, would engage in courting-like (i.e., grooming) behaviors with their victim prior to offending. Establishing an ongoing sexual relationship with a child allows preoccupied sexual offenders to be in control, to achieve some degree of intimacy, to satisfy sexual desires, and to avoid the fear and threat they feel in adult relationships.

In an attempt to determine the accuracy of Ward et al.'s (1995) theory, Marshall and Marshall (2002) evaluated both the attachment styles of incarcerated sexual offenders and the presence of grooming behaviors. They found that, as expected, offenders with a preoccupied adult attachment style chose a child victim, engaged in extensive preoffense grooming, and used either no coercion or, at most, very low levels of coercion. The grooming behavior of these offenders was remarkably like adult courting behavior.

Smallbone (2005) has recently extended theorizing about these issues to include relationships between the attachment (or intimacy-seeking), caregiving, and sexual systems. He points to the neurobiological proximity of these three systems and suggests that in men who do not find sexual and intimacy satisfaction with their adult partners but engage in caregiving behaviors toward a child, the activation of the neurobiological underpinnings of caregiving may facilitate the simultaneous activation of a desire for intimacy and sex. Smallbone's ideas fit well with the claims of many child molesters, particularly incest offenders, who report that engaging in caregiving activities with their victims made the offender feel close to the victim and gave the offender the affection and comfort he desired. If Smallbone is correct, then clearly a goal of treatment would require the offender to learn to distinguish these sets of needs.

Coping and Emotional Management

One of the basic and enduring tenets of the relapse prevention approach with sexual offenders (Marques, 1982; Pithers, Marques, Gibat, & Marlatt, 1983), even in its most recent revisions (Laws, Hudson, &

Ward, 2000), is that it is essential to teach clients to cope better with life's stressors and with their own emotional fluctuations. However, very little research has addressed either coping or emotional stability in these men. There are, fortunately, very extensive bodies of literature concerning people's general capacity to cope (Carpenter, 1992; Lazarus & Folkman, 1984; Zeidner & Endler, 1996) and their ability to express and modulate their emotions (Lewis & Haviland-Jones, 2000). Lazarus and Folkman (1984) suggest that coping involves "constantly changing cognitive and behavioral efforts to manage specific external and/or internal demands that are appraised as taxing or exceeding the resources of the person" (p. 141). It is essentially the capacity to respond to and recover from stress.

Endler and Parker (1999) have identified three characteristic coping styles: problem- (or task-) focused coping, emotion-focused coping, and avoidance-focused coping. Task-focused coping occurs when the person believes he/she can change things and involves a problem-solving approach to difficulties. An emotion-focused style involves either responding emotionally (e.g., sadness, anger, anxiety, depression) to the problem, or engaging in fantasized resolution, or indulging in excessive self-preoccupation (e.g., self-pity, seeing oneself as a victim). Finally, in avoidance-focused coping the person either distracts himself (e.g., watches television, gets intoxicated, engages in sex) or uses social diversion (e.g., speaks to a friend). The latter strategy of social diversion may prove to be an effective strategy as the friend may offer support or encourage the person to deal effectively with the problem. Some people do not deal effectively with problems and persist in emotion-focused or avoidance-focused coping, and often both.

To cope effectively with problems individuals need to have the specific skills required by each situation. Most of the coping training that is apparent in relapse prevention programs with sexual offenders is aimed at equipping the clients to deal with specific situations; for example, teaching clients to be assertive, helping them overcome situation-specific anxiety, training them in communication skills, or teaching them to recognize stress or risk provoking situations, and developing ways to avoid or escape these so-called "high risk situations." Very little appears to have been done to identify and modify general coping styles.

A small number of recent studies have shown that sexual offenders do indeed have deficient coping styles. Neidigh and Tomiko (1991) reported that when faced with problems, child molesters respond by either avoiding thinking about the issue or by engaging in self-denigration (i.e., an emotion-focused response). Cortoni (1998) used Endler and Parker's (1999) Coping Inventory for Stressful Situations. She found that child molesters in particular typically chose an emotion-focused response to problematic issues, a finding that has been replicated by others (Marshall,

Cripps, Anderson, & Cortoni, 1999; Marshall, Serran, & Cortoni, 2000; Serran, Firestone, Marshall, & Moulden, 2004).

Relevant to these issues are studies by Looman (1999) and by Proulx and his colleagues (McKibben, Proulx, & Lusignan, 1994; Proulx, McKibben, & Lusignan, 1996). These researchers have shown that when sexual offenders experience stress they are very likely to turn to deviant sex (in fantasy, pornography, or real life). Cortoni and Marshall (2001) also reported that sexual offenders typically use sex as a way of coping with problems, although in their study sexual offenders used both normative sex and deviant sex as ways to cope. Cortoni (1998) found that among sexual offenders deficient coping styles were most evident in those who turned to sex when faced with problems. Deficiencies in coping, then, appear to increase the risk that sexual offenders will seek out sex that may be deviant.

Effective coping reduces emotional distress, whereas ineffective coping increases emotional lability (Billings & Moos, 1984; Endler & Parker, 1999). Ward and his colleagues have suggested that sexual offenders have problems regulating their emotions as well as their behaviors (Keenan & Ward, 2003; Ward, 1999; Ward & Hudson, 2000). Ward's suggestion proposes that fluctuations in emotions, or dysregulated emotions, put sexual offenders at risk to reoffend. Recent reports indicate that, indeed, fluctuations in mood (i.e., the kind of response we might expect in people with poor coping skills) represent an acute dynamic risk factor for sexual offenders after their release into the community (Hanson & Harris, 2000; Harris & Hanson, 1999). Because stress induces transitory negative emotional responses (Endler & Parker, 1999; Folkman & Lazarus, 1986), and this is more pronounced and prolonged in those who lack effective coping skills or style (Billings & Moos, 1984; Mitchell, Cronkite, & Moos, 1983), then training in coping would seem to be an essential component of sexual offender treatment. However, even in the absence of stress some sexual offenders appear to be emotionally labile, so that assisting them in modulating their emotions should also be a goal of treatment.

Sexual Interests

In the early application of behavior therapy to men with paraphilias, including those who had sexually offended, the issue that was seen as central to their problems was their unusual sexual interests. More specifically, these clients were believed to have a sexual preference for their problematic sexual activities. Thus, modifying sexual preferences was considered to be the primary (or, in the view of some, the only) target of treatment with these clients (Bond & Evans, 1967).

First let us note that there are problems with the idea that sexual behavior is driven by trait-like preferences (i.e., preferences that endure over time and are present in all circumstances), despite the fact that our methods for assessing sexual interests (e.g., phallometriy or viewing time) relies on this notion (Marshall & Fernandez, 2003). If a man displays a greater response at assessment to deviant stimuli than to appropriate stimuli, he is deemed to have an enduring sexual preference for deviant sexual activities; if he shows greater arousal to appropriate stimuli, he is (cautiously) said to have an enduring preference for normative sex. However, sexual offenders typically report being in a cognitive, emotional, or physical state during the immediately preceding period and throughout their offense that differed from their usual states. This suggests the possibility that their deviant interests may emerge only when they are in one of these unusual states (e.g., angry, intoxicated, stressed, upset).

Research by Barbaree and his colleagues calls the trait notion into question. They have shown that both anger and intoxication affect sexual responding. In one study they showed that when normal males were angered by a woman, their sexual responses revealed quite different patterns (i.e., a preference for rape) than was evident at other times (Yates, Barbaree & Marshall, 1984). Intoxication by alcohol revealed similar changes in the sexual responses of normal males (Barbaree, Marshall, Yates, & Lightfoot, 1983). Because many rapists are either angry or intoxicated, and often both, preceding and during their assaults, it seems likely that testing their sexual preferences when they are calm and sober will tell us little about their offense-related sexual desires. Similarly, if Smallbone's (in press) theory, outlined in the section on social skills, is at all accurate, then many child molesters will only display deviant sexual behavior (and "preferences") when there is the simultaneous activation of the sexual, attachment, and caregiving systems. Now that an array of risk factors have been identified for sexual offenders (Doren, 2002; Hanson & Bussière, 1998), particularly risk factors that fluctuate (Hanson & Harris, 2000), we can be assured that our assessments of sexual interests are not embedded in a context (external and internal), that would allow us to make inferences about the transitory sexual responses that can be expected to occur immediately prior to and during an offense. The evidence adduced by Looman (1999) and by Proulx and his colleagues (McKibben et al., 1994; Proulx et al., 1996) indicating that in response to various mood altering events sexual offenders are likely to engage in deviant fantasizing, also suggests that our assessments of sexual interests are missing important elements.

Although in recent years alternative technologies have become available, phallometry (see Laws & Osborn, 1983, for a description of this procedure) has been the major basis for evaluating sexual interests both among normal males (Heiman, 1977; Rosen & Beck, 1988) and among sexual offenders (Barbaree, 1990; Marshall & Fernandez, 2003; McConaghy, 1993; Murphy & Barbaree, 1994). The results of phallometric assessments with sexual offenders, however, have not produced consistent results. Marshall and Fernandez (2003) provide detailed analyses of phallometric findings and the following simply summarizes their observations.

While some 50% of nonfamilial child molesters have been reported to show greater arousal to children than to adult sexual partners, this seemingly impressive result is in fact an overstatement. First, between 20% and 25% of all tested offenders display arousal so low to all stimuli that their results are discarded as meaningless. Second, clients who deny they committed an offense appear normal at phallometric assessment as do single-victim offenders. In fact it is only the multiple-victim nonfamilial child molesters who respond deviantly. Among father–daughter incest offenders only 18% to 20% appear deviant when the stimuli employed are visual images of children, although when audio-taped descriptions of sexual interactions are employed, incest offenders respond much like nonfamilial child molesters. With rapists the results have revealed significant inconsistencies. Some early studies found rapists to display deviant arousal (i.e., arousal to forceful, nonconsenting sex involving an adult female victim). However, later studies using larger samples were unable to discriminate rapists from various other comparison groups. Finally, most studies have failed to detect deviant arousal among exhibitionists.

While these results call into question the value of phallometry in discriminating populations, for those clients who display deviance phallometry can provide a baseline against which to infer the effects of treatment. Deviant arousal is also one factor that enters into a composite actuarial estimate of risk among sexual offenders (Hanson & Bussière, 1998; Quinsey, Rice, & Harris, 1995).

Alternatives to phallometry have been outlined with the most promising involving measures of viewing time. Abel and his colleagues have developed such a measure and they have provided evidence that a very significant number of child molesters display deviant responding on the test (Abel, 1995; Abel, Huffman, Warberg, & Holland, 1998; Abel, Lawry, Karstrom, Osborn, & Gillespie, 1994). There have been criticisms of Abel's measure (Fischer & Smith, 1999; Smith & Fischer, 1999) but in our view these criticisms are based on unrealistic expectations of a measure that is so early in its developmental stages. As something of a counter to these criticisms, an independent comparison of Abel's measure and phallometry revealed rather better results for the viewing time assessment (Letourneau, 2002).

EVIDENCE OF EFFECTIVENESS

There are two aspects to the evaluation of efficacy with programs like the present one that involve various interrelated targets associated with specific sets of procedures: (1) Do the procedures employed in treatment produce the desired effects? and (2) Does the overall program produce the desired effects? The former question we refer to as the attainment of within-treatment goals and is answered by measuring the specific target (e.g., self-esteem) prior to and after treatment. The primary overall evaluation of the program is its long-term effectiveness. In the present case, this can be phrased as: Does the program reduce the postrelease rate of reoffending? While this seems like a simple question, implying an obvious set of evaluation procedures, it turns out not to be so straightforward. Detailed discussion of the relevant issues concerning outcome evaluations with sexual offender programs will be presented in the section "Long-Term Treatment Outcome." Before we do that, we will examine the efficacy of each component.

Achievement of Within-Treatment Goals

While methodologically it might seem better to conduct these evaluations immediately before and immediately after the component in question, this does not make sense with our program. For example, while self-esteem is targeted as the initial step in treatment, work on enhancing self-esteem continues throughout treatment. In all components of treatment, clients are treated with respect and the therapist responds empathically to any signs of distress; the therapist is also rewarding and encourages progress and the expression of appropriate attitudes. All these features, as well as the possible re-initiation, if necessary, of some of the specific esteem-enhancing procedures, can be expected to progressively enhance self-esteem in addition to the enhancing effects of the client's own sense of achievement by the evident changes he is making. The same is true for all targets of treatment in a nonmodularized program. It would, therefore, be inappropriate to assess before and after each specific component since each component is simply meant to trigger the start of a process concerning each target that continues throughout treatment. Thus, the following appraisals were all made by assessing each treatment target before treatment was commenced, and again after treatment was complete. We will simply summarize the findings here. Readers who want more details can consult the original sources cited.

Although it was not an evaluation of our program, Webster et al. (2005) evaluated a similar approach to the modification of cognitive distortions. They found significant reductions in various aspects of these distortions as a result of treatment. The sexual offenders in this study displayed essentially normative attitudes, perceptions and beliefs after treatment. In addition, Marshall (1994) examined the effects on denial and minimizations of our treatment program. He showed that denial was all but eliminated and what minimizations remained after treatment were few and limited in degree. Finally, Thornton and Shingler (2001) have shown that adding a focus on modifying dysfunctional schema led to further reductions in offense-related distortions and beliefs, than did their previous component that simply focused on modifying the products of such schemas.

Marshall, Champagne, Sturgeon, and Bryce (1997) found that treatment in our program enhanced both self-esteem and the offenders' capacity for empathy as did an earlier study by Marshall, O'Sullivan, and Fernandez (1996). The relationship component of our treatment has been shown to both reduce loneliness and increase intimacy (Marshall, Bryce, Hudson et al., 1996), but as yet we have not examined changes in attachment styles.

Employing a quite similar approach to us in dealing with coping deficits, Rogers and Masters (1997) and Feelgood, Golias, Shaw, and Bright (2000) both demonstrated that treatment improved the coping styles of their clients. Serran et al. (2004) evaluated the coping component of our program and showed that sexual offenders markedly improved in their ability to identify effective ways of coping with potential risks and they displayed a more task-focused approach after treatment. These clients also showed an increased tendency to turn to their support groups for help as a result of treatment.

In a series of studies (Johnston, Hudson, & Marshall, 1992; Marshall, 1979; in press-a, -b, -c; Marshall & Barbaree, 1978; Marshall & Lippens, 1977), we have demonstrated the effectiveness of the various behavioral procedures we use to modify sexual interests. Other researchers have also shown some of these procedures to be effective (see Laws & Marshall, 1991, and Quinsey & Earls, 1990, for reviews). Finally, we have shown that our motivationally based approach enhances our clients' sense of self-efficacy, their hope for the future, and moves them in the appropriate direction along Prochaska and DiClemente's (1994) Stages of Change measure (Moulden, Marshall, & Marshall, 2005).

We have yet to examine the impact of the mood management aspects of our program and the effects of our program on the schemas of our clients. These projects are in process.

Long-Term Treatment Outcome

There was debate in the literature for some years regarding the efficacy of treatment for sexual offenders. Some authors expressed skepticism

(Quinsey, Harris, Rice, & Lalumière, 1993) at least in part because an earlier review (Furby, Weinrott, & Blackshaw, 1989) came to discouraging conclusions. During the last several years six meta-analytic reviews have appeared (Alexander, 1999; Dowden, Antonowicz, & Andrews, 2003; Gallagher, Wilson, Hirschfield et al., 1999; Hall, 1995; Hanson, Gordon, Harris et al., 2002; Löesel & Schmucker, 2005) that have provided quite positive appraisals. Hanson et al.'s (2002) study gathered 42 reports of treatment outcome with sexual offenders involving over 9000 subjects. These authors took care to select only those who met reasonable methodological standards and who provided a comparison group of untreated sexual offenders from the same setting. In addition, all studies relied on official recidivism data as the basis for determining effectiveness. Hanson et al. reported that considering only modern programs based on a cognitive behavioral approach with a relapse prevention component, the treated subjects had a sexual recidivism rate of 9.9% whereas the untreated group's sexual reoffense rate was 17.3%. Interestingly, Hanson et al. demonstrated that sexual offender-specific treatment also produced marked reductions in nonsexual reoffending. Treated subjects had a nonsexual recidivism rate of 28.7% whereas 41.7% of untreated subjects reoffended on nonsexual crimes. More recently, Löesel and Schmucker (2005) conducted a meta-analysis that involved 80 reports, many from Europe, that were not included in Hanson et al.'s study. They similarly report very encouraging results.

In response to the publication of Hanson et al.'s (2002) report, some critics, while expressing some degree of pleasure at the positive results, noted that the magnitude of the effects was not large (Berliner, 2002; Letourneau, 2004). We believe this is an incorrect interpretation of the data based apparently on ignorance of the magnitude of effects obtained in the treatment of other disorders or problems. As a result of these criticisms, Marshall and McGuire (2003) calculated the effect sizes of treatment for various medical disorders (e.g., myocardial infarcts, bypass surgery, angina, breast cancer, menopausal symptoms), as well as for nonsexual offenders. They report reasonably comparable effect sizes for sexual offender treatment and all the other disorders. In addition, both Prentky and Burgess (1990) and Marshall (1992) report that the effect of treatment of sexual offenders, even when the effect size is quite small, saves taxpayers considerable money, ranging well over U.S. $1 million for every 100 treated offenders.

In 1988 we (Marshall & Barbaree, 1988) reported an evaluation of our community-based clinic for child molesters. At the time 68 clients had completed treatment and been at risk for sufficient time to enter the appraisal. From our list of clients who had completed an assessment at our clinic but lived too far away to access our treatment program, we selected 58 who, on all risk factors and relevant demographics, matched our treated subjects. It is important to note that these untreated subjects were in fact referred by us to a nonspecialist treatment provider in their local community; whether they entered and completed this treatment, we were unable to determine. Using both official nationwide police (Royal Canadian Mounted Police, or RCMP) records and unofficial information derived from both police files and files kept by child protection agencies, the treated group sexually recidivated at a rate of 13.3% for the nonfamilial child molesters and 8.0% for the incest offenders. The reoffense rates for the untreated group were 42.9% for the nonfamilial offenders and 21.7% for the incest offenders. Using similar databases, we also evaluated our community program for exhibitionists (Marshall, Eccles, & Barbaree, 1991). In that study we found that 23.6% of the treated offenders recidivated while 57.1% of the matched untreated exhibitionists reoffended.

Finally, we (Marshall, Marshall, Malcolm et al., 2005) have recently completed an evaluation of the program described here, which in its present form has operated in a Canadian federal prison for 15 years. Of the 614 sexual offenders who have entered treatment, 95.8% completed the program. The majority of the 26 noncompleters were removed from the program as a result of factors over which neither the clients nor the treatment providers had control (e.g., death, deportation, or release from prison). Those released from prison while still in treatment were released at either their statutory (i.e., legally required) release date (i.e., two thirds of sentence completed), or because their full sentence had expired.

This outcome evaluation has yet to complete the follow-up of matched untreated subjects. However, based on the overall average risk levels of our clients, and using expected actuarial risk levels derived from the STATIC-99 (Hanson & Thornton, 1999) and the Levels of Service Inventory (Andrews & Bonta, 1995), we have estimated the expected recidivism rates of an untreated group to be 16.8% for sexual offenses and 40% for nonsexual crimes. In the evaluation of our 534 treated clients who had been at risk in the community for an average of 5.42 years, the total number of released offenders comprised 352 child molesters and 182 rapists. Of them 17 (14 child molesters and 3 rapists) had recidivated on a sexual crime, which reveals an overall sexual reoffense rate of 3.2% (4.0% of the child molesters and 1.6% of the rapists). For sexual offenders at this risk level, these results for sexual recidivism are among the best yet reported and clearly represent a lower-than-expected recidivism rate. Of the 17 sexual reoffenders among the treated subjects, none was a sexual sadist and only two scored above 20 on the Psychopathy Checklist–Revised, but none scored in the range (>30) Hare (1991) considers to be indicative of psychopathy. Of the total group of released treated sexual

TABLE 3.3   Treatment Outcome Data From Our Program

Observed and Expected Sexual and General Recidivism		
	SEXUAL RECIDIVISM	GENERAL RECIDIVISM
Expected	105 (16.8%)	248 (40%)
Observed	17 (3.2%)	84 (13.6%)

offenders, 13.6% reoffended on nonsexual crimes, including 5.2% who had committed a violent nonsexual crime. These rates of nonsexual crimes are substantially lower than the expected rate of 40% for nonsexual crimes. A statistical evaluation of the differences between the observed rates of sexual recidivism (n = 17, 3.2%) and general recidivism (n = 84, 13.6%) for the treated clients, and the expected rates derived from actuarial risk measures (n = 105.2, 16.8% and n = 248.4, 40%, respectively) revealed a clear beneficial effect for treatment, $\chi^2 (1) = 182.3$, $P < 0.001$. Table 3.3 describes the observed (or actual) numbers of both sexual and general reoffenders and compares them with the expected rates of reoffending.

Not only do these results mean our treatment program is saving potential victims from harm, it also means that it is significantly cost-effective. Marshall (1992) has previously estimated the costs that Canadian society incurs whenever a sexual offender reoffends after release from prison. These estimates were made in 1985 and were based on information provided by police and child protection agencies (their investigative costs), prosecuting attorneys (costs to prepare and present their case), the courts (average cost of a trial for such reoffenders), and prison authorities (to house a reoffender). The total cost per offender was CAN $200,000, which today is almost certainly an underestimate.

Our program treats a minimum of 60 clients per year at a total cost of CAN $205,000. Based on the actuarially estimated sexual reoffense rate (16.8%) and the observed rate (3.2%), we would expect 10.1 of every 60 of our treated clients to sexually reoffend whereas only 1.9 did. This means that each year our program prevents reoffending in approximately eight clients who would otherwise have committed a sexual reoffense. Multiplying this by the cost per reoffender, less the cost of operating the program, results in a financial saving to society of approximately CAN $1,395,000 per year. While these figures should not obscure the fact that our program saves many potential victims from suffering at the hands of sexual reoffenders, the obvious financial benefits of treating sexual offenders rebut any claims by governments that sexual offender treatment cannot be affordable.

Evidence gathered over 5 past five years in particular has demonstrated that treating sexual offenders, whether in prison or in the community, and preferably in both settings, can be effective even if some programs do not produce beneficial results. Clinicians and researchers working with sexual offenders are gradually getting closer to the goal of defining what is needed to effectively treat these problematic clients. This has only happened because of the close relationship between program development and empirical research. As long as this relationship continues we can expect programs to continually improve their effectiveness.

CHAPTER 4

Clinical Case Illustrations

ASSESSMENTS AND CASE FORMULATIONS

Two core aspects of the assessment of most clinical problems are (1) a series of interviews (structured or not) and (2) a battery of tests that purport to measure the salient features of the presenting disorder. These tests generally include a variety of relevant self-report measures as well as physiological evaluations. With many disorders the client is the one who arrives at the clinic complaining of one or more problems. It is the identification of these initial presenting complaints that initiates the series of interviews and tests aimed at fully elucidating the client's disorder so that appropriate treatment can be designed. In these cases where it is the client who begins the process of identifying the problems, we can expect most of these clients to respond honestly to the questions posed by the tests and by the interviewer. This, unfortunately, is not true with sexual offenders. Sexual offenders are, in almost all cases, referred by someone other than themselves, typically by an agency that has some degree of authority over the client. Most sexual offenders are initially somewhat reluctant clients who are hesitant to reveal anymore than they have to for fear that honest reporting of their problems will have the effect of increasing sanctions imposed on them. This means they are unlikely to be forthcoming at pretreatment interviews and are likely to be less than truthful in their responses to test questions. Nevertheless, many treatment programs for sexual offenders employ a large battery of self-report assessment measures. Table 4.1 describes some of the typical tests included in such batteries.

It has been suggested that one way around this problem is to use tests that have built-in measures of dissimulation (e.g., the MMPI) or to add to the assessment battery a measure that evaluates either impression management tendencies or the need to present in a socially desirable way. Unfortunately, the MMPI is a time-consuming test with most of the questions not of obvious relevance to the problems

TABLE 4.1   Relevant Assessment Instruments and Procedures

SELF-ESTEEM

General Self-Esteem
  Rosenberg's Measure   (Rosenberg, 1965)
  Coopersmith's Measure   (Coopersmith, 1967)

Specific Self-Esteem
  Body-Esteem Scale   (Franzoni & Shields, 1984)
  Social Self-Esteem Inventory   (Lawson, Marshall, & McGrath,
                                          1979)

LIFE HISTORY

Family Environment Scale   (Moos & Moos, 1981)
Childhood Attachment Questionnaire   (Hazan & Shaver, 1987)

COGNITIVE DISTORTIONS

Abel's Child Molester Cognitions   (Abel et al., 1989)
  Scale
Molest Scale   (Bumby, 1996)
Rape Scale   (Bumby, 1996)
Rape Myth Acceptance Scale   (Burt, 1980)
Hostility Toward Women Scale   (Check, 1984)
Justifications of Sex with Children   (Webster, Mann, Wakeling et al.,
                                          2005)
Young Schema Questionnaire   (Young & Brown, 2001)

EMPATHY

Empathy for Children   (Hanson & Scott, 1995)
Empathy for Women   (Hanson & Scott, 1995)
Child Molester Empathy Measure   (Fernandez, Marshall, Lightbody et
                                        al., 1999)
Rapist Empathy Measure   (Fernandez & Marshall, 2003)
Interpersonal Reactivity Test   (Davis, 1983)

COPING

Coping Inventory for Stressful   (Endler & Parker, 1990)
  Situations
Sex as a Coping Strategy   (Cortoni & Marshall, 2001)

SOCIAL FUNCTIONING

Assertiveness   (Keltner, Marshall, & Marshall, 1981)
  Social Response Inventory   (Rathus, 1973)
  Rathus Assertiveness Scale

Anger
  Buss-Durkee Hostility Inventory   (Buss & Durkee, 1957)
  State-Trait Anger Expression   (Spielberger, 1988)
    Inventory

TABLE 4.1   Relevant Assessment Instruments and Procedures
(continued)

Anxiety
  State-Trait Anxiety Inventory   (Spielberger, Gorsuch, & Lushene,
                                 1970)
  Fear of Negative Evaluations Scale   (Watson & Friend, 1969)
  Social Avoidance and Distress Scale   (Watson & Friend, 1969)

Problem-Solving   (D'Zurilla & Goldfried, 1971)

Social Supports Inventory   (Flannery & Weiman, 1989)

Relationships
  UCLA Loneliness Scale   (Russell, Peplau, & Cutrona, 1980)
  Miller's Social Intimacy Scale   (Miller & Lefcourt, 1982)
  Relationship Questionnaire   (Bartholomew & Horowitz, 1991)
  Relationship Styles Questionnaire   (Griffin & Bartholomew, 1994)
  Attachment History Questionnaire   (Pottharst, 1990)

SEXUAL INTERESTS

Clarke Sexual History   (Langevin, 1983)
  Questionnaire
Multiphasic Sex Inventory   (Nichols & Molinder, 1984)
Laws Card Sort   (Laws, 1986)
Wilson Sex Fantasy Questionnaire   (Wilson, 1978)
Phallometry   (Murphy & Barbaree, 1994)
Viewing Time   (Abel, 1995)

SUBSTANCE USE/ABUSE

Michigan Alcoholism Screening Test   (Selzer, 1971)
Drug Abuse Screening Test   (Skinner, 1982)

PSYCHOPATHY

Psychopathy Checklist-Revised   (Hare, 1991)

RELAPSE PREVENTION

Self-Monitoring Procedure   (McDonald & Pithers, 1989) STEP
Measures of Offense Chain   (Beckett et al., 1994)
Situational Competency Test   (Miner et al., 1989)

RECIDIVISM

General
  Level of Service Inventory-Revised   (Andrews & Bonta, 1995)

Violence
  Violence Risk Appraisal Guide   (Harris et al., 1993)

TABLE 4.1 Relevant Assessment Instruments and Procedures
(continued)

Sexual	
Minnesota Sex Offender Screening Tool	(Epperson et al., 1995)
Sex Offender Risk Appraisal Guide	(Quinsey et al., 1998)
Rapid Risk Assessment for Sexual Offense Recidivism	(Hanson, 1997)
STATIC-99	(Hanson & Thornton, 1999)
SOCIAL DESIRABILITY/IMPRESSION MANAGEMENT	
Marlow-Crowne Social Desirability Scale	(Crowne & Marlowe, 1960)
Paulhaus Balanced Inventory of Desirable Responding	(Paulhaus, 1991)

of sexual offenders. In addition, its resultant data, including responses to the questions assessing faking, etc., have not proved to be at all helpful with sexual offenders (see Marshall & Hall, 1995, for a detailed review). The currently available measures of social desirability or impression management seem to be no less transparent than other self-report measures. Sexual offenders rarely respond on these measures in a manner that differs from people with nothing to hide, even though they have clearly given dishonest responses on the rest of the test battery instruments. Thus, it is not meaningful to use such measures in order to correct, or detect, dissimulation on other instruments.

A further problem concerns the fact that most of the self-report instruments that typically comprise an assessment of sexual offenders have not been properly examined to determine their reliability and validity. To date, no one has developed interview strategies (structured or otherwise) for use with sexual offenders that are demonstrably reliable and valid. Even phallometric testing, which evaluates the magnitude of a client's sexual arousal to normative and appropriate sexual stimuli, has been criticized on psychometric grounds (Marshall & Fernandez, 2003) and, as we indicated in chapter 2, phallometry does not seem to identify as deviant more than a small percentage of sexual offenders. Indeed, the evidence on the reliability and validity of phallometric testing is so weak that some authors have declared phallometry to be unsuitable for routine clinical use (Marshall, 2005d), even though it may have a use in research.

The problems in the use of self-report measures with sexual offenders, then, concerns both their psychometric bases and the fact that they are so readily open to dissimulation by clients who have every reason to misrepresent themselves. Unfortunately, this has not deterred most treatment centers from developing test batteries for sexual offenders that are primarily based on self-report measures.

In the context of preparing for treatment, the purpose of testing is meant to both direct the focus of treatment (i.e., what should treatment target) and to provide a baseline against which post-treatment assessments can indicate treatment gains. In using test data to assist in determining treatment targets, the aim is to develop a case formulation for each client. Ward and his colleagues (Drake & Ward, 2003; Ward, Nathan, Drake et al., 2000) are strong advocates of a formulation-based approach to individual treatment planning with sexual offenders. Given the description of their particular case formulation approach, and our observations of its clinical application, it appears to consume a considerable amount of time and does not, in practice, appear to make much difference to how treatment is done or what is targeted in treatment. The aim of this approach is to produce a comprehensive theory of the origin of the individual's offending behavior and to identify all those factors that currently maintain these behaviors. From this comprehensive account, a specific set of individualized treatment targets will be generated and strategies to address these targets are designed and implemented. However, as we noted earlier in this book, most treatment programs for sexual offenders follow a manualized design in which a series of targets have well-organized and specified components aimed at modifying these targets. This makes it difficult to see how the results of a comprehensive formulation could be put into practice.

This problem has led Laws and Ward (2005) to argue that a "one size fits all" approach needs to be abandoned and replaced by individually designed treatment. This may be reasonable in clinics in which few sexual offenders are seen at any one time but in centers where there is a constant flow of high numbers of referrals, some more economically viable alternative is necessary. We agree that overly manualized programs are not the solution. However, we prefer a compromise between manualized approaches and the highly individualized treatment that appears to be recommended by Ward and his colleagues.

In our program we attempt to strike this compromise. While there is no doubt that each sexual offender has greater or lesser needs concerning each of the well-established targets that most programs address, this can readily be accommodated by employing a rolling approach to treatment. Such an approach, as we have already mentioned, allows the flexibility to spend more or less time on each treatment target as each client's need demands. The question still arises as to what strategy best determines the time and focus for each client on each treatment target. It seems unlikely to us that spending an exorbitant amount of time developing the kind of elaborately sophisticated, pretreatment, case formulation advocated by

Ward and his colleagues will produce a clear understanding of a client's problem sufficient to know exactly what should be the targets of treatment and how long should be spent on each target.

These criticisms, however, are not meant to fault the general approach of a formulation-based conceptualization of each client. Rather, our problem with Ward's suggestions is that he expects a comprehensive well-formulated conceptualization of each sexual offender's problems to be generated before treatment commences. Given what we have already said about the quite understandable reluctance of sexual offenders to be honest during an assessment process, we can expect that in order to produce a thorough and accurate case formulation, the trust of the client will have to be won before valid information can be expected to be forthcoming. Even with the use of very sophisticated motivational interviewing techniques (Miller & Rollnick, 1991), it seems unlikely to us that sexual offenders will develop a sufficient level of trust to divulge more than minimal aspects of their true problems prior to involvement in treatment.

For most sexual offenders establishing this trust will not only take time, it will also be contingent on the clinician demonstrating to the sexual offender that he has the client's interests at heart. Drapeau (2005) has shown that sexual offenders become more open and honest in expressing their problems when they feel they can trust the therapist and when they believe he/she has their interests in mind. From our experience this development of trust is unlikely to happen until treatment itself has progressed for several sessions. Thus, it seems to us that a case formulation should continue to evolve over time throughout treatment. Treatment is not only where the necessary trust is established, it is also the context in which offenders are challenged and where their emotions are activated. As noted in chapter 2, many of the important schema that direct sexually offensive behaviors are only activated when the client is either faced with challenges or is emotionally aroused. We would not, therefore, expect these problematic schemas to be activated, and, as a consequence, reveal their inappropriate products (i.e., attitudes, beliefs, behaviors, and aberrant sexual arousal) during pretreatment information-gathering interviews, much less on objective psychological or physiological tests.

Our experience with using self-report measures at pre- and post-treatment has been quite disappointing. The scores of most sexual offenders on such measures at pretreatment fall within the normative range. Those few whose responses revealed deviance were forthcoming at one or two interviews, which took far less time than scoring and interpreting a battery of tests. For the majority who appeared normal at pretreatment testing, their revelations in treatment contradicted this evidently false presentation. Furthermore, normative responding at pretreatment does not allow these clients to demonstrate treatment gains at post-treatment assessments, which is certainly not helpful to anyone including the clients, the therapists, and the subsequent decision makers who have to rely on post-treatment evaluations.

What then should we do? Traditionally behavior therapy rested on a functional analysis of the clients presenting problem and this approach is still alive and well (Haynes & O'Brien, 1990). A functional analysis essentially involves the application of scientific method to the single case. A combination of information from the client and from other sources (including test results) provides a basis on which the clinician generates hypotheses concerning the range and nature of the client's problem. These hypotheses are then tested by whatever means seem most suitable, and the formulation of the case (i.e., the set of hypotheses about what caused, or more importantly, what is maintaining the client's problematic behaviors) unfolds and evolves over time as additional information (usually from the client) becomes available. A crucial part of this hypothesis-generating and hypothesis-testing process is the delivery of treatment.

Given what we have noted about the likely unreliable responses of sexual offenders to self-report measures, it seems that the best sources of information to begin this process of case formulation using a modified version of functional analysis would include the following: information from victims, police, and prosecutors regarding the nature of the offenses and the circumstances surrounding them; the client himself; and, most importantly, his responses within the treatment group. On the basis of actuarial risk measures, all sexual offenders entering Correctional Service of Canada's (CSC) prisons are allocated to one of three levels of treatment, provided they do not have additional problems (e.g., psychoses, severe ill-health) that need to be attended to prior to entering sexual offender treatment. CSC provide three levels of treatment to which sexual offenders are allocated, depending on their actuarially estimated risk: high-risk offenders for whom treatment is prolonged and intense; moderate-risk offenders for whom treatment is less prolonged and less intense; and low-risk offenders who receive the lowest intensity and shortest duration treatment. In this process, needs are generally thought to be a reasonable match for risk, although instruments are employed to estimate needs. Each of these different levels of treatment has a corresponding program manual that is semi-structured and demands flexibility. This inbuilt flexibility allows the therapists to fully enact the skills known to be effective in the delivery of sexual offender treatment, and it also permits them to respond appropriately to the responsivity issues so essential to effective offender treatment (Andrews & Bonta, 1998). Information needed to determine the required risk-needs level of treatment is derived from official details of the offense (which police and prosecutors are required to provide) and the client's offense record (which is available to us), as well as his relevant life history details which are derived from a required presentence community appraisal and from the client's own account.

Our program is something of an oddity in CSC prisons since it is: (a) based on a rolling format, and (b) accepts offenders ranging in risk from high to low. Once a sexual offender is allocated to our program, we review this information and conduct a relatively brief interview aimed at determining his willingness to participate, his openness about his offenses, and his level of motivation and defensiveness. He then enters treatment where the first information-gathering step is to have him complete a written life history. All the prior information is combined with the details of his autobiography, to determine the first, but tentative, formulation of his problems. After the client has covered the segment dealing with self-esteem and has given his disclosure (i.e., his version of the offense and what led up to it), the case formulation is revised and outlined as a tentative pathway to offending. The pathway to offending is meant to illustrate not simply the steps the client took to access a victim and then offend, but also all of the factors (distal and proximal) that trigger the desire to offend. From this we infer problematic features of the client's behaviors, cognitions, and emotions that need attention and modification in treatment. In addition, our formulation at this stage determines the emphasis each client needs in each of the remaining treatment targets. If problems in relationships, for example, were one of the sets of factors that led to offending, then the client's intimacy skills and attachment style will be thoroughly explored and training in relationship skills will be emphasized. If this was not revealed to be an important factor, then although treatment will cover this topic, it will be dealt with in less detail.

As the client progresses through the subsequent treatment targets, this formulation is constantly revised as new information emerges. It occasionally happens, for example, that the formulation arising from the early steps in treatment does not point to deficits in coping skills but as he progresses in treatment, and particularly when we address coping styles, it may become apparent that the client has significant problems in this area of functioning. As a result, we adjust our formulation accordingly and expand our previously planned examination and treatment of coping skills. These adjustments to our case formulation continue throughout treatment and can be seen as an ongoing form of functional analysis. That is, our hypotheses about what caused and maintained the client's offending, and what needs to be targeted with vigor in treatment, are constantly adjusted (i.e., reformulated) with feedback derived from the client's responses to each treatment target, and, indeed, to any other events outside treatment. The final formulation emerges as we assist the client in defining his self-management plans, his release plans, and as he identifies the support groups that will help him re-enter society. This final formulation is articulated in our end-of-treatment report that also details the progress the client has made on each of the treatment targets. This continual process of reformulating the client's needs, and thereby adjusting the delivery of treatment, is more readily achieved within the context of a rolling program format because this approach provides the necessary flexibility to adjust treatment to meet newly identified needs.

THERAPIST RATING SCALE

At approximately halfway through treatment, and again at the end of treatment, the therapist completes our Therapist Rating Scale (see Appendix 1). This rating scale requires the therapist to estimate the client's present level of functioning, as manifest by within-treatment and within-the-institution behavior, on 17 features relevant to treatment targets. For each feature (e.g., empathy) the therapist is required to rate how well the client has demonstrated his understanding of the issue (i.e., his intellectual grasp of the concept and its implications) as well as rating the degree to which he has internalized what he has learned. The latter is inferred from the client's emotional responses and behavioral demonstrations relevant to each specific feature. The psychological tests administered at the end of treatment in most programs may reveal how well the client has grasped the relevant concept (i.e., he may be able to identify the responses that show he understands the issue) but give no information on how well he has integrated this understanding into his life. He may, for example, respond to an empathy measure showing a clear understanding of what empathy is and be able to respond in a seemingly appropriate way on post-treatment measures of empathy, but he may appear disinterested during treatment when either victim suffering is discussed or when a fellow group member displays distress. It is these overt, and not so overt, signs appearing throughout treatment that provide the basis for the therapist to make the ratings on how well the client has internalized what he appears to have learned. No testing we know of would readily allow such inferences to be made and, in any case, the wealth of information that clients provide, whether intentionally or not, during treatment should not be ignored. It is a tenet of assessment that the more information that is utilized in coming to conclusions, the more accurate is the likely resultant decision.

Contrary to the aim of conducting pre- and post-treatment tests to estimate treatment gains, we are not so interested in how much clients have improved as a result of treatment but rather we want to estimate how close to normative functioning they are on each of our treatment targets. Sexual offenders may show improvements over the course of treatment but they may still be at well below the level needed to function effectively. Positive changes on tests from pre- to post-treatment may, therefore, mistakenly be taken to indicate that the client has reached the goals of treatment when, in fact, his level of functioning remains poor. Our Therapist Rating Scale is meant to overcome this problem as it simply describes current levels of functioning rather than revealing changes with treatment.

To meet this demand, our Therapist Rating Scale is the basis for estimating end-of-treatment functioning. It has four levels of functioning on two dimensions (intellectual understanding and internalization) for each of 17 features and it is these four levels that provide the basis for rating the client. Level 1 indicates very poor quality functioning. If a client's understanding of the issue is rated as 1 this means he really does not understand the issue at all. If his emotional acceptance, or integration, of the issue is rated as 1, then despite what his intellectual rating may be, it is concluded that he does not display levels of functioning that would enable him to effectively adjust to an offense-free life. Depending on the issue and how well he has done on other targets, ratings of 1 mean that further treatment is required. Ratings of 2 indicate some grasp of the issue or some acceptance of it, but they also tell us that more work is needed. Again depending on the client's responses to other targets, ratings of 2 may indicate a need for further treatment. If the ratings on all other targets are satisfactory, two or three ratings of 2 may be acceptable for discharge without the need for further treatment in prison. Ratings of 3 are deemed adequate and are meant to match reasonably normative levels of functioning. Ratings of 4 are unusual and represent ideal levels of functioning. No clients have yet received uniform ratings at the end of treatment. Some features will be given 1, others will receive 2, and others may get ratings of 3 or 4; some features will be rated 3 on intellectual understanding but only 1 or 2 on emotional integration.

We (Marshall, Webster, Serran et al., 2004) have generated data on the inter-rater reliability of our scale and found all 17 items and both ratings (intellectual and emotional integration) to reach satisfactory levels. In addition, those clients who were identified as reoffenders in the outcome study of our program, all received overall ratings below acceptable standards and these were accompanied by cautions in our reports about their release. Combining the data on reliability with the data on the relationship between our ratings and outcome suggests that our Therapist Rating Scale has potential for more widespread use, but more psychometric data are needed. Several centers are now using this rating scale and have agreed to provide us with the resultant data so that we can eventually have a more secure empirical basis for the measure.

The following case descriptions will illustrate the ongoing process of case formulation, treatment delivery, final ratings, and long-term outcome. We have chosen cases that illustrate the types of clients we typically see in our prison setting (child molesters and rapists).

In our case formulation, we are not only looking for what we call background factors (or what some call "predisposing factors") and pathways to offending (or what some call "precipitating factors"), we are also seeking to identify the client's strengths (or what some call "protective factors"). Background factors are those that occur somewhat distal from the offense and may not, on their own, always trigger an offense. Typical background factors include: relationship difficulties, problems at work, financial problems, chronic drug or alcohol use, working long hours, a general sense of entitlement, persistently masturbating to deviant sexual fantasies or images, generally poor coping skills, chronic low self-worth, chronic loneliness, childhood abuse (physical, sexual, emotional) or neglect, persistent antisocial attitudes, general impulsivity, emotional dysregulation, ill health, and various other idiosyncratic factors.

Within our pathways to offending we identify immediate precipitators such as intoxication, acute emotional distress, sudden life stressors, emergence of situationally triggered negative schema (e.g., "All women are bitches," "Children (or this child) desire(s) sex with adults"), a narrowed exclusive focus on his own needs, an acutely triggered sense of entitlement, and a sense of hopelessness. Pathways to offending, however, also include the actual steps the offender takes to gain access to a victim. Opportunities to offend sometimes present themselves but more typically offenders seek them out. A child molester, for example, may spend many hours, days, weeks, or even months grooming a child as preparation to offend. This grooming may involve gift-giving, taking the child to shows or events, relaxing discipline, or giving special attention or affection. Child molesters invariably have to not only manipulate the child but also other adults in order to be alone with the victim. Rapists may cruise highways in their cars looking for hitchhikers, they may prowl neighborhoods at night, they may enter houses with the apparent intention of stealing to cover an intent to sexually assault, they may offer a woman a drive home in order to secure an opportunity to offend, they may ply a woman with alcohol or drugs to reduce her ability to resist, or they may physically attack a woman before raping her. Exhibitionists typically expose themselves either in a secluded area or while driving their cars. While the latter strategy seems certain to finally result in their identification, it does offer multiple opportunities to offend and this apparently compensates for the elevated risk. Very few exhibitionists expose themselves from the window of their home or apartment presumably because the risk of detection is high and the opportunities to expose may be few.

Once an offense has occurred, most perpetrators immediately respond with concerns about being reported. However, these responses usually occur only after the first offense (or first two offenses) and they rapidly diminish if their crime goes undetected. Over time, and with repeated offending, sexual offenders quite often become emboldened and less careful. As their fears of detection subside, sexual offenders are very likely to re-create the offense in their imagination, resulting in a pairing of the offense (or, more likely, an idealized version of the offense) with sexual arousal which may result in masturbating to ejaculation to these thoughts. Whether masturbation accompanies fantasies of the offense, the repeated repetition of the thoughts and associated sexual arousal will produce two results. First, these associations will serve to entrench a disposition to offend as a result of conditioning processes (see Laws & Marshall, 1990). Second, rehearsing deviant thoughts will, as Wright and Schneider (1997) quite rightly note, serve to enhance self-deception processes that excuse the offender from responsibility and entrench his distortions about the offense and the victim.

In developing our case formulation, all these issues (i.e., those involved in our client's background factors and pathways to offending) are crucial.

CLINICAL CASES

The following two cases are meant to illustrate some of the specific aspects of our treatment approach. In each case we could have elaborated details of the processes involved in every target of our overall treatment program; however, these two cases were chosen because each one illustrates, rather better than the other, the processes involved in the targets that were specifically relevant to each of the clients.

First Case

Stan (not his real name) was a 28-year-old Canadian-born male convicted of three sexual assaults (what in other jurisdictions would be called "rapes") for which he received a 5-year sentence to be served in a federal prison. He entered the Ontario Regional prison system of CSC and was sent to Millhaven Institution to complete the 4-month sexual offender assessment. This assessment uses a series of interviews which, along with extensive sources of official information, provide the basis for scoring several actuarial risk assessment and treatment needs instruments. In addition, sexual offenders are asked by the Millhaven Assessment Unit staff to participate in comprehensive phallometric assessments designed to detect their sexual interests in children, forced sex, and normative sex. From all of this information and assessment results, sexual offenders are allocated to one or another institution depending on their risk, needs, and potential institutional management problems. Almost all sexual offenders deemed to be at low/moderate and moderate risk are sent to Bath Institution as are some of the low-risk and some of the moderate/high-risk offenders. Stan was judged to be appropriate for Bath Institution.

Shortly after his arrival at Bath Institution, Stan was seen for two pretreatment interviews. Prior to these interviews, the interviewer reviewed the official documentation and the report from the Millhaven Assessment Unit. The official documentation revealed that Stan had committed three rapes, two by entering each victim's home at night and the other by attacking a lone woman in a dark narrow lane at the back of office buildings in a deserted downtown area. This information revealed not only the sexual details of the assaults but also that some degree of seemingly unnecessary violence was used. In addition, Stan had demanded that each of the two victims who were attacked in their homes make sexually explicit remarks that seemed aimed at degrading them; for example, one victim was required to describe herself as a "slut" who liked being raped, while the other was required to repeatedly utter disgusting colloquial descriptors of her genitalia and anus.

The police obtained DNA samples from Stan that matched semen found on the three victims. According to court documents, Stan pled guilty to the two sexual assaults that occurred in the victims' residences, but not to the other one despite the DNA evidence. The official documentation also included a detailed community assessment that described his family in rather ideal terms. His father was a senior accountant at a large business for 25 years; his mother was the assistant manager of a small local branch of a national bank; and his younger sister was a graduate student at a major university. The community report described the family as good citizens who were shocked to learn of Stan's offenses but were fully supportive of him.

Stan's offense record revealed additional nonsexual offenses: two break-and-enter convictions and one for damaging property. Details of the two break-ins bore strong similarities to the two rapes that involved entry to a residence. Stan's manner of gaining entry was the same and a lone adult female occupied each residence. The conviction for damaging property occurred during an argument between Stan and a woman with whom he had been living for 2 months. During the argument Stan became enraged and smashed some of her furniture but did not strike her. The relationship terminated after she called the police, and he was forcefully removed from the residence.

During the interviews, Stan provided few details of the two sexual offenses to which he had pled guilty at trial saying that he entered the houses to steal whatever he could find and that he had accidentally discovered a woman asleep on both occasions. Stan offered no reason why the victim who was assaulted in the alley had falsely claimed he raped her nor did he attempt to explain the presence of his DNA in her vagina. In fact, he was quite evasive about the sexual crimes except to say that he committed the break-and-enter offenses because he enjoyed the associated risks. When talking about these break-and-enters, Stan seemed rather boastful. According to Stan he held respectful attitudes toward women, had a number of good friends, got along well with his parents and sister, and had a well-paying job. When asked directly about the victims of his sexual assaults, Stan dismissed the possibility that they had suffered because he had not been forceful. This latter remark contradicted the reports by the victims.

After reviewing the official information and completing the interviews, a tentative formulation pointed to possible negative schemas about women (contrary to Stan's claims), more family problems than Stan was willing to admit to, a greater use of force in his offenses than he claimed, a lack of empathy for his victims, possible problems in controlling anger, and perhaps a low sense of self-worth given his boastfulness about some aspects of his crimes. Finally, the overall picture seemed inconsistent with Stan's relatively normative score on the PCL-R (he was scored as 16), and his crimes seemed at odds with the general picture of a man from a happy middle-class background who held a well-paying job and who otherwise appeared to be a respectable member of society. In fact we were left with more questions than answers, which is not at all unusual at this point in our typical development of a case formulation. It seemed, from Stan's responses at the interviews, that any number of further interviews or assessments would reveal little more than we knew at this point. We needed to secure Stan's confidence before any further accurate information was likely to be forthcoming.

At this point Stan entered treatment. The group had nine other offenders and one therapist. Each of the other clients was some way along in the process of treatment: two were near the beginning, having been in for only three sessions when Stan arrived; two were close to finishing and had done well; and the remaining five were some way along the process between these other four clients. Of the two other relatively new clients, one was a rather angry rapist who was still blaming his victim and who expressed negative views about women.

At Stan's first treatment session he was introduced to the group, told about confidentiality issues (both his and the therapist's), attendance and participation requirements, and asked to begin to write his autobiography.

He was shown the posters on the walls of the group room that identified each target of the program and described their broad content, and he was encouraged to seek advice of some of the more senior group members. Stan appeared hesitant and somewhat nervous at the first session so attention was directed toward other group members, and he was allowed to sit quietly and observe. At the second session Stan made some comments in response to remarks by others, but these were little more than agreements with what had been said and gave little insight into Stan's views. At the third session Stan was asked to describe aspects of his sense of self-worth.

To assist Stan, the therapist identified the following areas where self-esteem may or may not be strong: work, leisure and sport, general social functioning, relationships, sex, education, and an overall judgment about himself. It was thought that the issue of low self-esteem might be particularly relevant to Stan's offenses (given his boastfulness about his crimes) and to his ability to deal with various targets of treatment. For example, Marshall, Champagne, Brown, and Miller (1997) found a strong relationship among sexual offenders between low self-esteem and an expressed lack of empathy for victims, and Baumeister (1993) reported that people low in self-esteem typically have significant cognitive distortions and have difficulties in relationships.

Stan's initial response was that he was confident in all the areas listed, but with probing by the therapist and other group members, he gradually admitted to somewhat less-than-ideal levels of self-confidence in some areas. The therapist was left feeling unsatisfied with his understanding of Stan's position on this issue. As a result Stan was asked to indicate the three areas where he was most confident. He named work, education, and sex as areas of greatest confidence, describing himself rather boastfully as "a stud" when it came to sex. Before pursuing these areas, Stan was asked to describe positive features of himself in terms of relationships as well as leisure and sport, that is, two areas he had not mentioned as topics about which he felt confident. Stan was clearly caught off balance by these questions and appeared at a loss to point to any positive features. The therapist quickly offered assistance by indicating that Stan was able to converse easily and well and that would be helpful in relationships. This comment seemed to put Stan at ease, but he still struggled with identifying any positive features in either of the two areas. Stan admitted that he had always been poor at sports, and this seemed to affect him quite negatively. He became quiet and was obviously uncomfortable so the therapist congratulated him on his efforts and told him he had done well for his first try.

Stan was asked to write, before the next session, six positive characteristics of himself for each of the following four areas: work and sex

(areas where he claimed to be confident), and sport/leisure and relationships (areas where he did not seem confident). At the next session
the therapist read to the group Stan's lists of positive features. Stan
produced a long list of good qualities about himself concerning work.
In the group's discussion of these features it became clear that Stan had
worked long hours (at least 50 hours per week). When asked why he did
this Stan said it gave him satisfaction because it impressed his employer,
his fellow staff, and his father. It was clear his father's opinion was very
important to Stan, but he said he felt his father never fully approved of
him. Stan was then asked about what he did with his leisure time. This
line of questioning turned out to be productive, and the following is an
abbreviated transcript.

Therapist (T):	Stan, when you finish work, let's say at the end of the week on Friday, how do you feel?
Stan (S):	Okay, I guess. I feel satisfied.
T:	That you've done a good job?
S:	Yes.
T:	Do you feel you've earned your drinks at the bar?
S:	I do.
T:	That's good because you have. Could you elaborate a bit?
S:	Well, I feel I deserve to do what I want. You know, I put in long hours and I don't think I'm as appreciated as I should be.
T:	By whom?
S:	Well, by my bosses, I guess.
T:	But you said earlier that your work was satisfying because your boss was impressed.
S:	Well, he should be, but he doesn't show it.
Other client:	What about your father? You said your work impressed him.
S:	Oh, he never shows it, but I know he approves of good work habits.
T:	This is great, Stan. You're doing well. Back to the bit about feeling you deserve what you want. Can you say more about that please?
S:	I don't know. It seems to me if a person works long and hard that he should be able to have a good time.
T:	That seems fair. I notice in your written notes you didn't list anything under leisure. So you do not have any hobbies? Do you go to shows or ballgames?
S:	Not really. I don't have the time.

Other client:	What do you mean, you don't have the time? Everyone has spare time. What do you do in your spare time?
S:	My only spare time is the weekends. I don't really do anything except go to a bar on Saturday night. I need to rest on the weekend.
T:	Do you drink much on Saturday or on any other day?
S:	No. Maybe 4 or 5 beers over the course of a night.
T:	Good. That seems okay. If you don't do much with your spare time other than going to bars, how does that make you feel?
S:	Well, I just really pack a lot of fun into the time I do have.
T:	Like what?
S:	Well, I told you. I'm good at sex and I don't have a problem picking up women.
T:	That's interesting. Where do you pick them up?
S:	At bars.
Other client:	How easy is it?
S:	No problem really. I just say hello, buy them a drink, start a conversation, and it goes fine.
Other client:	I don't mean to be rude but you're an okay looking guy but not great and you come across as a bit full of yourself. Do women really go for that?
S:	Well, women who hang out at bars are not your everyday women you know. They are there for the same reason I am, to get laid.
Another relatively new client:	
	Yeah. I know the type.
T (to this client):	
	Can you tell me what you mean by this?

What the therapist wanted was Stan's view of women but guessed it would be less threatening to direct the question at the other client knowing that Stan would hear the man's response. The therapist wanted to see how Stan would respond to the other client's remarks. The therapist watched Stan's facial and bodily reactions as he listened to the other client.

Other client:	Most women who go to bars are sluts. It's easy to pick them up and you can just fuck them and forget them.

Stan was nodding.

T:	What does the group think of this view?

A discussion followed with most group members saying that women who go to bars alone are obviously lonely and probably looking for a nice guy. The group challenged the views of the other client, saying that he seemed contemptuous of women. Focusing on the other, more experienced, group member's views, allowed the challenges to be stronger than they might have been if Stan had been the focus. This tactic of seizing the chance to respond to another client's inappropriately supportive remarks has the advantage of allowing a new group member to vicariously absorb challenges without directly receiving them. Thus, the new group member is less likely to withdraw or simply become defensive. It is easy to lose the confidence of new clients if they are challenged too directly early on in treatment.

After this interchange with the other client Stan appeared to have relaxed and listened. The therapist then asked Stan what he was thinking.

S: Well, I think Charles's (the other client) views are a bit extreme. Not all women are sluts. You know I've had a relationship with one woman who wasn't like that at all.

T: Thanks. That's very interesting. I'm glad you can take a balanced view. We will come back to the nice women you mentioned in a bit, but first I want you to tell us a bit more about something you said earlier. You said that after working long hours you felt you deserved to enjoy yourself. What sort of things did you feel you deserved?

S: To have some fun.

T: What sort of fun?

S: Maybe sex mostly, I guess.

T: So when you went to the bar after work or on Saturday night, was it sex you were looking for?

S: Probably.

T: Anything else?

S: Talk to a few guys.

T: Did you ever go with friends?

S: Not too often. Mostly alone.

T: That's good but why alone?

S: My friends are married so they can't come to bars.

T: So you go alone to the bar, talk to a few guys you meet there, and try to pick up a woman?

S: I do pick up a woman if I want to.

T: What do you talk about with these guys?

S: Mostly about the women in the bar, which ones would be good in bed, which ones would be easy to pick up.

This discussion revealed several things. Among them it was clear that Stan felt entitled to meet his desires as a result of working long hours, and probably particularly because no one gave him the kind of direct approval for his work that he needed. Clearly, Stan also had quite negative views about women, although he noted at least one exception. As a result of this productive interchange, the formulation of Stan's case was expanded to include concerns about attitudes toward women, about a sense of entitlement particularly around sex, and also a need to be approved which, despite his best efforts (long hours at work), was not forthcoming. In addition, the case formulation was adjusted to include concerns about striking a better balance in Stan's life between work and play, an expansion of his circle of friends to include some with whom he could spend time, and a more creative use of leisure activities.

It is important for the reader to keep in mind that after the above interactions with Stan, the session shifted focus to another group member's issues. The therapist deliberately chose a client whose attitudes toward women had moved significantly from being similar to Stan's to being quite positive. This move had not been difficult since this other client's originally expressed attitudes were part of his initial defensiveness. Once the therapist had earned his trust this client's defensiveness was reduced, and he admitted that he blamed his victim (an adult female with whom he had been living) and cast all women in the same light to diminish his true responsibility for his offense. In examining this client's developing self-management plans (i.e., relapse prevention plans), the therapist deliberately asked him about his current feelings about women in general. Again, this was done to both compliment this client for his changed views and to provide Stan with a model of appropriate attitudes. Therapists leading group programs must always be aware that whichever client is the focus of a discussion, all group members are observing the process so the potential for vicarious learning is always present and such opportunities should not be missed.

The next step for Stan in treatment was for him to give an account of his offenses. We chose one of the two offenses that occurred after he broke into a house. Because he readily admitted to this offense, it seemed the best place to start as he could be reinforced for honesty and the details he might provide could help direct questioning about the other offenses. If we got sufficient details of this first offense, we might pass directly to the assault in the alley rather than probing too much about the other break-and-enter assault.

T: Stan, remember last session I asked you to prepare to give an account of one of your offenses and we decided that it would be the first of the two that resulted from your break-in. Could you start by telling us a bit about what was going on that day? Maybe you could tell us what you did that day; it was a Saturday, wasn't it?

S: Yeah, it was. I don't know exactly what you want, but I did the usual things I do on Saturdays.

T: What was that?

S: I tidied the apartment, went grocery shopping. You know, just the usual things.

T: Were you feeling differently than usual on a Saturday?

S: Well, I had a shitty week.

T: (Nods.) Tell me more.

S: It started with a blow-up with my father. He was ranting at me about my life. Saying I was going nowhere, not getting promoted at work, not being married, not settling down. Stuff like that. He's always judging me. Never says anything good about me.

T: Gosh, your dad seems hard on you. So you were still upset about that on the Saturday?

S: Yeah, but I also had a bad week at work. I couldn't seem to concentrate and messed up a few tasks and got told off by my boss who is a prick anyway.

T: Bit like your dad?

S: Yeah, I guess.

T: So you're feeling upset. Were you angry or depressed?

S: Bit of both. I also had arguments at work with almost everyone, particularly the office secretary who has always been a bitch to me.

T: This is good information. You are doing a great job. How did the day go on Saturday?

S: I just did the routine things, but I couldn't stop thinking about what a bad week it was. I felt pissed off and useless. I hadn't done anything right all week.

T: Let's get closer to the offense. What did you do on Saturday evening?

S: I thought about calling up a woman I had met at a bar the week before. We had sex and it was great so I thought I'd try again. I thought having sex would get my mind off the bad week. But she didn't answer her phone so I went to the bar where I met her hoping to see her again but she wasn't there.

T: So what did you do?

S: I stayed and drank. Drank too much actually, got a bit drunk. There was no one there to talk to except the bar man so about midnight I left.

T:	How drunk were you?
S:	Well, I was definitely over the legal limit for driving but I didn't have my car anyway. I could walk fine but I was kind of in a "I don't give a shit" mood. Booze does that to me if I drink too much.
T:	This is excellent. You are giving us valuable information. So what did you do?
S:	I walked up (unnamed) street to an area where I had broken into apartments before. Basement apartments or ground floor apartments are easy. Sooner or later you find one with an open window. It was summer so it was hot.
T:	Was this a regular routine to go searching for places to break into or do you only do this when you are drunk and upset?
S:	Yeah, usually only when I am drunk and pissed off.
T:	You're doing great. Keep it up. So tell us what happened next.

Stan gave a detailed account of how he searched for an apartment to break into, found one, and entered carefully through an open window.

T:	You are giving us the kind of detail we need. Good for you. So tell us what were you thinking and feeling after you got inside the apartment.
S:	I was shaking a bit, feeling a bit scared, but excited. I think I only wanted the excitement of it. I thought, I'll just steal something in case I get caught.
T:	You mean so that the police will think you were just a robber?
S:	Yeah. It would be hard to convince them I just broke in for the fun of it but that was true.
T:	Tell us what this excitement and the feeling of being a bit scared does for you.
S:	I don't know. Makes me forget about having a shitty week. Makes me feel in control. Something like that. I'm not really sure but I like it.
T:	Great. You have a good understanding of your feelings. You seem a bit excited telling us about the break-in. Am I right?
S:	I guess so, but it's not like when I'm doing it.
T:	Okay, I understand. Go on.

At this point several group members asked Stan about his feelings while in the house. They pushed him about sexual feelings, but he denied any strong sexual feelings. He maintained that the excitement generated by the risks of being caught was what he most clearly felt. Other group members had asked questions earlier in this process but for convenience we have left this out of the description because their questions and Stan's answers did not add anything to the unfolding dialogue. Stan was then asked to describe how he found the victim.

S:	I went to the bedroom. It was a single bedroom place. I looked in the bedroom and saw it was a woman alone in the bed. She looked to be asleep.
T:	Now what was going through your mind? What were you feeling?
S:	I guess I started to get horny. She looked so defenseless lying there. Ready for the taking.
T:	Good. You are being really clear. I see what you mean. Were you having any feelings other than sexual feelings? You said at first you were excited and scared. Were you still having those feelings?
S:	No. Weirdly enough I started to feel angry. Does that seem normal?
T:	Well, you had a lousy week. Maybe the excitement and feeling horny just got you so aroused it kicked in the anger.
S:	Yeah, that sounds okay. Thanks, that makes sense.
T:	Go on. You're doing great. It's okay that you were angry. We just want you to tell us what you were feeling. All feelings are understandable.
S:	It was a bit confusing really. Until I looked in at her in bed, I felt excited but in control. In fact, the feelings of control were strongest I think. But then when I saw her for some reason I started to remember what had happened during the week. I got angry and thought about that bitchy secretary at work and how no one appreciated me. It was really confusing and I thought, "Fuck it. I'll screw this bitch." So I just went ahead and did it.
T:	Stan, that was very, very good for your first account of your offense, wasn't it, guys? (Therapist looked around the group for confirmation and they all nodded in agreement.) Tell Stan what you thought was good about his account.

Each member of the group was asked to comment. The experienced clients gave a lot of positive feedback but one of the newer members started by pointing to features Stan had failed to mention. He was immediately stopped and reminded that his task was to give Stan positive feedback. After a client's first attempt at disclosure, no matter how poor it is, the group is required to comment only on the positive features so that the client leaves the group feeling he has done well. Our experience shows that this facilitates more open future accounts, whereas pointing to the inadequacies in the account seems to disappoint clients and makes them less accessible at subsequent sessions.

At Stan's two subsequent further elaborations of his disclosure, he essentially described all the details provided in the official records concerning the two break-in rapes. He was more reluctant to give details of the rape in the alley, but he did at least agree that he had committed this offense. It became clear that Stan considered this latter rape to be far worse than the other two and that Stan believed his father would disown him if he confessed to his father that he was responsible for this offense. Once Stan began to distance himself from his father and to recognize the destructive effects of his father's attitudes toward Stan, he seemed far more comfortable and admitted to the alleyway rape. This admission, however, was not made until toward the end of Stan's involvement in the program when he began to identify the avoidance aspects of his self-management plans.

As a result of these discussions Stan's case formulation was modified again. Concerns about his schemas involving women and about his low sense of self-worth were strengthened as were concerns about his relationship skills. In addition, it was clear that Stan had a far less positive relationship with his father than he first indicated, and this appeared to be related to his need for approval—a need that was not fulfilled by his father or by his boss or workmates. It also seemed clear that his long hours at work were meant to achieve this external approval but that it was an unsuccessful strategy. This raised the possibility that a change of employment might be useful.

Stan's subsequent offense accounts and his participation in each of the subsequent targets of treatment were good. He had most difficulty in the relationship component partly because of his recurring, but fluctuating, negative attitudes toward women. This schema seemed to be activated less and less frequently over treatment sessions as Stan's self-confidence grew and as he progressively came to distance himself from his father's influence. It appeared that this schema about women was triggered only when Stan felt angry or disappointed. He profited considerably from both the relationship component and particularly from the exercises on coping style and coping skills. Indeed, more time was spent with Stan on these issues than on any other topic.

Stan's responses to the earlier Millhaven Assessment Unit's phallometric appraisal displayed a normative profile. After our experience with Stan in the early stages of treatment, when his anger and self-denigration were more evident, it seemed clear that any deviant sexual responses by Stan at phallometric assessment would be unlikely to be evident unless he was similarly angry or upset. As noted earlier in this book, Yates, Barbaree, and Marshall (1984) demonstrated that having a woman make normal males angry markedly enhanced their otherwise normative phallometric responses to rape. We expect that had such a manipulation of Stan's anger been implemented, he would have shown deviant overall arousal to rape at the phallometric appraisal. We are not, however, suggesting that these strategies be adopted when phallometrically assessing sexual offenders as this would obviously present problems for institutional management and place citizens at risk when such assessments were conducted in community-based clinics. The point here is that it is the activation of usually dormant schemas that is relevant to understanding a client's offending behavior and that the usual methods of assessing clients does not involve such activation. During therapy, however, when clients are allowed to become somewhat upset, as happened with Stan, these dormant schemas are activated and can be addressed. As a result of these considerations, Stan was advised to implement satiation procedures (see description in chapter 2) immediately after masturbating to orgasm. Stan said he usually masturbated to appropriate sexual thoughts unless he was angry or depressed when he would think about raping a woman, usually by re-creating one of his offenses. By the end of treatment, Stan said these deviant fantasies no longer generated arousal even when he was upset.

Stan's final self-management plans included a list of positive lifestyle changes such as: the generation of a list of leisure activities (e.g., regular swimming and exercise, photography, Saturday night outings to theater or cinema, joining a book club); the development of more effective friendships and relationships; part-time schoolwork with the hope of developing alternative job skills; taking greater care with what he eats (in the past he had relied on fast foods); and reducing his working hours to a normal level (35–40 hours per week). In addition, Stan's self-management plans included some avoidance elements. For example, Stan agreed that he should not go to bars alone or allow himself to be alone when intoxicated, and he should structure things so that he cannot wander the streets at night alone. Stan developed contacts in the community so that when he left prison he could immediately enter a community-based sexual offenders' program to continue treatment for at least the first 6 months, and he also contacted a community program aimed at enhancing relationship skills. Also, prior to leaving prison, Stan voluntarily completed an anger management program, and he agreed that should angry feelings become difficult to control he would immediately contact a therapist to get help.

Stan's support groups were limited as he wished to separate himself from his parents, although his sister has remained one of his supports, and he believed that associating with his old friends (such as they were) would likely lead him back to risky behaviors. However, Stan did develop a good group of professional supports by contacting these people while still in prison. Stan's warning signs were sensibly related to his self-management plans, and his release plans were sensible. Stan was fully aware of the fact that he would be at some risk to reoffend for the foreseeable future, but he was sensibly optimistic about the future.

At the end of treatment the therapist completed the Therapist Rating Scale on Stan. Table 4.2 describes the results of these ratings. As a result of the ratings it was recommended that Stan enter our Maintenance Program in the 6 months prior to his likely release in order to revaluate him and to do further work on the issues (i.e., coping skills, self-esteem, control over impulses, and emotional regulation) that received less than satisfactory ratings. Stan was also required to complete the institutional

TABLE 4.2   Stan's Ratings on the Therapist Rating Scale

TARGETS	LEVEL FOR INTELLECTUAL UNDERSTANDING	LEVEL FOR EMOTIONAL ACCEPTANCE/ DEMONSTRATION
1. Acceptance of responsibility	3	3
2. General empathy	3	3
3. Empathy for victim	3	3
4. Prosocial attitudes	3	3
5. Adequate coping skills/styles	2	2
6. Adequate social skills	4	3
7. Positive self-esteem	3	2
8. Control over impulses	3	2
9. Good emotional regulation	3	2
10. Control over anger/aggression	3	3
11. Control over substance use	2	2
12. Normative sexual views/ interests	3	3
13. Understanding of risk factors	3	3
14. Quality of self- management plans	3	3
15. Quality of supports	2	2
16. Quality of release plans	3	3
17. Commitment to maintenance	3	3

Substance Abuse Program. After completion of these two additional programs, Stan's functioning was close to normative on all issues.

To date Stan has been in the community for 3 years and has not had any further contact with the law. At his last contact with his parole officer, when parole requirements had expired, Stan reported the development of new friends, a budding romantic relationship, and a new, more satisfying job.

Second Case

Robert (not his real name) was a 32-year-old unemployed delivery van driver who was charged and convicted of two counts of sexual interference and received a 3-year sentence to be served in a federal prison. He entered the Ontario Regional prison system of the CSC and was judged to be appropriate for Bath Institution where our main program operates.

Robert was seen for two pretreatment interviews after his arrival at Bath Institution. According to official documentation regarding the offense, the victim was a 4-year-old female child. The parents of the victim were close friends of Robert and his wife, Jody (not her real name), and Robert was babysitting when he offended. The offenses included kissing, fondling, oral sex, digital penetration, and attempted vaginal intercourse. Robert's wife, Jody, remained supportive of him following the offenses, although she expressed a determination to improve their relationship, and she said she expected Robert to make changes.

During the interviews, Robert provided few details of the sexual offenses and instead focused on external issues. Specifically, Robert reported a wide range of health-related complaints and other stressors in his life. Robert noted that he was unemployed at the time of the offenses due to health-related problems. However, Robert appeared disconnected from his emotions, as he found it difficult to identify how he felt in relation to the problems in his life. When questioned specifically about the offenses, Robert admitted to touching the victim but claimed that she initiated the sexual contact. He described the victim as a sexually aggressive child who "came on" to him. He also minimized the abuse by claiming that the sexual offenses occurred less frequently than described by the victim, and he denied attempting intercourse. These attitudes and beliefs are typical of many men who molest children.

During the initial interviews Robert also placed some blame on his wife. He said they rarely had sex (he estimated once per month) and that they often argued. Robert said that because he was out of work (injured back) he spent a lot of time alone and that he masturbated quite frequently, usually because he was bored and because he felt sexually unsatisfied with his wife. His description of his relationship revealed that he expected his wife to still do most of the household chores, despite the fact that she was employed and he was not working. When Robert complained about the lack of sex, his wife said she was too tired after working all day and then making supper and cleaning the house. She apparently asked him to do more chores but he responded indignantly, "Those are women's jobs." It was clear that Robert was very demanding of his wife and he appeared to have little sympathy for her.

As a result of these interviews and the information from the files, our tentative case formulation identified the following as targets for treatment: a failure to take responsibility for his actions, a possible sense of entitlement about sex, a fragile sense of self-worth, poor coping strategies, constrained emotional expression, and inadequate relationship skills. A sexual attraction to children was also a possible problem but an earlier phallometric assessment revealed normative sexual interests. However, we held the possibility that this might emerge as a target once Robert became confident enough to be truthful about this.

When Robert entered our open-ended program, the other nine group members were at different stages of treatment and already had experience with several treatment-related issues. Two group members had adult female victims and the other clients had child victims.

After having been given information about confidentiality and the group rules, Robert was required at the second session to provide a disclosure detailing his offenses, the following brief account serves to illustrate Robert's initial position.

Therapist (T): Go ahead, Robert, and tell us about your offense.

Robert (R): It was a difficult time in my life; I was going through a lot. My health wasn't good, and that was stressful. I was off work because I hurt my back, and so Tina's [the victim, not her real name] parents regularly brought her over to be babysat by my wife and I. My wife was working on most of the occasions, so I was at home alone with Tina. One day I lay down with Tina to take a nap and I fell asleep. When I woke up, Tina was cuddling next to me and she had taken off her pyjamas. Then she kissed me on the lips. The same thing happened again later, but that time we ended up touching each other. That happened maybe once a month or so. That's it.

The therapist and group members asked questions aimed at getting further details of the abuse. Robert denied having any sexual thoughts about the victim and instead stated that he "had been taken off guard and was unable to resist" her advances. Then the therapist turned to Robert.

T: Robert, that was a good first attempt.
                (Turns to the group.)
                What do each of you think about Robert's disclosure?

The group members complimented Robert on his efforts, but they added that they looked forward to a further disclosure that they hoped would provide additional details, particularly of the role Robert played in the offense. As can be seen, Robert was not yet ready to accept responsibility for his offenses.

Robert was reinforced for admitting to his offenses, which he had been unable to do in the past, but was given the feedback that he needed to accept far more responsibility in his next attempt at disclosure. He was told that his version blamed the victim. Like many of our clients, Robert was surprised and stated that he did not intend to blame the victim. The other group members suggested to Robert that he had problems and issues he had to address and that he needed to be honest in order to do so. Through further discussion it was determined that Robert's feelings of shame were preventing him from fully accepting what he had done. This issue was addressed through helping Robert to distinguish himself from these specific aspects of his behavior. He was also given work aimed at increasing his self-esteem. For example, Robert was required to examine the schemas that undermined his sense of self-worth. His major problematic schema about himself was that "he was a failure at everything" and was therefore, an inadequate person. Robert became aware that this schema distorted his perceptions of himself and prevented him from making positive changes in his life. With encouragement from the therapist and the other group members, Robert began to challenge this schema by replacing it with more appropriate ways of interpreting his behavior and life. After some practice at this, Robert not only reported improved self-esteem, he also functioned in a far more confident manner than he had shown earlier. Robert also reported that he no longer saw himself as a failure, but rather, he recognized that as long as he did the best he could with each situation, he felt satisfied. As Robert progressed on these issues, he was able to accept progressively more responsibility for his actions and stopped blaming the victim.

Throughout Robert's disclosure and the self-esteem component, he seemed emotionally flat when describing problematic issues. In particular, when Robert was describing his offenses and when he spoke about his relationship with his wife, he was emotionally distant. Robert clearly had problems expressing his feelings and this appeared to be exacerbated when he was discussing difficult issues.

The next step was to have Robert produce a written autobiography. The following discussion occurred during Robert's presentation of his autobiography.

T:	Robert, you mention in your autobiography that you felt "unwanted" by your parents. Can you tell us more about this?
R:	It just felt to me like they didn't care.
T:	I see. What told you this, Robert?
R:	They always paid attention to my younger brother or my older brother, but never me.
T:	It sounds like you felt unnoticed.
R:	Yeah, that's right. I mean, they weren't abusive or anything, but I just seemed to get ignored, you know, lost in everything else that was happening.
Other client:	What about friends at school?
R:	Well, I had problems with reading and writing. I failed grade 1, and I was put in special classes. I felt really different from the other kids, I just didn't fit in. I just played by myself.
Other client:	You must have felt really lonely.
R:	Yeah, I was a loner. The other kids rejected me and called me a "weirdo." When I got older, I got involved with the wrong crowd. We got into trouble, got into drugs, you know.
T:	That's interesting, Robert. Were you less lonely doing that?
R:	Well, I thought I fit in, but then I accidentally overdosed and nearly died. I decided it wasn't worth the risk. I decided I wanted to change my life, so I did. I quit using drugs, got a job, and decided I wanted a family. That would make me feel complete.
T:	You are doing a good job, Robert. Very good identification of your feelings. I'd like you to think about how those experiences influenced your adult relationships, especially with your wife.

Robert reported he met his first girlfriend Kim (not her real name) shortly after giving up his negative lifestyle. Robert jumped into the relationship without getting to know the woman because he was desperate to have a relationship and family. She had a daughter from a previous relationship and Robert said this thrilled him because he had a "ready-made family." Robert later discovered that Kim had cheated on her previous boyfriend, which he described as devastating news. He immediately left the relationship without ever addressing the issue. Robert was questioned in the group about his relationship with his current wife, Jody.

T: Robert, tell us about your relationship with Jody. How you met, what the relationship was like, those kinds of things.

R: Well, I met Jody about a year after I left Kim. Jody was a friend of my roommate, and we spent several months together as friends before going out. Then, we got involved in a relationship and a year later we got married. Things were good at first, but then they started to go downhill.

T: Good. Can you tell us more about that last part—how everything was going well at first, but then started going downhill?

R: Well, at first the relationship was great. Jody and I got along really well. We didn't fight; we had a great sex life. After a while, I ended up losing my job because of health problems, and Jody had to work, and we started having financial problems. Those things led to a lot of stress. Then, Jody found out she was pregnant.

T: Wow, that's a lot to handle. How were you feeling?

R: Well, I thought everything was going downhill, but then I figured once we had the baby, things would be great. I wanted to be a dad more than anything. Things were really rough, Jody was really ill during the pregnancy and our sex life disappeared. I thought she wasn't paying enough attention to me.

T: So tell me how you felt about the fact that things were going rough and that your sex life had stopped?

R: I thought she didn't love me and wasn't committed to the relationship.

T: And how did you feel?

R: I felt unwanted and unloved. I felt inadequate, like a failure. Like when I was younger. I also thought about Kim's unfaithfulness and wondered if Jody would do the same.

T: Good for recognizing that, Robert. You mentioned some time earlier that part of the reason sex was infrequent was because your wife said she was too tired after working all day. Could you say more about that?

R: Yeah, she always complained that she had to work all day and then cook the meals and clean up and so on. But lots of women we knew did that so I don't know why she complained.

T: That's interesting, Robert. I am wondering if you felt worried that your wife was out working? Did it bother you?

R: Yeah, probably. She was the one making the money, and it seemed she didn't need me. I believed I was going to lose

	her, that scared me, and I didn't know what to do. Also I needed sex. I was doing my best to do my part in the relationship but I was getting nothing back. I felt I deserved better. So I focused on the victim, paid attention to her. She was nice to me, liked to cuddle, made me feel good. That's how come the sex started with her.
Other client:	I can relate to that. I felt jealous when my wife started working and spending time with her friends. I never talked to her about it, I just let my feelings build inside. Did you ever tell your wife how you felt?
R:	No—I didn't talk to her about how I felt. I think I thought it wouldn't matter, that maybe if I talked about the problems, they would get worse and it would be better if I ignored them. Also it makes me nervous to talk about problems. My parents never talked about their problems and they sure had some, but they managed to stay married.
T:	Okay—that's important. I have an assignment for you. I want you to talk to Jody and ask her how she felt about that time in your relationship, prior to and during the offending, when all of the stressors were happening.

This exercise turned out to be a good one for Robert, as he became far more aware of the effects on Jody of working, being pregnant, and feeling sick. Apparently she told him this at a moment when their visit was making him feel good about their relationship so it had a greater effect than in the past when Robert was far more self-focused. Jody told him that when she got home she just wanted to relax and had no energy to do anything else. Robert began to see how his avoidance of problems, unrealistic expectations, and self-focus led to the deterioration of the relationship.

This discussion illustrated some important issues for Robert, which are frequently seen in group members. First, Robert felt comfortable with the "honeymoon" phase of the relationship and expected these initial feelings to remain. When those feelings faded and problems developed, Robert was ill-equipped to deal with issues.

During group discussions, the therapist addressed these issues by helping Robert to understand that the initial strong and romantic feelings in a relationship typically fade, and in relationships where the couple work at issues, these feelings are replaced by more enduring and deeply satisfying feelings. It was also clear that Robert equated sex with intimacy, and as a result, he concluded that less sexual activity implied his wife did not love him. This belief was challenged. It became apparent that the stress brought on by these changes in their relationship triggered Robert's previous negative beliefs about himself and left him feeling insecure in the relationship.

In terms of his relationship style, Robert identified himself as anxious-ambivalent, a style characterized by a negative view of self but a positive view of others. Robert was preoccupied with his relationship and placed unrealistic expectations on his spouse. Robert expected his partner always to meet his needs for attention and affection, and he ignored her weariness and sickness. When he thought his needs were not being met, Robert sought to meet them inappropriately. It was during this time that Robert offended. The therapist focused on Robert's thoughts and feelings about himself to help him understand how these feelings and beliefs were negatively affecting his relationship with his wife.

T:	Robert, you told us that your first partner had cheated on her prior boyfriend. How did you feel when she told you that?
R:	I was devastated. I felt as though my entire life had fallen apart. My trust was destroyed.
T:	Wow … that seems like an overgeneralization from just one partner.
R:	Well, in that relationship I wanted a family so badly—I thought it would make me happy, if I had a family.
T:	So you believed your partner [Kim] and her daughter would fulfill your needs?
R:	I never thought about it like that before, but I guess so.
Other client:	It sounds like you expected everything to be perfect.
T:	(Addressed the other group member.) That's a good point—what suggested that to you?
Other client:	Well, I know I thought if I had a relationship, my life would be perfect, but I found out that it just wasn't the case. I thought I'd never feel lonely, that I would be happy, and sometimes I was. I've now learned that nobody else can do that for me. Robert reminds me of myself in that way.
T:	Good for you. What do you think about that, Robert?
R:	Well, I guess it makes sense. Looking back I can see that I was expecting a perfect family, that if I had that, it would make my life worthwhile. I'd at least be succeeding at something. I wish things could be perfect but I guess they never are.
T:	That also fits with our earlier discussions where you told the group you "felt like a failure." These things are all fitting together.
Other client:	Robert, did you feel the same way in other aspects of your life?

R: Well, yeah I did. I lost my job and that was really rough for us, financially.

T: Any other examples?

R: I can't really think of any....

T: That's interesting you say that. At the beginning of our discussion, you described feeling completely destroyed when you felt the trust was broken in your earlier relation ship with Kim. (Therapist turns to the group.) What thoughts do you guys have about that?

The group affirmed the therapist's comments and it was concluded that Robert was clearly insecure about relationships and, therefore, easily devastated.

Further discussion indicated that Robert felt mistrustful and insecure, although these feelings generally only arose when Robert felt threatened. Robert was afraid of conflict so when he and Jody argued, he thought she didn't love him and that she might leave. As a result, Robert responded to conflict by withdrawing. His wife responded by arguing with him more forcefully in the beginning, but eventually she had so many responsibilities she just ignored him. Robert noted that he ended up feeling unimportant and a failure. These feelings were enhanced when he lost his job and developed health problems. These issues placed a great deal of pressure on Robert's wife and they began to withdraw from one another. They no longer spent time engaged in mutually enjoyable activities nor did they communicate their feelings.

During a later discussion, Robert began to integrate his understanding of how he behaved in the relationship, why this was problematic, and what needed to change.

R: By not allowing myself to trust Jody, you know, because of my past experiences, I didn't ever really tell her how I felt. I was afraid, I always thought in the back of my mind that she would let me down or be unfaithful. It made things worse, because I thought she should just know how I felt.

T: How do you see things differently now, Robert?

R: Well, I know it was the way I was looking at things. I ended up setting myself up. When my wife was pregnant, she felt really sick and we stopped having sex. She was working and didn't have as much time for me, and I thought she didn't love me anymore.

T: How did you handle those thoughts and feelings?

R: I kept them inside; I didn't say anything.

T: So you didn't question those beliefs, and you didn't talk
                about them. What would that do, guys (turning to the group),
                keeping things like that inside?

Other client: Well, I'd say it would make the feelings worse.

R: That's exactly it, I felt even more unwanted and unloved.
                Then I'd start feeling sad and thinking that my relationship
                would end and I'd be all alone. When Tina [the victim] came
                over, I forgot about those feelings. I always felt accepted
                and loved by her.

T: Excellent insight, Robert. You are making some really im-
                portant links here. Can you see how you were trying to meet
                your needs through the offenses against Tina?

R: Yes, I think I see it.

T: Can you explain it to the group, Robert?

R: Well, when she snuggled with me, I used that for my benefit—I
                felt good, and wanted. The affection was really nice. After a
                few times, it was like I saw it sexually, I saw her sexually.

T: Why do you think you decided to sexually abuse Tina?

R: Well, I don't think I actually decided. It was more that I felt
                comfortable with Tina and I was in control—I no longer felt
                powerless in my life. And I convinced myself that sex was
                what Tina wanted. Of course I know now that wasn't true but
                at the time I guess I wanted to believe it. Also, Tina looked
                up to me, I knew she wouldn't say anything and I was also
                alone with her.

Other client: Do you think it was because she was so young, that it made
                it easier?

R: Maybe. Yeah, I think so.

T: That's a good point. Children are pretty affectionate, trust-
                ing, and accepting, aren't they? Were you worried about
                being rejected by Tina when you touched her sexually?

R: Actually … no. Tina liked the attention I gave her, and I used
                that to my advantage. As I spent more and more time with
                her it made it easier to offend. But, I'd always feel guilty af-
                terwards, and I noticed I'd withdraw even more from Jody,
                because I had this secret. And I couldn't look Tina's parents
                in the eye after I'd molested her.

T: I'm really glad you identified that, Robert. What that sug-
                gests to me is that there were moments during the time you
                were offending when you recognized it was your responsi-
                bility and that you were abusing the trust placed in you by
                Jody and by Tina's parents. Most importantly, you are now
                quite well aware of this.

It took some more work for Robert to be able to develop a full understanding of the issues but he displayed a determination and commitment to treatment that was not previously evident. As Robert developed his sense of self-worth, he was able to challenge his schema of being a failure and being unwanted. Robert was asked to become more involved in activities in the institution in order to develop some stronger interpersonal relationships and a better sense of self-esteem.

Next, we worked on what Robert needed to do to develop a healthier approach to relationships. A discussion was held regarding the features of healthy relationships. The therapist pointed out the importance of developing a relationship based on equality and shared interests. Robert was required to identify how he could improve his relationship with Jody.

T: What are you doing now, Robert, to make your relationship healthier?

R: I express myself now. I tell Jody how I feel.

T: So, you are trying harder to communicate particularly about feelings. That's great, Robert. How are you finding that's going?

R: Actually, I'm feeling good about it. We're planning to attend marital counseling when I get out, because there are lots of issues we need to address.

T: That's realistic. It is really important to address conflicts in a timely manner, so they don't get worse. Communication will make all aspects of your relationship more satisfying.

R: That's definitely something I've learned.

T: I know there are many issues the two of you need to address, but you also need to have enjoyable times together. It doesn't sound like you gave time to that before.

R: No, that's true. We didn't.

T: Perhaps you should make a list of enjoyable things you could share as well as some you could each enjoy individually. You could ask Jody if she would like to do the same thing, and the pair of you could then compare your lists, and pick some new activities.

R: Yes, that sounds like a good idea.

Robert still had a lot of work to do in this area. His relationship was far from stable, but his attitudes were much improved and with a better understanding and approach to his relationship, Robert was in a position to build a healthy relationship with Jody.

The research we described in chapter 3 revealed that sexual offenders are more likely to use ineffective coping strategies such as those involved in coping styles identified as emotion focused (e.g., dwelling on negative emotions, feeling sorry for oneself, and fantasizing) or avoidance focused (e.g., masturbation or sexual activity, ignoring the problem, or substance abuse). During our initial interviews with Robert, and throughout the initial group sessions, it was apparent that Robert used both emotion-focused and avoidance-focused strategies. As Robert progressed through treatment, we learned more about his specific coping strategies, which were affected by his negative beliefs about himself, his failure to address problems, and his poor relationship style. The characteristic coping styles outlined in the literature were described by the therapist, and Robert readily identified avoidance as his main style of coping.

R:	Now I can see that I had poor coping skills. I didn't deal with problems. I kept everything inside, you know, I thought I needed to deal with everything alone.
T:	What was that about, Robert? Why did you think you couldn't talk about your problems?
R:	I felt nobody cared, but I was also used to avoiding talking about emotions. I think I said earlier that my mother and father always avoided emotional stuff. Even when they were angry or upset, they would pretend there was no problem.
Other client:	Did you also think there was something wrong with you if you weren't able to solve your problems yourself?
R:	Yes, it was that whole failure complex I had.
T:	Wow! Congratulations, Robert. It takes strength to admit to that. Tell us more about those feelings, what it means to "feel like a failure."
R:	It seemed as though everything I did went to shit. It always seemed that whenever I started to feel happy, everything would fall apart. I felt like I couldn't do anything right.
T:	I think it takes strength to be able to ask for help, and you've done that in here, Robert.

Robert began to address the problems with his coping style. He recognized that avoidance was a harmful strategy, in that it increased his stress and left him feeling unhappy and dissatisfied. Robert also realized that holding in his emotions was bad for him. The therapist pointed out that doing so typically causes health problems and she pointed to Robert's poor health. He seemed surprised about this connection between holding in emotions and health difficulties but said it made good sense to him and he noted that both his parents, who were emotionally unexpressive, had poor health. Robert was encouraged to express positive feelings as a first step toward the goal of becoming comfortable with expressing his feelings. This proved to be reasonably easy for Robert and he reported back to the group that he actually enjoyed saying nice things to people. He said it made him feel good. Once Robert was accustomed to expressing positive feelings, he was able to begin talking about negative feelings. Robert reported that, as a result of these efforts, he was less likely to perceive remarks or actions by others as directed at him in a negative manner. He was also more able to dismiss an issue as unimportant when it truly was trivial. Robert attributed these new feelings and perceptions to enhanced self-confidence and a greater hope for the future, but he also recognized that they were a result of his practice at expressing his feelings. As Robert began to actively and appropriately deal with problems, he felt more in control of his life.

Robert was asked to develop his release and self-management plans, and he adopted a positive focus in the development of the latter. Robert stated that continued treatment (sexual offender treatment as well as other types of counseling) was his primary goal. Robert noted that throughout his life he has felt unimportant and ignored. Robert became aware that it is his responsibility to challenge such beliefs as well as behaviors that undermine his effective functioning. He declared that he intended to focus on continuing his "journey of self-improvement." Part of this involved upgrading his education in pursuit of a better, more satisfying job that could accommodate his health problems. Robert participated in schooling at the institution and developed a sense of confidence about his capacity to learn. He decided to apply to college and take college courses in the general arts after release from prison.

Robert's primary goal was to build a positive relationship with his wife and son. Robert was committed to attending marital counseling with his wife to further improve their communication and to give them guidance in addressing the many issues they faced. Due to the many years of an unbalanced, stressful lifestyle, Robert struggled to include balance in his life. The group members and therapist helped Robert to develop some leisure activities he could include as a part of a balanced lifestyle. Robert reported that he had been involved in a band in the past (writing songs and playing guitar) and this was something he wanted to get involved in again. Robert noted that he was feeling far more optimistic about his life than he had when he was first incarcerated.

Robert expressed a strong commitment not to reoffend. He recognized that by managing his risk factors and living a healthy, balanced lifestyle, he would be in a stronger position to ensure he met this goal. Robert recognized that while he would always be at risk, there were things he could do to reduce this risk. Living a satisfying, positive life, seeking support, and coping effectively were critical parts of Robert's new approach but so also was his need to avoid risks. Robert planned to avoid unsupervised contact with underage females. He identified having access to potential victims as a high-risk situation and he made the decision not to place himself in such a position. Robert discussed this issue with his wife and reported that she planned to help him meet this goal by ensuring that Robert was never alone with young girls. They both agreed not to babysit anymore. Robert noted that if he experienced any inappropriate sexual thoughts in the future, he would discuss them with a therapist.

Table 4.3 describes our final end-of-treatment ratings of Robert on the Therapist Rating Scale. As can be seen, Robert made sufficient progress to be ready for release. He expressed an intention to continue with treatment in the community and his wife supported this. We supported this intention as Robert clearly needed to do more work on most issues. Robert's coping capacity remained restricted and his emotional expression was limited. His self-management plans, particularly his good life goals and the means by which he might achieve them, were limited and needed further development. Also, Robert's supports were essentially restricted to his wife and parole officer so involvement in community treatment was essential to help Robert reestablish himself in the community and broaden his supports. Although Robert's expressions of self-confidence markedly improved, he still did not accept compliments in a convincing way. Overall, Robert progressed well, and we were confident that with further community treatment he would make even more gains.

CONCLUSIONS

The two cases described in this chapter were meant to illustrate our approach to the specific treatment targets as well as our ways of encouraging and reinforcing the clients for their small steps toward the goals of treatment. We chose these two cases partly because one was a rapist and one was a child molester, but also because they had different issues that needed to be emphasized in treatment. Of course, both clients completed the processes and procedures involved in every target of treatment, but we only illustrated those targets that in each case seemed the most important. We did not go through the precise details of the procedures described in detail in chapter 2 since they are essentially self-explanatory. It is the manner in which clients are engaged in the treatment process that we wanted to illustrate, since we believe (and, as we have seen, evidence supports this belief) that the manner in which treatment is delivered is crucial and yet this is rarely described. Indeed, the sexual offender literature describes little more than a set of procedures without

TABLE 4.3 Robert's Ratings on the Therapist Rating Scale

TARGETS	LEVEL FOR INTELLECTUAL UNDERSTANDING	LEVEL FOR EMOTIONAL ACCEPTANCE/ DEMONSTRATION
1. Acceptance of responsibility	3	3
2. General empathy	2	2
3. Empathy for victim	3	3
4. Prosocial attitudes	3	2
5. Adequate coping skills/styles	2	2
6. Adequate social skills	2	2
7. Positive self-esteem	3	2
8. Control over impulses	3	3
9. Good emotional regulation	2	2
10. Control over anger/aggression	3	3
11. Control over substance use	3	3
12. Normative sexual views/ interests	3	3
13. Understanding of risk factors	3	3
14. Quality of self-management plans	2	2
15. Quality of supports	2	3
16. Quality of release plans	3	3
17. Commitment to maintenance	3	3

outlining the best way to deliver these procedures or how to engage the clients in the process. We hope our descriptions of the two cases serve as illustrations of our overall approach to effectively engaging sexual offenders in treatment.

CHAPTER **5**

Complicating Factors

These are two general sets of factors that could, and at times do, complicate the appropriate treatment of sexual offenders: particular characteristics of the offenders, and legal or institutional issues. We will discuss each of these separately, although in practice they are sometimes entangled.

PROBLEMATIC CHARACTERISTICS OF THE OFFENDERS

Denial

Some sexual offenders declare that they did not commit the offense for which they are incarcerated. If these deniers appear likely to change their stance in response to vigorous challenging, then we place them in our regular treatment program. This approach has proved to be successful in getting these clients to admit to having offended (Marshall, 1994). If the denial appears entrenched, and if they declare they will not do a program designed to challenge their stance, then these clients are offered a place in our Deniers' Program (for a detailed description see Marshall, Thornton, Marshall et al., 2001). This program was developed because men who refuse to enter our regular program (where aspects of denial are challenged) would otherwise eventually be released from prison as untreated sexual offenders, which places them at risk to reoffend. Briefly, this Deniers' Program targets the same issues as are addressed in the regular program except for disclosure of the offense. Participants in the Deniers' Program are truthfully informed that their denial will not be challenged. We tell them we are going to help them identify the factors (internal and external) that put them in a position to be "falsely" accused and "wrongfully" convicted, so that they can then develop strategies to avoid putting themselves in a position to be falsely accused again. We also indicate that the program will help them develop the skills and attitudes that will allow them to lead more satisfying lives. Our experience has been that these men, once convinced we are not going to trick them into admitting, enter enthusiastically into treatment and typically generate excellent relapse preventions plans. An evaluation of the effectiveness of this program is presently under way.

A variation on the issue of denial (or at least the avoidance of responsibility) concerns those clients who claim to have suffered a loss of memory for the events surrounding and including their offense. When sexual offenders report no recall of their crime it means we cannot be sure they are taking responsibility for their actions. It also means we would not be able to assist them in formulating their offense pathways and, as a consequence, they could not design effective self-management plans. Loss of memory then could be a serious block to effective treatment. In response to this problem, we have developed a strategy to assist these offenders (see Marshall, Serran, Marshall, & Fernandez, 2005; Serran & Marshall, 2005). These "amnesic" clients (whether genuine or not) are provided with a method to facilitate recall that is derived from the body of experimental literature on memory recovery processes (Kihlstrom & Barnhardt, 1993; Shiekh, Hill, & Yesavage, 1987; Wilkinson, 1988; Wilson, 1987). Essentially, this requires them to contextualize the offense by recalling whatever details they can of the day of their crime. They start from the moment they got out of bed on the morning of the offense, recalling details of the bedroom, and what they did immediately thereafter. As they gradually reconstruct the day in its details, the steps to offending and details of the offense itself should gradually return. We (Marshall, Serran, Marshall, & Fernandez, 2005) have demonstrated the effectiveness of this procedure with 22 clients, some of whom appeared to have genuinely lost their memory of the offense as a result of head injury or alcoholic blackout. All 22 recovered sufficient details of the offense to proceed with treatment. Thus, we do not have to exclude these clients from treatment.

Sadists

Sexual sadists present particular difficulties. First, the diagnosis of sexual sadism is problematic and appears to be quite unreliably applied in practice (Marshall, Kennedy, & Yates, 2002), and even in a controlled field trial, the interdiagnostician reliability was very poor (Marshall, Kennedy, Yates, & Serran, 2002). The primary feature of these offenders that causes problems is their presumed sexual arousal to the physical and psychological suffering of their victims. This tendency to be sexually aroused by these features might be elicited during treatment both directly (as they discuss details of their own offense) and vicariously (as they listen to the disclosures of others). In fact, some clinicians have suggested to us that the discussion of offense details might have this effect on all treatment participants. Perhaps surprisingly, this possibility of sexual arousal has not been apparent in treatment (either by overt signs of arousal or by evident distraction). We avoid discussing most of the sexual details of offenses, examining only those that need clarification. For example, many offenders avoid mentioning offense behaviors such as forcefulness, threats, anal sex, or unusual sexual activities. To ensure they take full responsibility, we question them about these features when they appear in the official records but are not mentioned in the clients' disclosure. Even so, we take care to do so in an objective manner and we avoid going into too much detail or spending more time than is necessary on these details.

The aspect of treatment with these clients that appears to raise the greatest concern among therapists is when empathy is the focus. As noted in the relevant section of chapter 2, we do our best to deal with the potential problem that might arise due to the fact that alerting sexual sadists to suffering of the victim may defeat the purpose of empathy training. Despite all these potential problems, we have not experienced insurmountable difficulties with sexual sadists and none of these offenders who have completed our program (admittedly few) and been released have reoffended.

Health Problems

Occasionally health problems can present difficulties. We do our best to accommodate these issues and we work cooperatively with the health unit. The institution, and our treatment room in particular, has legally mandated provisions for disabled offenders and the health unit carefully administers medications and monitors their effects. Interference with cognitive functioning and rapid exhaustion are not uncommon effects of various illnesses or side effects of medications. We are as accommodating as possible to these difficulties and since our program is open-ended, these clients can, if necessary, spend longer in treatment. Sometimes it is necessary for disabled or chronically ill clients to take a break from treatment which the rolling feature of our program allows us to readily accommodate. In addition, other group members invariably offer assistance to these clients and this facilitates their continued and active involvement in treatment.

Comorbid Disorders

Other than the above-mentioned features, the presence of comorbid disorders can be a complicating factor. Marshall (in press-a) has reviewed the literature on comorbid diagnoses among sexual offenders. Considerable research has been devoted to describing the presence of comorbid disorders in these offenders, but precious little advice is offered in the literature on how to deal with this in treatment, except for substance disorders (Lightfoot & Barbaree, 1993).

Levenson (2004) reported that some 60% of the 450 sexual offenders in her study had at least one comorbid disorder, although this included other paraphilias. Various authors have reported mood disorders in 3% to 95% of sexual offenders, psychoses in 2% to 16%, anxiety disorders in 3% to 38%, and personality disorders in over 35% of these offenders (see Marshall, 2005a, for details). In addition, Bownes (1992) found that 57% of sexual offenders had some form of sexual dysfunction, and 35.8% were reported to have attention deficit/hyperactivity disorder (Kafka & Hennen, 2002). For all these comorbid disorders, except the personality disorders, a referral is made to psychiatry where the appropriate medications can be provided and monitored. Severely disturbed clients are assigned to a special institution that caters specifically to their needs and also typically provides them with sexual offender treatment once the intensity of their other disorders are reduced and they are stabilized.

Personality Disorders

Personality disorders have been consistently reported to be present among sexual offenders at rates that appear well above those in the general population (Marshall, in press-a). For example, Firestone, Bradford, Greenberg, and Larose (1998) identified personality disorders of various kinds in 52% of sexual offenders and Fazel, Hope, O'Donnell, and Jacoby (2002) report that 33% of sexual offenders had one or another personality disorder. Sjöstedt, Grann, Långström, and Fazel (2003) examined the general (nonoffender) population records in Sweden over a 12-year period and found a prevalence rate for personality disorders of only 0.2%, clearly indicating that the observed rates for sexual offenders reported in the literature are extremely high. The types of personality disorders that are most consistently identified among sexual offenders are antisocial personality disorders, with rates as high as 40% (Motiuk & Porporino, 1992), borderline personality disorder, and narcissistic personality disorder. The latter disorder has been particularly evident in Catholic clergy who have sexually offended (Marshall, in press-b).

One type of sexual offender who presents complications for all treatment providers is the psychopathic client. The diagnostic manual describes these clients as suffering from antisocial personality disorder, but the concept of "psychopathy" has proved to be more useful for research purposes, and Hare (1991, 2003) has provided a valuable and reliable measure of this concept. Extensive research has established that these clients have personality characteristics that are thought to make them resistant to treatment and disruptive to others in group therapy. Hare (2003) points to the egocentricity, grandioseness, and manipulative nature of psychopaths, who, Hare says, are emotionally labile but affectively shallow, lacking in empathy, and unable to form effective bonds with others. These sorts of features could be expected to make it difficult to establish an appropriate therapeutic relationship with these clients and to engage them in a genuine effort to change. Indeed, a commonly expressed sentiment suggests that psychopathic sexual offenders are untreatable (Meloy, 1995; Reid & Gacono, 2000) or possibly made worse by treatment (Prendergast, 1991).

Recent research by Barbaree, Langton, and Peacock (2005) at least demonstrated that their sexual offender program did not increase the reoffense rate of psychopathic clients. In fact, Barbaree, Seto, Langton, and Peacock (2001) report no relationship between PCL-R scores and recidivism in treated sexual offenders. Hildebrand, de Ruiter, and de Vogel (2004), on the other hand, found that psychopaths who entered treatment had higher postrelease rates of recidivism (55%) than did untreated nonpsychopaths (23%). However, of the 17 psychopaths in Hildebrand et al.'s study, who also displayed deviant sexual arousal and had the highest recidivism rates (82%), only 1 completed treatment; the remaining 16 were removed because of disturbed relations between them and the treatment staff. We now know that sexual offenders must not only complete treatment but also satisfactorily achieve the goals of treatment (e.g., reduced cognitive distortions, enhanced empathy, elimination of deviant sexual responding, generating of effective relapse prevention plans) if they are to effectively reduce their risk of recidivism (Marques, Weideranders, Day et al., 2005). If Hildebrand et al. had developed strategies to gain the cooperation of these clients, perhaps the psychopaths would have completed treatment and been at less risk to reoffend. In this regard some clinicians have suggested that psychopathic offenders need to be aggressively confronted over their manipulative tactics. Unfortunately, for this idea, punitive responses (which is how sexual offenders perceive confrontation; see Drapeau, 2005) have been shown to make psychopaths even more oppositional (Schmauk, 1970; Stewart, 1972) and, therefore, more intractable to treatment.

For the purposes of organizing the delivery of treatment, we consider all sexual offenders who score 20 and above on Hare's Psychopathy Checklist–Revised (Hare, 1991) to be sufficiently problematic to warrant concern. If they are willing to enter treatment then we select no more than two (and usually only one) to participate in group therapy at any one time. This tends to reduce any negative influence they might otherwise have on the group and appears to attenuate their oppositional, disruptive, and manipulative behaviors. In addition, we respond to cooperation and progress by all clients with immediate self-relevant rewards, and psychopaths are said to be motivated almost entirely by the fulfillment of short-term needs. The fact is, those relatively few clients who present problems in our treatment program have as frequently been those who score below 20 on the PCL-R as those whose scores are in the somewhat more psychopathic range. Perhaps our efforts to devise ways to motivate each and every offender accounts for this, but for whatever reason our treatment outcome data reveal that only two of our recidivists scored more than 20 on Hare's (1991) PCL-R and none scored in the range (>30) that Hare considers necessary to define a client as a psychopath.

In our program, the personality disordered sexual offenders are not offered specialized treatment and are rarely placed on medications even though there is evidence that medications can be helpful with personality disorders (Sperry, 1999). Several authors have described recent approaches to the psychological treatment of personality disordered clients. Young (1999; Young, Klosko, & Weishaar, 2003) describes an approach aimed primarily at modifying the dysfunctional schemas of these clients; Greenberg's (Greenberg & Pavio, 1997; Greenberg, Rice, & Elliott, 1993) program aims at regulating the emotions of personality disordered clients; and Sperry's (1999) more comprehensive program targets schemas, emotional regulation, and various other aspects of their functioning such as self-esteem, social and relationship problems, impulse control, empathy, and their ability to cope with stress. More specifically Buschman and van Beek (2003) have developed a cognitive behavioral approach to the treatment of personality disordered sexual offenders. Table 5.1 summarizes the targets identified in the above approaches as requiring attention in treatment.

As the reader will recall, all of these issues are targets in our sexual offender program, so we simply adjust our approach to the specific needs of personality disordered clients. This is one aspect of the way we put into practice the "responsivity principle," which is essential to the effectiveness of any program with any type of offender (Andrews & Bonta, 1998). We have not had any significant problems in accommodating personality disordered clients, and our outcome data do not suggest that they are more likely than other sexual offenders to reoffend. It appears that our accommodations to these clients are effective.

TABLE 5.1   Treatment Targets for Personality Disordered Clients

1. Schemas: Challenges and examination of early origins

   a. Entitlement/self-centeredness—overindulgent parents or the failure of parents to encourage self-responsibility

   b. Abuse/mistrust—abuse in childhood

   c. Insufficient self-control/self-discipline—parents fail to model self-control, set limits, or inadequate discipline

   d. Unloveability/defectiveness—parents who were either emotionally indifferent or punitive

   e. Abandonment/instability—parental inconsistency or parental loss

   f. Dependency/incompetence—parents fail to encourage independence, self-sufficiency, or competence

2. Style/temperament: Deficits/problems in the following

   a. Cognitive distortions

   b. Anger management

   c. Empathy training

   d. Relationship training

   e. Impulse control

   f. Coping

   g. Self-esteem

   h. Social skills

   i. Emotional awareness/regulation

   j. Self-destructive acts

LEGAL AND INSTITUTIONAL FACTORS

Clinicians working with sexual offenders function in a context where they have obligations not only to their offender clients. Indeed, it could reasonably be said that such clinicians have three sets of clients: the offenders themselves; the justice or correctional system that refers offenders and pays for their treatment; and society whose members are the potential future victims of the offenders. So long as our clients do well in treatment, we serve all three of these clients. However, in those cases where the offender's progress in treatment has not beensatisfactory, clinicians must struggle with the need to fulfill their obligations to their sexual offender clients while at the same time being straightforward to prison authorities about their potential risk to reoffend. Decision makers (e.g., parole boards, courts) rely, to varying degrees, on treatment reports about sexual offenders, and their decisions can affect the safety of society, so treatment reports must spell out the details of any failure to progress despite the fact that such comments may not seem to serve the desired interests of the sexual offender client. Thus, the wishes of the referring agency and the wishes of the client (as well as the safety of society) may often clash and the clinician must attempt to balance these sometimes conflicting responsibilities.

This issue is best handled, we believe, by establishing at the outset with each client where the limits of confidentiality lie. Clients should be told very clearly what issues will be addressed in the final report on treatment and what things the clients might reveal in treatment that would require the therapist to report the details to authorities. Most jurisdictions, for example, have laws that require the reporting of abuses of children that have come to attention even if by way of treatment. Thus, if a sexual offender in treatment reveals either past or ongoing sexual abuse of a child, this must be immediately reported to the police. This can put a therapist in a difficult situation unless he/she has made reporting obligations clear. If, of course, the client indicates past abuse without providing sufficient details, then reporting the matter might be considered moot since the authorities would be unable to proceed with an investigation. In working with our Deniers' group, this issue of the boundaries of confidentiality can be particularly problematic for those clients who are appealing their conviction. Should they reveal information that indicates guilt, the therapist could be placed in an awkward legal and professional dilemma. We avoid this by telling clients that if they are considering admitting to aspects of the crime, they must immediately withdraw from the Deniers' program; to date, we have not had to face this problem but no doubt it will arise sooner or later.

The final complication that occurs in working with sexual offenders happens when treatment is delivered in an institutional, and particularly in a prison, setting. A common sentiment that is apparent in the behavior of some prison administrators and some prison staff is to be punitive toward all inmates, a sentiment that reflects the view of the general public. Inmates in prisons are not typically treated with the respect that we might expect to be provided to clients in other settings (for example, in hospitals or in homes for the elderly). Exactly why the climate in some prisons has developed in this way is beyond the scope of the interests of this book. The fact is that when such a climate prevails it presents a problem that reduces the ability of treatment providers to do their job properly. The notion that rewarding any aspect of the behavior of sexual offenders might be useful is not readily apparent to most prison staff, so treatment providers must work to overcome entrenched attitudes if they wish to provide effective treatment in such settings.

Alec Spencer, the one-time governor (or warden) of a large prison in Scotland that exclusively housed sexual offenders, had the wisdom to realize that for the rehabilitation of these offenders to be effective, the attitudes and behaviors of all staff had to change. Almost single-handedly, and without much executive support, Spencer radically changed the way his staff worked with sexual offenders. Treatment was provided within a context in which all staff were directly supportive and rewarding of the offenders' attempts at change. Interestingly, after a short period of implementing this way of functioning, prison staff reported greater job satisfaction. He has described the ways in which this was implemented in a book that all prison administrators should read (Spencer, 1998).

Fortunately for us, the context in which our program is delivered in Correctional Service of Canada's Bath Institution operates according to the same principles that Spencer describes and has so for many years. However, the usual prison settings require that treatment providers do more than just offer treatment. They must also work respectfully with administrators and prison staff to win their confidence and get them to cooperate in ways that are supportive of the efforts of the treatment providers and the offenders. Clearly it is possible to achieve this goal, and our outcome data defy the suggestions made by some skeptics that treatment cannot effectively be conducted in prisons.

CHAPTER 6

Maintenance and Follow-Up Strategies

REGISTERS AND PUBLIC NOTIFICATION

One approach to reduce the risk sexual offenders present on their release from prison was developed in the United States. Actually there are two aspects to this approach that typically go hand in hand: a sexual offender register and public notification of an offender's release. A sexual offender registry requires all sexual offenders to have their names, addresses, occupations, and some other (but variable across jurisdictions) personal information recorded in an officially kept register.

The first such register was established in California in 1947, but all U.S. states now have similar registers. Unfortunately, compliance with the requirements of these registers is far from complete with rates varying from 50% to over 80% compliance across states (Center for Sex Offender Management, 1999). Although Ontario is presently the only Canadian province with a compulsory sexual offender register, the Canadian federal government is in the process of establishing a national register. The compliance rate for initial registration in Ontario is over 90%, but the required subsequent notification of changes of address and the required yearly check-ins fall well below that compliance rate. As Wilson and Picheca (in press) suggest, those sexual offenders who maintain compliance with the register are likely the ones who will not reoffend, so in the absence of ensuring full compliance, these registers may not be achieving their purported goal (i.e., reduction of risk). Of course, they clearly serve the political goal of seeming to be strict with sexual offenders and perhaps also the barely submerged aim of continued punishment. The greatest value of these registers may not be so much their impact on recidivism, but rather their usefulness to police investigating sexual offenses where the offender has not yet been identified. The police can use the register to check for sexual offenders who live in the area of the crime and whose prior modus operandi or victim choice fit the features of the current crime.

The other related tactic concerns public notification when a sexual offender is released from prison. In some jurisdictions in the United States, public notification involves the public display of the offender's photograph, address, and workplace. These public displays may appear on the Internet or as posters in public places. Presumably, public notification is meant to reduce the risk these offenders pose by alerting the community in advance of a possible crime. Unfortunately, to date, there is no evidence that public notification achieves this goal. Given the difficulty of recognizing a person (in this case someone we have never otherwise met) from just one photograph, the likelihood of mistaken identification not only seems probable, it has actually occurred. These notifications have also resulted in occasional acts of vigilante justice. Other than these obviously drastic errors, and the lack of evidence for the value of public notification, there is every reason to suppose that such tactics might actually decrease public safety when sexual offenders return to the community. We know that stress and its subsequent mood fluctuations increase the likelihood that a sexual offender will commit another offense (Hanson & Harris, 2000; Pithers, Beal, Armstrong, & Petty, 1989), and it seems certain that public notification alone would increase the offender's stress levels. The additional harassment that sometimes follows public notification would markedly increase the offender's stress levels and mood fluctuations, and, thereby, increase his risk to reoffend.

Perhaps the primary problem with both sexual offender registers and public notification is that both, all too often, involve all sexual offenders. Sexual offenders are an extremely heterogeneous group on all aspects of their functioning that have been examined. Most particularly, actuarial risk assessment instruments have been used to allocate sexual offenders to various levels of risk based on the match between each individual's features and data collected on thousands of prior sexual offenders whose reoffense rates are known (see Doren, 2002, and Hanson and Morton-Bourgon, 2004, for a discussion of such actuarial risk instruments). Therefore, to respond to all sexual offenders as if they are the same makes no empirical sense and it is difficult to see the sense in treating them all the same at release from prison. Is public safety really increased by the community knowing there are low-risk sexual offenders in its midst? We doubt it. In fact it is not known what level of risk should be required for public notification to be useful. At the moment it would perhaps be wise to require public notification for all high-risk or persistently repetitive offenders. This is the way public notification has been applied in Canada. Similarly, it seems somewhat pointless to require all such offenders to have their name and information placed on an official register. In Canada, for example, there are no statutes of limitation on sexual offenses, so a man who molested a child 30 years ago, but has been prosocial ever since, can be convicted and imprisoned for that historical crime. It seems absurd to place him on a sexual offender register or to notify the public of his release.

There are, in addition, problems regarding who should be allowed access to the information held on sexual offender registers. Law enforcement officials should, it seems obvious, have ready access to these registers, but only for the purposes of pursuing potential suspects in a crime. The other potentially valuable purpose of a sexual offender register would be in the screening of applicants for jobs or volunteer work where access to, or power over, potential victims might be involved. But how are the appropriate organizations to be provided with the relevant information? Obviously, allowing public access to the registers would not only abrogate the rights to privacy of those offenders whose names are on the register, but might also result in the abuse of the registrant or provide the basis for blackmail schemes. Our suggestion is that concerned employers or volunteer organizations should require applicants to obtain a letter from the register indicating that their names are not on the list. Persons who know their names are on the register will, under these conditions, presumably withdraw their application. This strategy would appear to protect the privacy of individuals as well as protect from harm the potential victims.

Fortunately, there are other alternatives to the management of risk when sexual offenders are returned to the community. These alternatives are aimed not only at reducing the offender's risk to harm, but they are also intended to assist the offender in reassimilating into society in a way that maximizes his likelihood of achieving the goals of a better, more personally and socially satisfying life.

RELEASE OR DISCHARGE PROCEDURES

To describe these approaches, it is necessary to outline the procedures that are followed in the jurisdictions where our program operates when a sexual offender is released from conditions of confinement. All Canadian sexual offenders who are given a sentence of 2 years or more are sent to prisons under the jurisdiction of Correctional Service of Canada (CSC). Almost all offenders convicted of child molestation or of sexual assault (what used to be called rape) on an adult receive a sentence of more than 2 years and thus end up in a CSC prison. Very few exhibitionists receive a federal prison sentence but instead are either placed on probation or, if they are a repeat offender, they may be given a term to be served in a provincial prison. All exhibitionists who are either given probation or a short (<2 years) sentence are the responsibility of the province rather than the federal government and are seen primarily in outpatient clinics.

Sexual offenders housed in CSC prisons can be released before their sentence expires (called "Warrant-of-Expiry Date," or WED) under conditions imposed by the National Parole Board. They can be released on Day Parole (i.e., placement in a community-based halfway house with curfew requirements) after one sixth of their sentence, or on Full Parole after one half of their sentence. Full Parole involves direct release of offenders into the community but with certain restrictions placed on various aspects of their behavior, as well as on the type of job or leisure activity they may choose and the location of their residence. These types of release are usually conditional on the sexual offender having successfully completed specialized treatment, which is available to every sexual offender in CSC prisons. In the case of sexual offenders whose scores on actuarial risk assessments place them in the highest risk category, a gradual release program is usually instituted. This typically involves stepwise movement from a maximum security prison to a medium security institution and then to a minimum security setting, with each move contingent on the offender having progressed satisfactorily in treatment and having complied with institutional rules. Once in a minimum security setting, the next step might involve escorted short-term passes into the community, followed (if successful) by unescorted absences. After successful completion of these passes, a high-risk offender will be placed in a half-way house until he demonstrates effective functioning, at which time he may be moved fully into the community.

All offenders must be released after two thirds of their sentence is completed unless it can be shown that they constitute a real threat to commit another offense (i.e., there are reasonable grounds to believe they will) that will likely cause serious harm. This release at two thirds of the sentence is called the "Statutory Release Date." Release at this time still allows the imposition of conditions that must be met or parole will be revoked and the offender will be returned to prison where he may be held until WED. If an offender can be shown to meet the criteria of constituting a real threat to harm someone, he may be refused any form of parole and held until WED. The National Parole Board does its best to avoid holding offenders to WED as no jurisdictional control can then be exerted over such an offender when he is returned to the community; he can live where he chooses and with whom he chooses, he can take any job, associate with whomever he wishes, he need not attend treatment, and he cannot be monitored.

Recently, concern over sexual offenders held until WED brought about changes in sentencing practices that allowed judges to impose, at the time of initial sentencing, an additional period of 10 years supervised probation to be served after WED. Therefore, the judge has to decide if the offender constitutes sufficient concerns to be likely to be held until WED. This, of course, requires some guesswork (albeit informed guesswork) on the part of the judge, and it seems likely that such decisions will be mistaken occasionally both in terms of overestimating and underestimating future risk. The judge could, on the other hand, decide that a convicted sexual offender meets criteria at sentencing that justifies the application of a "Dangerous Offender" designation. This latter designation (which is applied infrequently) functions as an indeterminate sentence with the requirement that if the offender is ever released he must be on lifetime supervision with strict release conditions including extended treatment involvement.

RISK MANAGEMENT

Sexual offenders released on parole or under conditions of extended probation are assigned to an informed parole or probation officer whose responsibility it is to ensure the offender is complying with his parole conditions and that he is not doing anything that might increase his risk. The detailed post-treatment reports from prison-based programs are provided to parole supervisors. These reports describe the factors that might put the client at risk to reoffend and they include recommendations for further treatment of various kinds. Thus, the parole supervisor knows what to monitor and where to send the client for further help. In addition to having available to them the reports from prison-based treatment that describe static risk factors, supervising parole officers now have available a list of dynamic factors that they need to monitor. Hanson and Harris (2000), on the basis of extensive work with parole and probation officers, have been able to identify sets of stable dynamic risk factors (i.e., those features of the client that are potentially changeable and that are subsumed by most of the targets addressed in treatment) as well as acute factors (e.g., sudden mood changes, temporary relationship problems) that Hanson and Harris have shown to indicate an acute elevation in risk. These factors alert parole officers to take immediate steps to reduce the client's risk. The implementation and widespread dissemination of this information has occurred only recently, so we await emerging evidence of how the availability of this knowledge has affected parole officers' work and what effect this has had on recidivism.

All sexual offenders released to the community for whom actuarial measures place them at moderate/high or high risk to reoffend are required to be assessed by a community-based specialized sexual offender program. Caution almost invariably requires all such high-risk sexual offenders to enter community treatment and participate effectively. Most moderate risk sexual offenders are similarly required to participate in an assessment and many are required to enter treatment. Very few low/moderate or low-risk sexual offenders are required to complete community treatment. However, all released sexual offenders may be required to participate in other types of treatment programs such as substance abuse, anger management, relationship counseling, or parenting skills programs.

As part of prison-based treatment, all sexual offenders must not only describe their own personal risk factors that are then sent on to the parole supervisor but are also required to identify two groups of people in the community who can, and have agreed to, provide support to the offender upon his release. One of these groups involves professionals with whom the client will be involved upon release. Typical members of this support group include the offender's supervising parole officer, the therapist running the community-based sexual offenders' program, treatment providers of other programs, the clients' religious advisor (if appropriate), and any other professional with whom the offender may be involved. The other support group includes members of the client's family, friends, members of his church (if relevant), and possibly coworkers. In the case of family and friends, it is carefully determined prior to release that they are able to function as effective supports. For some offenders, their family either does not believe the client is guilty or the family believes the client has learned his lesson and is no longer at risk. It is only when family members or friends clearly accept the client's guilt and his need to avoid risks that they are deemed to be useful support group members. Members of both support groups are provided with the offender's list of factors and circumstances that might place him at risk so they can properly monitor his behaviors and provide him with appropriate support and direction. When support groups function as they are supposed to, the evidence suggests they effectively reduce the risk of recidivism (Wilson & Picheca, in press).

The community supervision provided by informed parole officers varies in intensity, depending on the client's level of risk to reoffend as determined by actuarial risk measures. High and high/moderate risk offenders receive the most intensive supervision, including unannounced visits to the client's home or work and random urine tests for alcohol and other drugs. The intensity of the supervision for high-risk sexual offenders is maintained typically for the several months after release and gradually reduced as the offender demonstrates his adherence to his parole conditions. For moderate risk sexual offenders the intensity of supervision is lower and is usually reduced more rapidly than with the higher-risk offenders. With the lowest-risk sexual offenders, supervision is typically markedly less intense and less prolonged.

Required involvement in treatment matches the levels of supervision. High-risk offenders are required to effectively participate in a specialized community treatment program for as long as is deemed necessary by the director of the community program in consultation with the parole supervisor. Most moderate-risk sexual offenders also enter treatment but usually for less time than the higher risk clients. Very few low-risk offenders participate in community treatment. Some offenders, particularly the sexual sadists and other very dangerous offenders (i.e., those whose risk is high and who, if they do reoffend, can be expected to do considerable harm), will almost certainly be stabilized on an antiandrogen prior to release and will be required to be maintained on this medication for an indefinite period of time after release.

Supervision, involvement in treatment, and the use of support groups are necessary to maintain offenders' motivation to remain offense-free after release from prison (Barrett, Wilson, & Long, 2003; Stirpe, Wilson, & Long, 2001). When used appropriately, these measures increase the likelihood that sexual offenders will succeed in their attempts to effectively reenter society (Wilson, Stewart, Stirpe et al., 2000).

Wilson and Picheca (in press) describe the development of a specific "Circles of Support and Accountability" (COSA) for those sexual offenders who are held until WED before release to the community. As noted earlier, release at WED does not allow continued involuntary supervision and no legal controls can be exerted over the offender concerning where he lives, what work or volunteer activities he engages in, where he spends his leisure time, or what intoxicants he chooses to use. In other words, no conditions can be imposed on such offenders nor can they be required to use support groups, despite the fact that in many cases clients want such help or would be willing to take it if it were offered. Wilson and Picheca and their colleagues actively sought out community volunteers for specific offenders released at WED who had agreed to participate in a support group program. Modeling their approach on what is done with offenders released on parole, Wilson and Picheca formed two support groups: professionals (whom they describe as the "outer" group) and a group comprising of community volunteers (the "inner" group). In the latter group, one volunteer (the primary support) meets with the offender daily during the initial period of his return to the community. The other members of the inner group meet at least weekly with the offender during this early period. Over time, and as the offender shows that he is functioning well and carefully following his plan to avoid reoffending, the frequency of contacts is reduced. The professional or outer group's task is to provide support and consultation to the inner group but do not themselves meet with the offender.

This COSA program has been shown to be effective (Wilson & Picheca, in press), and its success has prompted the development of similar programs across Canada. More recently, post-release support programs, modeled on Wilson and Picheca's COSA, have been implemented in the United States and United Kingdom and several other countries have expressed interest in developing similar programs.

We believe that requiring moderate- and high-risk sexual offenders to form effective support groups, whose assistance is monitored, and to participate effectively in treatment provides the basis of the best post-release strategies for sexual offenders. Indeed, for the low-risk sexual offenders, provision of the support groups should be sufficiently effective not to require community treatment. Combined with careful and effective supervision by appropriately trained parole or probation officers, these strategies should markedly reduce any tendencies to return to offending and should contribute to the enhancement of the sexual offenders' fulfillment of their good lives plans.

Therapist Rating Scale

INSTRUCTIONS FOR THERAPIST RATINGS

Each of the 17 topics is to be rated on each of the two categories (i.e., intellectual understanding, and emotional acceptance/demonstration), according to your considered opinion of how well the client is functioning on each topic. Level 4 is meant to describe "optimal" functioning, level 3 is considered to be "satisfactory," level 2 is "marginal," and level 1 is "unsatisfactory." The descriptors under each category for each topic are meant to provide possible descriptors for report writing. It is expected that the levels will vary both across topics (e.g., a client may be at level 4 for intellectual understanding of General Empathy and at level 2 for intellectual understanding of Prosocial Attitudes) as well as between categories (e.g., within the topic General Empathy, a client may be at level 4 for intellectual understanding and at level 2 for emotional acceptance/demonstration). Do your best to avoid "halo effects" (i.e., try to avoid being influenced by your overall impression of the client as either having done well or poorly in treatment). If you do not get variability in the rated levels across the various topics and categories, then you may need to reconsider your ratings.

The rating form that follows is to be used for each client. The profile form can be used to plot the ratings—use different colors (or a broken versus unbroken lines) for plotting the different categories (i.e., intellectual understanding and emotional acceptance/demonstration).

RATINGS FORM		
TARGETS	LEVEL FOR INTELLECTUAL UNDERSTANDING	LEVEL FOR EMOTIONAL ACCEPTANCE/ DEMONSTRATION
1. Acceptance of responsibility		
2. General empathy		
3. Empathy for victim		
4. Prosocial attitudes		
5. Adequate coping skills/styles		
6. Adequate social skills		
7. Positive self-esteem		
8. Control over impulses		
9. Good emotional regulation		
10. Control over anger/aggression		
11. Control over substance use		
12. Normative sexual views/ interests		
13. Understanding of risk factors		
14. Quality of self-management plans		
15. Quality of supports		
16. Quality of release plans		
17. Commitment to maintenance		

PROFILE OF POST-TREATMENT RATINGS

Name of Client: _____

Identification Number: _____

Center: _____

Rater: _____

Level

Level																		
4																		Optimal
3																		Satisfactory
2																		Marginal
1																		Unsatisfactory

1 2 3 4 5 6 7 8 9 10 11 12 13 14 15 16 17

Targets

POST-TREATMENT RATINGS BY THERAPISTS

1. Acceptance of Responsibility

Level 4

a. Intellectual understanding
  i. Makes extensive connections of issues leading up to offense
  ii. Presents all information competently and confidently
  iii. Demonstrates thorough understanding of skills and concepts involving personal responsibility
  iv. Always identifies and discusses issues of responsibility
  v. Considers all available information/strategies to understand and accept responsibility
  vi. Shows exceptional regard for analyzing and evaluating responsibility
  vii. Confidently able to apply situational analyses to other group members appropriately

b. Emotional acceptance/demonstration
  i. Independently admits and accepts responsibility for offense
  ii. Demonstrates insightful self awareness for his involvement
  iii. Demonstrates complete and sound remorse for actions
  iv. Able to admit to full disclosure with clarity and competence
  v. Responds to official records responsibly and maturely
  vi. Fully understands and accepts historical descriptor of offense as "bad action" not "bad self"
  vii. Demonstrates strong interest and concern to challenge/assist others in group to accept their responsibility

Level 3

a. Intellectual understanding
  i. Makes thoughtful connections of issues leading up to offense
  ii. Presents most information competently and confidently
  iii. Demonstrates proficient understanding of skills and concepts involving personal responsibility
  iv. Usually identifies and discusses issues of responsibility
  v. Considers most available information/strategies to understand and accept responsibility
  vi. Shows careful regard for analyzing and evaluating responsibility
  vii. Reasonably able to apply situational analyses to other group members appropriately

b. Emotional acceptance/demonstration
  i. Routinely admits and accepts responsibility for offense

ii. Demonstrates consistent self-awareness for his involvement
iii. Demonstrates sound remorse for actions
iv. Able to admit to disclosure with some clarity and competence
v. Responds appropriately to official records (i.e., no denial)
vi. Accepts historical descriptor of offense as "bad action" not "bad self"
vii. Demonstrates some interest to challenge/assist others in group to accept their responsibility

Level 2

a. Intellectual understanding
    i. Makes a few connections of issues leading up to offense
    ii. Presents information hesitantly
    iii. Demonstrates basic understanding of skills and concepts involving personal responsibility
    iv. Needs encouragement to identify and discuss issues of responsibility
    v. Considers only some information/strategies to understand and accept responsibility
    vi. Shows adequate regard for analyzing and evaluating responsibility
    vii. Shows some development in ability to apply situational analyses of other group members
b. Emotional acceptance/demonstration
    i. Sometimes admits and accepts responsibility for offense
    ii. Demonstrates adequate self-awareness for his involvement
    iii. Demonstrates only some remorse for actions
    iv. Able to admit to disclosure with some clarity and competence
    v. Sometimes responds appropriately to official records (i.e., no denial)
    vi. Needs encouragement to accept historical descriptor of offense as "bad action" not "bad self"
    vii. Demonstrates little interest to challenge/assist others in group to accept their responsibility

Level 1

a. Intellectual understanding
    i. Makes limited connections of issues leading up to offense
    ii. Needs assistance to present information
    iii. Demonstrates an emerging understanding of skills and concepts involving personal responsibility

     iv. Rarely participates in identifying and discussing issues of responsibility

     v. Reluctantly considers information/strategies to understand and accept responsibility

     vi. Shows insufficient regard for analyzing and evaluating responsibility

     vii. Beginning to show a development in ability to apply situational analyses of other group members

b. Emotional acceptance/demonstration
   i. Rarely admits and accepts responsibility for offense
   ii. Demonstrates limited self-awareness for his involvement
   iii. Demonstrates minimal remorse for actions
   iv. Unable to admit to disclosure with clarity and competence
   v. Responds inappropriately to official records (i.e., no denial)
   vi. Needs assistance/support to accept historical descriptor of offense as "bad action" not "bad self"
   vii. Rarely demonstrates interest to challenge/assist others in group to accept their responsibility

2. General Empathy

Level 4

a. Intellectual understanding
   i. Always listens attentively when others are speaking
   ii. Consistently allows others to express their opinions without interrupting
   iii. Fully understands/determines which behaviors are acceptable or unacceptable in response to others
   iv. Consistently able to identify/describe/interpret own feelings/ emotions
   v. Consistently able to identify/describe/interpret feelings/ emotions of others (both in and outside of group)
   vi. Readily able to perceive and then verbalize the perspective of other group members or others outside the group
   vii. Consistently respectful of the rights, property, and opinions of others (both in and outside of group)

b. Emotional acceptance/demonstration
   i. Always expresses appropriate affect in response to others' emotions (both within and outside of the group)
   ii. Has insightful understanding of other group members' experiences/feelings

   iii. Able to adopt with maturity, the perspective of someone with whom he is in conflict (e.g., parole officer)

   iv. Sincerely expresses/demonstrates a desire to alleviate distress in other group members

   v. Confidently shows exceptional ability to comfort other group members when distressed

   vi. Confidently and with understanding is able to adopt others' perspectives during a highly emotional situation

Level 3

a. Intellectual understanding
   i. Usually listens attentively when others are speaking
   ii. Routinely allows others to express their opinions without interrupting
   iii. Continually able to understand/determine which behaviors are acceptable or unacceptable in response to others
   iv. Usually able to identify/describe/interpret own feelings/emotions
   v. Usually able to identify/describe/interpret feelings/emotions of others (both in and outside of group)
   vi. Frequently able to perceive and then verbalize the perspective of other group members or others outside the group
   vii. Routinely is respectful of the rights, property, and opinions of others (both in and outside of group)

b. Emotional acceptance/demonstration
   i. Regularly expresses appropriate affect in response to others' emotions (both within and outside of the group)
   ii. Often spontaneously verbalizes an understanding of other group members' experiences/feelings
   iii. Able to adopt appropriately the perspective of someone with whom he is in conflict (e.g., parole officer)
   iv. Competently expresses/demonstrates a desire to alleviate distress in other group members
   v. Skillfully attempts to comfort other group members when distressed
   vi. Usually able to adopt and understand others' perspectives during a highly emotional situation

Level 2

a. Intellectual understanding
   i. Sometimes listens attentively when others are speaking
   ii. Sporadically allows others to express their opinions without interrupting

    iii. Developing an ability to understand/determine which behaviors are acceptable or unacceptable in response to others

    iv. Sometimes able to identify/describe/interpret own feelings/emotions

    v. Sometimes capable of identifying/describing/interpreting the feelings/emotions of others (both in and outside of group)

    vi. Adequately able to perceive and then verbalize the perspective of other group members or others outside the group

    vii. Shows a development in being respectful of the rights, property, and opinions of others (both in and outside of group)

b. Emotional acceptance/demonstration

    i. Sometimes expresses appropriate affect in response to others' emotions (both within and outside of the group)

    ii. Beginning to verbalize an understanding of other group members' experiences/feelings

    iii. Learning to adopt appropriately, the perspective of someone with whom he is in conflict (e.g., parole officer)

    iv. Adequately expresses/demonstrates a desire to alleviate distress in other group members

    v. Adequately attempts to comfort other group members when distressed

    vi. Inconsistently able to adopt and understand others' perspectives during a highly emotional situation

Level 1

a. Intellectual understanding

    i. Rarely listens attentively when others are speaking

    ii. Needs reminders to allow others to express their opinions without interrupting

    iii. Emerging in his ability to understand/determine which behaviors are acceptable or unacceptable in response to others

    iv. Hesitant to identify/describe/interpret own feelings/emotions

    v. Relies on peers to identify/describe/interpret feelings/emotions of others (both in and outside of group)

    vi. Needs assistance to perceive and then verbalize the perspective of other group members or others outside the group

    vii. Has limited respect for the rights, property, and opinions of others (both in and outside of group)

b. Emotional acceptance/demonstration

    i. Rarely expresses appropriate affect in response to others' emotions (both within and outside of the group)

   ii. Rarely verbalizes an understanding of other group members' experiences/feelings

   iii. With assistance, is able to adopt the perspective of someone with whom he is in conflict (e.g., parole officer)

   iv. Hesitantly expresses/demonstrates a desire to alleviate distress in other group members

   v. Relies on peers to comfort other group members when distressed

   vi. Rarely able to adopt and understand others' perspectives during a highly emotional situation

3. Empathy for Victim

Level 4

a. Intellectual understanding
   i. Confidently able to identify/describe a wide variety of short- and long-term effects of sexual abuse on victims (general)
   ii. Always participates in discussions of victim empathy/harm within group
   iii. Insightfully challenges victim-related cognitive distortions in other group members
   iv. Able to adopt perspective of victim(s) with ease
   v. Consistently applies knowledge/understanding of effects of sexual abuse to own victim(s)
   vi. Outstanding at identifying others victimized by his behavior (e.g., the "ripple effect")
   vii. All written assignments reflect a sensitivity and understanding of the negative effects of sexual abuse on own victim(s)
   viii. Written assignments consistently exclude selfish or self-serving sentiments and statements

b. Emotional acceptance/demonstration
   i. Consistently expresses appropriate affect during discussions of victim harm (general victims)
   ii. Consistently expresses appropriate affect during discussions of victim harm (own victim)
   iii. Independently verbalizes remorse and guilt for his abusive behavior
   iv. Always desists from shifting blame/responsibility to own or others' victim(s)
   v. Consistently expresses a realistic understanding of relationship and victim(s) (e.g., does not "romanticize" relationship)

    vi. Makes insightful connections between experiences of other group members' victim(s) and experiences of own victim(s)

Level 3

a. Intellectual understanding
    i. Competently able to identify/describe a wide variety of short- and long-term effects of sexual abuse on victims (general)
    ii. Regularly participates in discussions of victim empathy/harm within group
    iii. Persistently challenges victim-related cognitive distortions in other group members
    iv. Able to adopt perspective of victim(s) with some ease
    v. Routinely applies knowledge/understanding of effects of sexual abuse to own victim(s)
    vi. Proficient at identifying others victimized by his behavior (e.g., the "ripple effect")
    vii. Written assignments capably reflect a sensitivity and understanding of the negative effects of sexual abuse on own victim(s)
    viii. Written assignments usually exclude selfish or self-serving sentiments and statements

b. Emotional acceptance/demonstration
    i. Usually expresses appropriate affect during discussions of victim harm (general victims)
    ii. Usually expresses appropriate affect during discussions of victim harm (own victim)
    iii. Appropriately verbalizes remorse and guilt for his abusive behavior
    iv. Usually desists from shifting blame/responsibility to own or others' victim(s)
    v. Routinely expresses a realistic understanding of relationship and victim(s) (e.g., does not "romanticize" relationship)
    vi. Makes thoughtful connections between experiences of other group members' victim(s) and experiences of own victim(s)

Level 2

a. Intellectual understanding
    i. Adequately able to identify/describe a variety of short- and long-term effects of sexual abuse on victims (general)
    ii. Adequately participates in discussions of victim empathy/harm within group

   iii. Hesitantly challenges victim-related cognitive distortions in other group members

   iv. Sporadically able to adopt perspective of victim(s)

   v. Occasionally applies knowledge/understanding of effects of sexual abuse to own victim(s)

   vi. Shows development at identifying others victimized by his behavior (e.g., the "ripple effect")

   vii. Written assignments irregularly reflect a sensitivity and understanding of the negative effects of sexual abuse on own victim(s)

   viii. Written assignments sometimes exclude selfish or self-serving sentiments and statements

b. Emotional acceptance/demonstration

   i. Inconsistently expresses appropriate affect during discussions of victim harm (general victims)

   ii. Inconsistently expresses appropriate affect during discussions of victim harm (own victim)

   iii. Learning to verbalizes remorse and guilt for his abusive behavior

   iv. Sporadically desists from shifting blame/responsibility to own or others' victim(s)

   v. Sometimes expresses a realistic understanding of relationship and victim(s) (e.g., does not "romanticize" relationship)

   vi. Makes a few thoughtful connections between experiences of other group members' victim(s) and experiences of own victim(s)

Level 1

a. Intellectual understanding

   i. Unable to identify/describe a wide variety of short- and long-term effects of sexual abuse on victims (general)

   ii. Rarely participates in discussions of victim empathy/harm within group

   iii. Rarely challenges victim-related cognitive distortions in other group members

   iv. Needs assistance to adopt perspective of victim(s)

   v. Beginning to apply knowledge/understanding of effects of sexual abuse to own victim(s)

   vi. Hesitant at identifying others victimized by his behavior (e.g., the "ripple effect")

   vii. Written assignments rarely reflect a sensitivity and understanding of the negative effects of sexual abuse on own victim(s)

   viii. Written assignments rarely exclude selfish or self-serving sentiments and statements

b. Emotional acceptance/demonstration
   i. Rarely expresses appropriate affect during discussions of victim harm (general victims)
   ii. Rarely expresses appropriate affect during discussions of victim harm (own victim)
   iii. Verbalizes limited remorse and guilt for his abusive behavior
   iv. With assistance, is beginning to desist from shifting blame/ responsibility to own or others' victim(s)
   v. Has difficulty expressing a realistic understanding of relationship and victim(s) (e.g., does not "romanticize" relationship)
   vi. Makes minimal connections between experiences of other group members' victim(s) and experiences of own victim(s)

4. Prosocial Attitudes

Level 4

a. Intellectual understanding
   i. Independently challenges others displaying antisocial attitudes
   ii. Insightfully links antisocial attitudes to offending behavior
   iii. Clearly links antisocial attitudes to life difficulties
   iv. Readily recognizes antisocial attitudes in others, in the media, etc.
   v. Makes mature prosocial attitudes part of RPP (Relapse Prevention Plans), e.g., not to associate with other criminals
   vi. Firmly sees importance of having a job—ideally a satisfying job/ career
   vii. Clearly values and understands the importance of family and friends
   viii. Respectfully accepts that police, corrections, parole board, etc. have an important job to do
b. Emotional acceptance/demonstration
   i. Confidently uses a wide variety of positive social skills, e.g., does not make inappropriate jokes about women and children
   ii. Always uses appropriate language, e.g., does not use "girl" for "woman"
   iii. Always gets along with parole officer and other prison staff and shows appropriate respect to authority
   iv. Consistently demonstrates self-awareness, e.g., doesn't collude with other group members when they express antisocial attitudes
   v. Participates fully in social development, e.g., becomes involved with groups that foster prosocial attitudes (e.g., Toastmasters, AA)

vi. Always acts responsibly to promote well-being of group, e.g., reports to therapists or turns in offenders who are being antisocial

vii. Readily accepts parole board decisions (as fair)

Level 3

a. Intellectual understanding

i. Regularly challenges others displaying antisocial attitudes

ii. Competently links antisocial attitudes to offending behavior

iii. Appropriately links antisocial attitudes to life difficulties

iv. Competently recognizes antisocial attitudes in others, in the media, etc.

v. Usually makes thoughtful prosocial attitudes part of RPP (Relapse Prevention Plans), e.g., not to associate with other criminals

vi. Typically sees importance of having a job—ideally a satisfying job/career

vii. Appropriately values and understands the importance of family and friends

viii. Appropriately accepts that police, corrections, parole board, etc. have an important job to do

b. Emotional acceptance/demonstration

i. Uses a wide variety of positive social skills, e.g., does not make inappropriate jokes about women and children

ii. Routinely uses appropriate language, e.g., does not use "girl" for "woman"

iii. Often gets along with parole officer and other prison staff and shows appropriate respect for authority

iv. Usually demonstrates self-awareness, e.g., doesn't collude with other group members when they express antisocial attitudes

v. Often participates in social development, e.g., becomes involved with groups that foster prosocial attitudes (e.g., Toastmasters, AA)

vi. Routinely acts responsibly to promote well-being of group, e.g., reports to therapists or turns in offenders who are being antisocial

vii. Usually accepts parole board decisions (as fair)

Level 2

a. Intellectual understanding

i. Capable of challenging others displaying antisocial attitudes

ii. Adequately links antisocial attitudes to offending behavior

    iii. Inconsistently links antisocial attitudes to life difficulties
    iv. Recognizes a few antisocial attitudes in others, in the media, etc.
    v. Makes improved prosocial attitudes part of RPP (Relapse Prevention Plans), e.g., not to associate with other criminals
    vi. Sometimes sees importance of having a job—ideally a satisfying job/career
    vii. Occasionally values and understands the importance of family and friends
    viii. Adequately accepts that police, corrections, parole board, etc., have an important job to do

b. Emotional acceptance/demonstration
    i. Uses a few positive social skills, e.g., does not make inappropriate jokes about women and children
    ii. Occasionally uses appropriate language, e.g., does not use "girl" for "woman"
    iii. Inconsistently gets along with parole officer and other prison staff while showing appropriate respect for authority
    iv. Irregularly demonstrates self-awareness, e.g., doesn't collude with other group members when they express antisocial attitudes
    v. Sometimes participates in social development, e.g., becomes involved with groups that foster prosocial attitudes (e.g., Toastmasters, AA)
    vi. Needs encouragement to promote well-being of group, e.g., reports to therapists or turns in offenders who are being antisocial
    vii. Sometimes accepts parole board decisions (as fair)

Level 1

a. Intellectual understanding
    i. Incapable of challenging others displaying antisocial attitudes
    ii. Needs assistance to link antisocial attitudes to offending behavior
    iii. With assistance links antisocial attitudes to life difficulties
    iv. Rarely recognizes antisocial attitudes in others, in the media, etc.
    v. Makes limited prosocial attitudes part of RPP (Relapse Prevention Plans), e.g., not to associate with other criminals
    vi. Rarely sees importance of having a job—ideally a satisfying job/career
    vii. Needs assistance to value and understand the importance of family and friends
    viii. Has limited acceptance that police, corrections, parole board, etc. have an important job to do

b. Emotional acceptance/demonstration
    i. Uses a limited number of positive social skills, e.g., does not make inappropriate jokes about women and children
    ii. Developing more appropriate language, e.g., does not use "girl" for "woman"
    iii. Hesitant to get along with parole officer and other prison staff while showing some respect to authority
    iv. Demonstrates limited self- awareness, e.g., doesn't collude with other group members when they express antisocial attitudes
    v. Needs assistance to participate in social development, e.g., becomes involved with groups that foster prosocial attitudes (e.g., Toastmasters, AA)
    vi. Has difficulty promoting well-being of group, e.g., reports to therapists or turns in offenders who are being antisocial
    vii. Rarely accepts parole board decisions (as fair)

5. Adequate Coping Skills/Styles

Level 4

a. Intellectual understanding
    i. Completely understands the difference between effective and ineffective coping strategies
    ii. Skillfully identifies his typical ways of reacting to stressful and difficult situations
    iii. Accurately identifies how his typical ineffective coping strategies in the past have led to an increase of problems and/ or his offending behavior
    iv. Clearly understands the importance of addressing in a constructive manner the various stressful situations that inevitably arise in life
    v. Has independently developed a wide variety of effective strategies to deal with stressors.
    vi. Skillfully and accurately differentiates between situations that he can or cannot control
    vii. Confidently recognizes the importance of being flexible in his strategies to deal with problems and stressful situations
b. Emotional acceptance/demonstration
    i. Able to consistently identify various stressors in his life as they arise
    ii. Accurately analyzes the various contributors to his feelings of stress/distress

   iii. Consistently demonstrates an ability to identify and resolve the stressors that are under his control
   iv. Adept at cognitively reframing those stressors that are not within his control (e.g., parole hearing)
   v. Consistently demonstrates a skillfull utilization of a repertoire of coping strategies that effectively addresses a range of situations
   vi. Thoroughly modifies his strategies as needed to suit a given difficult situation or stressor
   vii. Fully evaluates the effectiveness of his strategies to address problems/stressors

Level 3

a. Intellectual understanding
   i. Sufficiently understands the difference between effective and ineffective coping strategies
   ii. Effectively identifies his typical ways of reacting to stressful and difficult situations
   iii. Appropriately identifies how his typical ineffective coping strategies in the past have led to an increase of problems and/or his offending behavior
   iv. Aptly understands the importance of addressing in a constructive manner the various stressful situations that inevitably arise in life
   v. Has competently developed a wide variety of effective strategies to deal with stressors
   vi. Meaningfully differentiates between situations that he can or cannot control
   vii. Competently recognizes the importance of being flexible in his strategies to deal with problems and stressful situations
b. Emotional acceptance/demonstration
   i. Able to aptly identify various stressors in his life as they arise
   ii. Competently analyzes the various contributors to his feelings of stress/distress
   iii. Routinely demonstrates an ability to identify and resolve the stressors that are under his control
   iv. Capable of cognitively reframing those stressors that are not within his control (e.g., parole hearing)
   v. Usually demonstrates a utilization of a repertoire of coping strategies that effectively addresses a range of situations
   vi. Effectively modifies his strategies as needed to suit a given difficult situation or stressor

vii. Competently evaluates the effectiveness of his strategies to address problems/stressors

Level 2

a. Intellectual understanding
  i. Adequately understands the difference between effective and ineffective coping strategies
  ii. Learning to effectively identify his typical ways of reacting to stressful and difficult situations
  iii. Shows improvement at identifying how his typical ineffective coping strategies in the past have led to an increase of problems and/or his offending behavior
  iv. Adequately understands the importance of addressing in a constructive manner the various stressful situations that inevitably arise in life
  v. Has developed a few effective strategies to deal with stressors
  vi. Adequately differentiates between situations that he can or cannot control
  vii. Developing the ability to recognize the importance of being flexible in his strategies to deal with problems and stressful situations

b. Emotional acceptance/demonstration
  i. Learning to identify various stressors in his life as they arise
  ii. Moderately able to analyze the various contributors to his feelings of stress/distress
  iii. Occasionally demonstrates an ability to identify and resolve the stressors that are under his control
  iv. Somewhat capable of cognitively reframing those stressors that are not within his control (e.g., parole hearing)
  v. Sometimes demonstrates a utilization of a repertoire of coping strategies that effectively addresses a range of situations
  vi. Demonstrates improvement at modifying his strategies as needed to suit a given difficult situation or stressor
  vii. Learning to evaluate the effectiveness of his strategies to address problems/stressors

Level 1

a. Intellectual understanding
  i. Has difficulty understanding the difference between effective and ineffective coping strategies
  ii. Beginning to identify his typical ways of reacting to stressful and difficult situations

    iii. Shows little improvement at identifying how his typical ineffective coping strategies in the past have led to an increase of problems and/or his offending behavior

    iv. Needs assistance to understand the importance of addressing in a constructive manner the various stressful situations that inevitably arise in life

    v. With assistance, is learning a few effective strategies to deal with stressors

    vi. Needs assistance to differentiate between situations that he can or cannot control

    vii. Developing a recognition of the importance of being flexible in his strategies to deal with problems and stressful situations

b. Emotional acceptance/demonstration

    i. With assistance is able to identify a few stressors in his life as they arise

    ii. Rarely able to analyze the various contributors to his feelings of stress/distress

    iii. Rarely demonstrates an ability to identify and resolve the stressors that are under his control

    iv. Needs assistance to cognitively reframe those stressors that are not within his control (e.g., parole hearing)

    v. Rarely demonstrates a utilization of a repertoire of coping strategies that effectively addresses a range of situations

    vi. Demonstrates minimal improvement at modifying his strategies as needed to suit a given difficult situation or stressor

    vii. Has difficulty learning to evaluate the effectiveness of his strategies to address problems/stressors

6. Adequate Social Skills

Level 4

a. Intellectual understanding

    i. Readily identifies the general skills needed to function effectively

    ii. Insightfully distinguishes between anxiety and lack of skills

    iii. Adeptly identifies specific skills he should enact in particular situations (e.g., being assertive with someone)

    iv. Respectfully understands the skills involved in intimate relationships

    v. Accurately distinguishes various levels of intimacy (i.e., romantic partners, friendships, acquaintances)

    vi. Thoroughly understands boundaries and interpersonal space

      vii. Fully recognizes the consequences of emotional loneliness
    viii. Completely understands the need to take time in forming
         relationships
  b. Emotional acceptance/demonstration
       i. Demonstrates refined social skills within and outside the group
      ii. Not anxious
     iii. Respectively assertive
     iv. Readily role-plays appropriate skills for specific context
      v. Always acts appropriately toward friends and acquaintances
     vi. Behavior consistently reveals separation of different levels
        of intimacy
     vii. Maintains appropriate boundaries and interpersonal space
    viii. Shows no signs of avoiding others
     ix. Always respectful of relationships (i.e., does not rush them)

Level 3

  a. Intellectual understanding
       i. Routinely identifies the general skills needed to function
        effectively
      ii. Competently distinguishes between anxiety and lack of skills
     iii. Aptly identifies specific skills he should enact in particular
        situations (e.g., being assertive with someone)
     iv. Effectively understands the skills involved in intimate
        relationships
      v. Able to distinguish various levels of intimacy reasonable well
        (i.e., romantic partners, friendships, acquaintances)
     vi. Effectively understands boundaries and interpersonal space
     vii. Generally recognizes the consequences of emotional loneliness
    viii. Sufficiently understands the need to take time in forming
        relationships
  b. Emotional acceptance/demonstration
       i. Demonstrates appropriate social skills within and outside
        the group
      ii. Not often anxious
     iii. Usually respectively assertive
     iv. Voluntarily role-plays appropriate skills for specific context
      v. Routinely acts appropriately toward friends and acquaintances
     vi. Behavior typically reveals a separation of different levels of
        intimacy
     vii. Usually maintains appropriate boundaries and
        interpersonal space
    viii. Shows few signs of avoiding others

    ix. Sufficiently respectful of relationships (i.e., does not rush them)

Level 2

a. Intellectual understanding
    i. Sometimes identifies the general skills needed to function effectively
    ii. Adequately distinguishes between anxiety and lack of skills
    iii. Hesitantly identifies specific skills he should enact in particular situations (e.g., being assertive with someone)
    iv. Moderately understands the skills involved in intimate relationships
    v. Able to distinguish various levels of intimacy with some assistance (i.e., romantic partners, friendships, acquaintances)
    vi. Adequately understands boundaries and interpersonal space
    vii. Sometimes recognizes the consequences of emotional loneliness
    viii. Inconsistently understands the need to take time in forming relationships

b. Emotional acceptance/demonstration
    i. Demonstrates basic social skills within and outside the group
    ii. Sometimes anxious
    iii. Developing some appropriate assertiveness
    iv. Hesitantly role-plays appropriate skills for specific context
    v. Shows improvement in acting appropriately toward friends and acquaintances
    vi. Occasionally, behavior reveals a separation of different levels of intimacy
    vii. Sometimes maintains appropriate boundaries and interpersonal space
    viii. Shows some signs of avoiding others
    ix. Developing respect of relationships (i.e., does not rush them)

Level 1

a. Intellectual understanding
    i. Rarely identifies the general skills needed to function effectively
    ii. Demonstrates incomplete distinction between anxiety and lack of skills
    iii. Relies on peers to identify specific skills he should enact in particular situations (e.g., being assertive with someone)
    iv. Has difficulty understanding the skills involved in intimate relationships
    v. Unable to distinguish various levels of intimacy (i.e., romantic partners, friendships, acquaintances)

vi. Inadequately understands boundaries and interpersonal space
vii. Uncertain about the consequences of emotional loneliness
viii. Demonstrates limited understanding for the need to take time in forming relationships
b. Emotional acceptance/demonstration
  i. Demonstrates a lack of social skills within and outside the group
  ii. Anxious
  iii. Developing limited appropriate assertiveness
  iv. Reluctantly role-plays appropriate skills for specific context
  v. Shows minimal improvement in acting appropriately toward friends and acquaintances
  vi. Rarely, behavior reveals a separation of different levels of intimacy
  vii. Rarely maintains appropriate boundaries and interpersonal space
  viii. Shows signs of avoiding others
  ix. Beginning to develope respect of relationships (i.e., does not rush them)

7. Positive Self-Esteem

Level 4

a. Intellectual understanding
  i.   Acknowledges at least 6 positive qualities about self with ease
  ii. Clearly understands the advantages of positive self-esteem
  iii. Fully understands the disadvantages of low self-esteem
  iv. Readily identifies ways to enhance and maintain positive self-esteem
  v.   Easily recognizes when self-esteem drops
  vi. Insightfully identifies areas of self-esteem that need continuing work
  vii. Readily identifies defensive styles in self
  viii. Readily identifies defensive styles in others
b. Emotional acceptance/demonstration
  i.   Always displays self-confidence
  ii. Displays exceptional supportive behavior to others who have low self-esteem
  iii. Identifies low self-esteem in others and offers suggestions for improvements in a sophisticated way
  iv. Respectfully encourages others to enhance their self-confidence
  v.   Consistently not defensive
  vi. Independently identifies and discourages defensiveness in others

Level 3

a. Intellectual understanding
  i. Acknowledges at least 4 positive qualities about self
  ii. Competently understands the advantages of positive self-esteem
  iii. Has a good understanding of the disadvantages of low self-esteem
  iv. Thoughtfully identifies ways to enhance and maintain positive self-esteem
  v. Often recognizes when self-esteem drops
  vi. Reasonably adept at identifying areas of self-esteem that need continuing work
  vii. Usually identifies defensive styles in self
  viii. Usually identifies defensive styles in others
b. Emotional acceptance/demonstration
  i. Typically displays self-confidence
  ii. Displays sufficient supportive behavior to others who have low self-esteem
  iii. Identifies low self-esteem in others and offers suggestions for improvements in an appropriate way
  iv. Skillfully encourages others to enhance their self-confidence
  v. Usually not defensive
  vi. Appropriately identifies and discourages defensiveness in others

Level 2

a. Intellectual understanding
  i. Needs encouragement to acknowledge at least 2 positive qualities about self
  ii. Adequately understands the advantages of positive self-esteem
  iii. Has a basic understanding of the disadvantages of low self-esteem
  iv. Sometimes identifies ways to enhance and maintain positive self-esteem
  v. Sometimes recognizes when self-esteem drops
  vi. Capable of identifying areas of self-esteem that need continuing work
  vii. Occasionally identifies defensive styles in self
  viii. Occasionally identifies defensive styles in others
b. Emotional acceptance/demonstration
  i. Inconsistently displays self-confidence
  ii. Displays moderate supportive behavior to others who have low self-esteem

iii. Learning to identify low self-esteem in others and offer suggestions for improvements
iv. Inconsistently encourages others to enhance their self-confidence
v. Occasionally not defensive
vi. Learning to identify and discourage defensiveness in others

Level 1

a. Intellectual understanding
   i. Needs assistance to acknowledge any positive qualities about self
   ii. Has difficulty understanding the advantages of positive self-esteem
   iii. Has a limited understanding of the disadvantages of low self-esteem
   iv. Rarely identifies ways to enhance and maintain positive self-esteem
   v. Rarely recognizes when self-esteem drops
   vi. Reluctant to identify areas of self-esteem that need continuing work
   vii. Beginning to identify defensive styles in self
   viii. Beginning to identify defensive styles in others
b. Emotional acceptance/demonstration
   i. Rarely displays self-confidence
   ii. Displays insufficient supportive behavior to others who have low self-esteem
   iii. Needs assistance to identify low self-esteem in others and offer suggestions for improvements
   iv. Needs assistance to encourage others to enhance their self-confidence
   v. Defensive
   vi. Has difficulty learning to identify and discourage defensiveness in others

8. Control Over Impulses

Level 4

a. Intellectual understanding
   i. Confidently makes impulse control part of RPP (Relapse Prevention Plans)
   ii. Always recognizes when others are being impulsive
   iii. Consistently recognizes emotional precursors to impulsivity
   iv. Readily links impulsivity to offending behavior

     v. Generates strategies to deal with impulsivity in a refined way
    vi. Respectfully challenges others about their impulsivity
   vii. Confidently knows and describes the steps and strategies to control impulsive behavior

b. Emotional acceptance/demonstration
     i. Continually pursues positive approaches to overcome set backs, i.e., does not give up when given a set back
    ii. Consistently refrains from collusion with other group members
   iii. Responds with maturity when challenged
   iv. Persistently catches self being impulsive, then stops
    v. Works respectfully to foster a positive relationship with parole officer
   vi. Demonstrates consistency to use steps and strategies to control impulsive behavior
  vii. Independently interacts effectively with others (with no institutional charges)

Level 3

a. Intellectual understanding
     i. Carefully makes impulse control part of RPP (Relapse Prevention Plans)
    ii. Usually recognizes when others are being impulsive
   iii. Routinely recognizes emotional precursors to impulsivity
   iv. Appropriately links impulsivity to offending behavior
    v. Generates strategies to deal with impulsivity accurately
   vi. Thoughtfully challenges others about their impulsivity
  vii. Capably knows and describes the steps and strategies to control impulsive behavior

b. Emotional acceptance/demonstration
     i. Actively pursues positive approaches to overcome set backs, i.e., does not give up when given a set back
    ii. Routinely refrains from collusion with other group members
   iii. Responds appropriately when challenged
   iv. Usually catches self being impulsive, then stops
    v. Works competently to foster a positive relationship with parole officer
   vi. Demonstrates concern to use steps and strategies to control impulsive behavior
  vii. Interacts effectively with others (with no institutional charges)

Level 2

a. Intellectual understanding
  i. Hesitantly makes impulse control part of RPP (Relapse Prevention Plans)
  ii. Sometimes recognizes when others are being impulsive
  iii. Recognizes a few emotional precursors to impulsivity
  iv. Occasionally links impulsivity to offending behavior
  v. Learning to generate strategies to deal with impulsivity
  vi. Occasionally challenges others about their impulsivity
  vii. Learning to recognize and describe the steps and strategies to control impulsive behavior

b. Emotional acceptance/demonstration
  i. Shows some independence to pursue positive approaches to overcome set backs, i.e., does not give up when given a set back
  ii. Inconsistently refrains from collusion with other group members
  iii. Responds hesitantly when challenged
  iv. Occasionally catches self being impulsive, then stops
  v. Works adequately to foster a positive relationship with parole officer
  vi. Demonstrates some interest to use steps and strategies to control impulsive behavior
  vii. Occasionally interacts effectively with others (with no institutional charges)

Level 1

a. Intellectual understanding
  i. Has difficulty making impulse control part of RPP (Relapse Prevention Plans)
  ii. Rarely recognizes when others are being impulsive
  iii. Rarely recognizes a few emotional precursors to impulsivity
  iv. Needs assistance to link impulsivity to offending behavior
  v. Needs assistance to generate strategies to deal with impulsivity
  vi. Relies on peers to challenge others about their impulsivity
  vii. Beginning to learn to recognize and describe the steps and strategies to control impulsive behavior

b. Emotional acceptance/demonstration
  i. Shows little independence to pursue positive approaches to overcome set backs, i.e., does not give up when given a set back
  ii. Rarely refrains from collusion with other group members
  iii. Reluctant to respond when challenged
  iv. Rarely catches self being impulsive, then stops

     v. Beginning to work to foster a positive relationship with
       parole officer
    vi. Demonstrates minimal interest to use steps and strategies to
       control impulsive behavior
   vii. Rarely interacts effectively with others (with no
       institutional charges)

9. Emotional Regulation

Level 4

a. Intellectual understanding
     i. Confidently identifies when he is experiencing an emotional
      response
    ii. Thoroughly and confidently labels his emotional responses
   iii. Consistently understands that emotions are not value-laden
     (i.e., negative emotions are not bad)
   iv. Readily identifies that the way he thinks about or interprets a
     situation typically dictates the resulting emotional state
    v. Accurately recognizes how his various emotional states impact
     on his thinking patterns
   vi. Independently acknowledges how his general emotional
     disposition on a particular day will affect his behavioral
     responses to situations
   vii. Skillfully distinguishes all the various emotional states
     associated with his offending behavior
b. Emotional acceptance/demonstration
     i. Insightful when allowing himself to experience and process an
     emotion without negating or minimizing it
    ii. Consistently shows an ability to regulate his behavior
     regardless of his emotional state
   iii. Accurately and completely discusses his emotional states as
     opposed to experiencing his emotions as "good" or "bad"
   iv. Confidently shares his emotions in relevant situations
    v. Consistently checks out his thinking and perceptions with
     others to minimize and manage his negative emotional state
   vi. Thoroughly consults with appropriate others before acting
     when he is experiencing a negative emotional state
   vii. Always maintains flexibility and acceptance of feedback when
     experiencing a negative emotional state

Level 3

a. Intellectual understanding
  i. Competently identifies when he is experiencing an emotional response
  ii. Carefully and thoughtfully labels his emotional responses
  iii. Appropriately understands that emotions are not value-laden (i.e., negative emotions are not bad)
  iv. Generally identifies that the way he thinks about or interprets a situation typically dictates the resulting emotional state
  v. Competently recognizes how his various emotional states affect his thinking patterns
  vi. Appropriately acknowledges how his general emotional disposition on a particular day will affect his behavioral responses to situations
  vii. Skillfully distinguishes most emotional states associated with his offending behavior
b. Emotional acceptance/demonstration
  i. Appropriately allows himself to experience and process an emotion without negating or minimizing it
  ii. Usually shows an ability to regulate his behavior regardless of his emotional state
  iii. Meaningfully discusses his emotional states as opposed to experiencing his emotions as "good" or "bad"
  iv. Effectively and appropriately shares his emotions in relevant situations
  v. Usually checks out his thinking and perceptions with others to minimize and manage his negative emotional state
  vi. Effectively consults with appropriate others before acting when he is experiencing a negative emotional state
  vii. Typically maintains flexibility and acceptance of feedback when experiencing a negative emotional state

Level 2

a. Intellectual understanding
  i. Adequately identifies when he is experiencing an emotional response
  ii. Needs encouragement to label his emotional responses
  iii. Adequately understands that emotions are not value-laden (i.e., negative emotions are not bad)
  iv. Learning to identify that the way he thinks about or interprets a situation typically dictates the resulting emotional state

     v. Adequately recognizes how his various emotional states affect his thinking patterns

    vi. Inconsistently acknowledges how his general emotional disposition on a particular day will affect his behavioral responses to situations

   vii. Shows improvement when distinguishing the various emotional states associated with his offending behavior

b. Emotional acceptance/demonstration

     i. Learning to experience and process an emotion without negating or minimizing it

    ii. Occasionally shows an ability to regulate his behavior regardless of his emotional state

   iii. Beginning to discuss his emotional states as opposed to experiencing his emotions as "good" or "bad"

   iv. Hesitantly shares his emotions in relevant situations

    v. Occasionally checks out his thinking and perceptions with others to minimize and manage his negative emotional state

   vi. Shows improvement by consulting with appropriate others before acting when he is experiencing a negative emotional state

   vii. Shows some independence to develop flexibility and acceptance of feedback when experiencing a negative emotional state

Level 1

a. Intellectual understanding

     i. Incompletely identifies when he is experiencing an emotional response

    ii. With assistance, is able to label his emotional responses

   iii. Has difficulty understanding that emotions are not value-laden (i.e., negative emotions are not bad)

   iv. Needs assistance to identify that the way he thinks about or interprets a situation typically dictates the resulting emotional state

    v. Has limited recognition of how his various emotional states affect his thinking patterns

   vi. Inconsistently and with some reluctance acknowledges how his general emotional disposition on a particular day will affect his behavioral responses to situations

   vii. Shows limited improvement when distinguishing the various emotional states associated with his offending behavior

b. Emotional acceptance/demonstration
   i. With assistance, is learning to experience and process an
       emotion without negating or minimizing it
   ii. Shows a limited interest to regulate his behavior regardless of
       his emotional state
   iii. Needs assistance to discuss his emotional states as opposed to
       experiencing his emotions as "good" or "bad"
   iv. Reluctantly shares his emotions in relevant situations
   v. Rarely checks out his thinking and perceptions with others to
       minimize and manage his negative emotional state
   vi. With some assistance, is beginning to consult with appropriate
       others before acting when he is experiencing a negative
       emotional state
   vii. Shows limited interest to develop flexibility and acceptance of
       feedback when experiencing a negative emotional state

10. Control Over Anger and Aggression—Anger Management

Level 4

a. Intellectual understanding
   i. Confidently differentiates between actual feelings of anger,
       and other feelings mislabelled as anger
   ii. Fully able to separate the feelings of anger from the behavioral
       expression of aggression, does not see them as inextricably linked
   iii. Thoroughly and meaningfully discusses the benefits of
       resolving conflicts appropriately, including the recognition of
       the inherent difficulties in doing so
   iv. Insightfully identifies and explains situations that trigger
       his anger
   v. Readily acknowledges that he experiences short-term reward for
       anger and accompanying aggression, but that inevitably, long-
       term negative consequences outweigh these short-term rewards
   vi. Fully recognizes his defense mechanisms and how he uses
       them (e.g., blaming, rationalizing, justifying)
   vii. Independently has developed a wide variety of effective
       strategies to prevent and manage his anger
b. Emotional acceptance/demonstration
   i. Consistently listens to feedback and/or questions from others
       without reacting in an angry fashion
   ii. Always asks questions or seeks clarification to prevent himself
       from jumping to angry conclusions

    iii. Sincerely seeks assistance and cooperation from others in dealing with conflicts

    iv. Accurately recognizes when he is angry, and consistently demonstrates anger management techniques in those situations (e.g., time-out, self-talk strategies)

    v. Respectfully communicates with others and seeks assistance as needed when experiencing anger

    vi. Always takes time to consider responses rather than expressing impulsive retorts when angry

    vii. Consistently verbalizes ownership of his own angry feelings

Level 3

a. Intellectual understanding

    i. Skillfully differentiates between actual feelings of anger, and other feelings mislabelled as anger

    ii. Effectively separates the feelings of anger from the behavioral expression of aggression, does not see them as inextricably linked

    iii. Meaningfully discusses the benefits of resolving conflicts appropriately, including the recognition of the inherent difficulties in doing so

    iv. Competently identifies and explains situations that trigger his anger

    v. Usually acknowledges that he experiences short-term reward for anger and accompanying aggression, but that inevitably, long-term negative consequences outweigh these short-term rewards

    vi. Effectively recognizes his defence mechanisms and how he uses them (e.g., blaming, rationalizing, justifying)

    vii. Has developed a variety of effective strategies to prevent and manage his anger

b. Emotional acceptance/demonstration

    i. Continually listens to feedback and/or questions from others without reacting in an angry fashion

    ii. Routinely asks questions or seeks clarification to prevent himself from jumping to angry conclusions

    iii. Adeptly seeks assistance an cooperation from others in dealing with conflicts

    iv. Effectively recognizes when he is angry, and routinely demonstrates anger management techniques in those situations (e.g., time-out, self-talk strategies)

    v. Effectively and appropriately communicates with others and seeks assistance as needed when experiencing anger

    vi. Routinely takes time to consider responses rather than expressing impulsive retorts when angry

   vii. Routinely verbalizes ownership of his own angry feelings

Level 2

a. Intellectual understanding

     i. Adequately differentiates between actual feelings of anger, and other feelings mislabelled as anger

    ii. Hesitant to separate the feelings of anger from the behavioral expression of aggression, does not see them as inextricably linked

   iii. In a somewhat meaningful way discusses the benefits of resolving conflicts appropriately, including the recognition of the inherent difficulties in doing so

    iv. Shows improvement identifying and explaining situations that trigger his anger

     v. Occasionally acknowledges that he experiences short-term reward for anger and accompanying aggression, but that inevitably, long-term negative consequences outweigh these short-term rewards

    vi. Developing more recognition of his defence mechanisms and how he uses them (e.g., blaming, rationalizing, justifying)

   vii. Developing effective strategies to prevent and manage his anger

b. Emotional acceptance/demonstration

     i. Sometimes listens to feedback and/or questions from others without reacting in an angry fashion

    ii. Occasionally asks questions or seeks clarification to prevent himself from jumping to angry conclusions

   iii. Needs encouragement to seek assistance and cooperation from others in dealing with conflicts

    iv. Becoming more skillfull at recognizing when he is angry, and demonstrates improvement of anger management techniques in those situations (e.g., time-out, self-talk strategies)

     v. Sometimes communicates effectively and appropriately with others and seeks assistance as needed when experiencing anger

    vi. Occasionally takes time to consider responses rather than expressing impulsive retorts when angry

   vii. Hesitant to verbalize ownership of his own angry feelings

Level 1

a. Intellectual understanding

     i. Inadequately differentiates between actual feelings of anger, and other feelings mislabelled as anger

   ii. Needs assistance to separate the feelings of anger from the behavioral expression of aggression, does not see them as inextricably linked

  iii. Has difficulty discussing the benefits of resolving conflicts appropriately, including the recognition of the inherent difficulties in doing so

  iv. Rarely identifies and explains situations that trigger his anger

   v. Reluctantly acknowledges that he experiences short-term reward for anger and accompanying aggression, but that inevitably, long-term negative consequences outweigh these short-term rewards

  vi. Beginning to learn to recognize his defence mechanisms and how he uses them (e.g., blaming, rationalizing, justifying)

 vii. Developing basic strategies to prevent and manage his anger

b. Emotional acceptance/demonstration

   i. Rarely listens to feedback and/or questions from others without reacting in an angry fashion

  ii. Rarely asks questions or seeks clarification to prevent himself from jumping to angry conclusions

  iii. Has difficulty seeking assistance and cooperation from others in dealing with conflicts

  iv. Has difficulty recognizing when he is angry, and demonstrates limited improvement of anger management techniques in those situations (e.g., time-out, self-talk strategies)

   v. Rarely communicates with others and seeks assistance as needed when experiencing anger

  vi. Rarely takes time to consider responses rather than expressing impulsive retorts when angry

 vii. Beginning to verbalize ownership of his own angry feelings

11. Control Over Substance Abuse

Level 4

a. Intellectual understanding

   i. Thoroughly discusses the cognitive distortions that contributed to and which would facilitate a return to substance abuse

  ii. Consistently displays a well-developed understanding of the positive and negative, and short-term and long-term consequences of substance abuse

iii. Readily takes responsibility for his substance abuse and does not attribute his sexual offending to the substance abuse problem

iv. Accurately views substance abuse as a behavior under his control instead of a disease beyond his control

v. His behavioral chain about his substance abuse is integrated in a refined way with his offending pathway and concurrent self-management plan

vi. Respectfully recognizes that substance abuse programming does not constitute a "cure" and that ongoing self-monitoring and self-management are required

vii. Thoughtfully and extensively discusses the value of ongoing substance abuse maintenance work

b. Emotional acceptance/demonstration

i. Voluntarily adheres to a program of random urinalysis; results consistently show no substance use

ii. Skillfully and consistently applies strategies designed to prevent a resurgence of the cues associated with substance abuse (e.g., emotional regulation, alternate activities)

iii. Expertly challenges his own and other offenders' cognitive distortions that support substance abuse

iv. Consistently demonstrates that he is implementing steps to organize his current situation to include activities and relationships to prevent substance abuse while incarcerated

v. Consistently demonstrates that he is implementing steps to organize his future plans to include activities and relationships that effectively preclude a lifestyle involving substance abuse upon his return to the community

vi. Effectively utilizes institutionally based resources to master his ability to manage his substance abuse problem before his release

vii. Thoroughly discusses his struggles and successes in dealing with cravings and independently seeks appropriate support when necessary

Level 3

a. Intellectual understanding

i. Skillfully discusses the cognitive distortions that contributed to and which would facilitate a return to substance abuse

ii. Routinely displays a well-developed understanding of the positive and negative, and short-term and long-term consequences of substance abuse

iii. Appropriately takes responsibility for his substance abuse
and does not attribute his sexual offending to the substance
abuse problem

iv. Competently views substance abuse as a behavior under his
control instead of a disease beyond his control

v. His behavioral chain about his substance abuse is
meaningfully integrated with his offending pathway and
concurrent self-management plan

vi. Appropriately recognizes that substance abuse programming
does not constitute a "cure" and that ongoing self-monitoring
and self-management are required

vii. Thoughtfully discusses the value of ongoing substance abuse
maintenance work

b. Emotional acceptance/demonstration

i. Voluntarily adheres to a program of random urinalysis; results
routinely show no substance use

ii. Skillfully applies strategies designed to prevent a resurgence
of the cues associated with substance abuse (e.g., emotional
regulation, alternate activities)

iii. Actively challenges his own and other offenders' cognitive
distortions that support substance abuse

iv. Routinely demonstrates that he is implementing steps to
organize his current situation to include activities and
relationships to prevent substance abuse while incarcerated

v. Often demonstrates that he is implementing steps to organize
his future plans to include activities and relationships that
effectively preclude a lifestyle involving substance abuse upon
his return to the community

vi. Effectively utilizes institutionally based resources to improve his
ability to manage his substance abuse problem before his release

vii. Meaningfully discusses his struggles and successes in dealing
with cravings and independently seeks appropriate support
when necessary

Level 2

a. Intellectual understanding

i. Capably discusses the cognitive distortions that contributed to
and which would facilitate a return to substance abuse

ii. Occasionally displays a moderate understanding of the
positive and negative, and short-term and long-term
consequences of substance abuse

    iii. Sometimes takes responsibility for his substance abuse and does not attribute his sexual offending to the substance abuse problem

    iv. Adequately views substance abuse as a behavior under his control instead of a disease beyond his control

    v. His behavioral chain about his substance abuse is somewhat integrated with his offending pathway and concurrent self-management plan

    vi. Learning to recognize that substance abuse programming does not constitute a "cure" and that ongoing self-monitoring and self-management are required

    vii. Developing more meaningful discussions about the value of ongoing substance abuse maintenance work

b. Emotional acceptance/demonstration

    i. Adheres to a program of random urinalysis; results sometimes show no substance use

    ii. Shows interest to apply strategies designed to prevent a resurgence of the cues associated with substance abuse (e.g., emotional regulation, alternate activities)

    iii. Inconsistently challenges his own and other offenders' cognitive distortions that support substance abuse

    iv. Occasionally demonstrates that he is implementing steps to organize his current situation to include activities and relationships to prevent substance abuse while incarcerated

    v. Adequately demonstrates that he is implementing steps to organize his future plans to include activities and relationships that effectively preclude a lifestyle involving substance abuse upon his return to the community

    vi. Utilizes institutionally based resources to develop management of his substance abuse problem before his release

    vii. Sometimes discusses his struggles and successes in dealing with cravings and occasionally seeks appropriate support when necessary

Level 1

a. Intellectual understanding

    i. Needs assistance to discuss the cognitive distortions that contributed to and which would facilitate a return to substance abuse

    ii. Rarely displays an understanding of the positive and negative, and short-term and long-term consequences of substance abuse

    iii. Has difficulty taking responsibility for his substance abuse and does not attribute his sexual offending to the substance abuse problem

    iv. Beginning to view substance abuse as a behavior under his control instead of a disease beyond his control

    v. His behavioral chain about his substance abuse is inconsistent with his offending pathway and concurrent self-management plan

    vi. Beginning to recognize that substance abuse programming does not constitute a "cure" and that ongoing self-monitoring and self-management are required

    vii. Developing some ongoing discussions about the value of ongoing substance abuse maintenance work

b. Emotional acceptance/demonstration

    i. Reluctant to participate in a program of random urinalysis; results sometimes show no substance use

    ii. Rarely shows an interest to apply strategies designed to prevent a resurgence of the cues associated with substance abuse (e.g., emotional regulation, alternate activities)

    iii. Has difficulty challenging his own and other offenders' cognitive distortions that support substance abuse

    iv. Demonstrates limited interest in implementing steps to organize his current situation to include activities and relationships to prevent substance abuse while incarcerated

    v. Needs assistance to implement steps to organize his future plans to include activities and relationships that effectively preclude a lifestyle involving substance abuse upon his return to the community

    vi. Rarely utilizes institutionally based resources to develop management of his substance abuse problem before his release

    vii. Shows little interest to discuss his struggles and successes in dealing with cravings and rarely seeks appropriate support when necessary

12. Normative Sexual Views/Interests

Level 4

a. Intellectual understanding

    i. Phallometric testing reveals normative responding

    ii. Has thorough understanding of the range of normative sexual behaviors

   iii. Has solid understanding of the range of non-normative
       sexual behaviors
   iv. Always clear about appropriate age range of potential
       sexual partners
    v. Fully understands the importance of equality in sexual relations
   vi. Has clear understanding of women's, men's, and children's
       sexuality
  vii. Has solid understanding of ways in which he can reduce
       occurrence of deviant fantasies
 viii. Readily identifies the risks posed by pornography or cybersex use

b. Emotional acceptance/demonstration
    i. If pretreatment phallometric responding was deviant,
      independently seeks out and uses arousal reconditioning or
      medications to correct this
   ii. Consistently expresses prosocial attitudes about sex
  iii. Consistently identifies inappropriate sexual attitudes in others
  iv. No evidence from others (e.g., security staff, other inmates,
     case management officers, partners) of participation in deviant
     interests (e.g., watching children's TV, enthusiasm for sexual
     harassment or sexual assault on TV)
   v. Always behaves appropriately toward women and children
     at visits
  vi. Respectfully expresses egalitarian views
 vii. Consistently speaks protectively about children
viii. Independently reports using deviant arousal reducing
     procedures if necessary

Level 3

a. Intellectual understanding
    i. Phallometric testing usually reveals normative responding
   ii. Has appropriate understanding of the normative sexual
     behavior range
  iii. Has good understanding of the range of non-normative
     sexual behaviors
  iv. Is clear about appropriate age range of potential sexual partners
   v. Effectively understands the importance of equality in sexual
     relations
  vi. Has good understanding of women's, men's, and children's
     sexuality
 vii. Has reasonable understanding of ways in which he can reduce
     occurrence of deviant fantasies

    viii. Proficiently identifies the risks posed by pornography or cybersex use

b. Emotional acceptance/demonstration

    i. If pretreatment phallometric responding was deviant, competently seeks out and uses arousal reconditioning or medications to correct this

    ii. Generally expresses prosocial attitudes about sex

    iii. Usually identifies inappropriate sexual attitudes in others

    iv. Routinely has no evidence from others (e.g., security staff, other inmates, case management officers, partners) of participation in deviant interests (e.g., watching children's TV, enthusiasm for sexual harassment or sexual assault on TV)

    v. Typically behaves appropriately toward women and children at visits

    vi. Appropriately expresses egalitarian views

    vii. Usually speaks protectively about children

    viii. Voluntarily reports using deviant arousal reducing procedures if necessary

Level 2

a. Intellectual understanding

    i. Phallometric testing sporadically reveals normative responding

    ii. Has adequate understanding of the normative sexual behavior range

    iii. Has some understanding of the range of non-normative sexual behaviors

    iv. Is somewhat clear about appropriate age range of potential sexual partners

    v. Adequately understands the importance of equality in sexual relations

    vi. Has basic understanding of women's, men's, and children's sexuality

    vii. Has some understanding of ways in which he can reduce occurrence of deviant fantasies

    viii. Adequately identifies the risks posed by pornography or cybersex use

b. Emotional acceptance/demonstration

    i. If pretreatment phallometric responding was deviant, sometimes seeks out and uses arousal reconditioning or medications to correct this

    ii. Occasionally expresses prosocial attitudes about sex

    iii. Sometimes identifies inappropriate sexual attitudes in others

    iv. Some evidence from others (e.g., security staff, other inmates, case management officers, partners) shows participation in deviant interests (e.g., watching children's TV, enthusiasm for sexual harassment or sexual assault on TV)
    v. Behaves more appropriately toward women and children at visits
    vi. Is improving at appropriately expresses egalitarian views
    vii. Sometimes speaks protectively about children
    viii. Needs encouragement to report using deviant arousal reducing procedures

Level 1

a. Intellectual understanding
    i. Phallometric testing rarely reveals normative responding
    ii. Has inadequate understanding of the normative sexual behavior range
    iii. Has limited understanding of the range of non-normative sexual behaviors
    iv. Unclear about appropriate age range of potential sexual partners
    v. Has an emerging understanding the importance of equality in sexual relations
    vi. Has limited understanding of women's, men's, and children's sexuality
    vii. Has minimal understanding of ways in which he can reduce occurrence of deviant fantasies
    viii. With assistance identifies risks posed by pornography or cybersex use
b. Emotional acceptance/demonstration
    i. If pretreatment phallometric responding was deviant, rarely seeks out and uses arousal reconditioning or medications to correct this
    ii. Rarely expresses prosocial attitudes about sex
    iii. Needs assistance to identify inappropriate sexual attitudes in others
    iv. Evidence from others (e.g., security staff, other inmates, case management officers, partners) shows participation in deviant interests (e.g., watching children's TV, enthusiasm for sexual harassment or sexual assault on TV)
    v. Learning to behave appropriately toward women and children at visits
    vi. Learning to expresses egalitarian views
    vii. Hesitantly speaks protectively about children

    viii. Needs assistance to report using deviant arousal reducing
         procedures

13. Understanding Risk Factors

Level 4

a. Intellectual understanding
    i. Clearly identifies relevant life history events (childhood,
       adolescent, adult experiences)
    ii. Accurately identifies preoffense factors that disposed him
       to offend (stress, depression, low self-esteem, relationship
       problems, use of intoxicants)
    iii. Fully understands the role his attitudes had in his offense chain
    iv. Fully aware of how he set up things so that he could offend
       (i.e., accepts that he planned the offense)
    v. Considers all available information/strategies to understand
       and accept responsibility; carefully considers all feedback
       from therapist and other group members
    vi. Identifies all the steps in his own decision making
    vii. Accurately able to apply these analyses to other group
       members appropriately; clearly helps other group members
       identify their risk factors
b. Emotional acceptance/demonstration
    i. Readily demonstrates self awareness of acts leading to offense
    ii. Specifically identifies thoughts, feelings, and behaviors that led
       up to and produced his offense
    iii. Takes full responsibility—does not blame his offending on any
       of his risk factors (e.g., alcohol)
    iv. Makes an exceptional effort to challenge his own negative
       attitudes
    v. Completely recognizes emotional precursors to risks
    vi. Immediately willing to take other perspectives into account
    vii. Always practises positive approach—doesn't "test" himself

Level 3

a. Intellectual understanding
    i. Meaningfully identifies relevant life history events (childhood,
       adolescent, adult experiences)
    ii. Effectively identifies preoffense factors that disposed him
       to offend (stress, depression, low self-esteem, relationship
       problems, use of intoxicants)

    iii. Reasonably understands the role his attitudes had in his offense chain
    iv. Sufficiently aware of how he set up things so that he could offend (i.e., accepts that he planned the offense)
    v. Competently considers available information/strategies to understand and accept responsibility; carefully considers all feedback from therapist and other group members
    vi. Identifies most of the steps in his own decision making
    vii. Aptly able to apply these analyses to other group members appropriately; clearly helps other group members identify their risk factors

b. Emotional acceptance/demonstration
    i. Typically demonstrates self awareness of acts leading to offense
    ii. Meaningfully identifies thoughts, feelings, and behaviors that led up to and produced his offense
    iii. Usually takes full responsibility—does not blame his offending on any of his risk factors (e.g., alcohol)
    iv. Makes a strong effort to challenge his own negative attitudes
    v. Competently recognizes emotional precursors to risks
    vi. Usually willing to take other perspectives into account
    vii. Routinely practises positive approach—doesn't "test" himself

Level 2

a. Intellectual understanding
    i. Adequately identifies relevant life history events (childhood, adolescent, adult experiences)
    ii. Shows improvement at identifying preoffense factors that disposed him to offend (stress, depression, low self-esteem, relationship problems, use of intoxicants)
    iii. Adequately understands the role his attitudes had in his offense chain
    iv. Moderately aware of how he set up things so that he could offend (i.e., accepts that he planned the offense)
    v. Learning to consider available information/strategies to understand and accept responsibility; considers some feedback from therapist and other group members
    vi. Identifies a few of the steps in his own decision making
    vii. Hesitantly applies these analyses to other group members to appropriately help them identify their risk factors

b. Emotional acceptance/demonstration
    i. Sometimes demonstrates self awareness of acts leading to offense

    ii. Making advances to identify thoughts, feelings, and behaviors that led up to and produced his offense

   iii. Occasionally takes full responsibility—does not blame his offending on any of his risk factors (e.g., alcohol)

   iv. Makes a basic effort to challenge his own negative attitudes

    v. Adequately recognizes emotional precursors to risks

   vi. Shows an willingness to take other perspectives into account

  vii. Occasionally practices positive approach—doesn't "test" himself

Level 1

a. Intellectual understanding

    i. Reluctantly identifies relevant life history events (childhood, adolescent, adult experiences)

   ii. Shows limited improvement at identifying preoffense factors that disposed him to offend (stress, depression, low self-esteem, relationship problems, use of intoxicants)

   iii. Beginning to understand the role his attitudes had in his offense chain

   iv. Insufficiently aware of how he set up things so that he could offend (i.e., accepts that he planned the offense)

    v. Needs assistance to consider available information/strategies to understand and accept responsibility, to carefully consider all feedback from therapist and other group members

   vi. Identifies a limited number of the steps in his own decision making

  vii. Reluctantly applies these analyses to other group members to appropriately help them identify their risk factors

b. Emotional acceptance/demonstration

    i. Rarely demonstrates self awareness of acts leading to offense

   ii. Beginning to make advances to identify thoughts, feelings, and behaviors that led up to and produced his offense

   iii. Rarely takes any responsibility—does not blame his offending on any of his risk factors (e.g., alcohol)

   iv. Makes a minimal effort to challenge his own negative attitudes

    v. Incompletely recognizes emotional precursors to risks

   vi. Shows limited interest to take other perspectives into account

  vii. Rarely practises positive approach—doesn't "test" himself

14. Quality of Relapse Prevention Plan

Level 4

a. Intellectual understanding
   i. Generates a sophisticated list of strategies to avoid risks
   ii. Generates sophisticated list of appropriate responses should risk factors occur
   iii. Generates sophisticated list of positive leisure activities
   iv. Independently sets realistic short- and long-term goals
   v. Has complete and realistic release/discharge plans (e.g., job, accommodation, etc.)
   vi. Identifies an excellent support group
   vii. Generates a sophisticated set of warning signs (for himself and for others) that might indicate he is not following RPP
   viii. Readily able to apply these analyses to other group members appropriately—recognizes whether plans are realistic or not
b. Emotional acceptance/demonstration
   i. Sincerely motivated to follow relapse plan
   ii. Confidently identifies positive and negative consequences of choices
   iii. Clearly identifies new, effective strategies to address the risk factors he identified previously
   iv. Confident in his ability to use/learn new skills
   v. Fully accepts that he controls his own behavior
   vi. Independently willing to make sacrifices in order to follow RPP
   vii. Always provides supportive feedback to others

Level 3

a. Intellectual understanding
   i. Generates a proficient list of strategies to avoid risks
   ii. Generates a proficient list of appropriate responses should risk factors occur
   iii. Generates a proficient list of positive leisure activities
   iv. Capably sets realistic short- and long-term goals
   v. Has appropriate release/discharge plans (e.g., job, accommodation, etc.)
   vi. Identifies a good support group
   vii. Generates a sound set of warning signs (for himself and for others) that might indicate he is not following RPP
   viii. Satisfactorily able to apply these analyses to other group members appropriately—recognizes whether plans are realistic or not

   b. Emotional acceptance/demonstration
- i. Sufficiently motivated to follow relapse plan
- ii. Meaningfully identifies positive and negative consequences of choices
- iii. Thoughtfully identifies new, effective strategies to address the risk factors he identified previously
- iv. Reasonably confident in his ability to use/learn new skills
- v. Aptly accepts that he controls his own behavior
- vi. Generally willing to make sacrifices in order to follow RPP
- vii. Usually provides supportive feedback to others

Level 2

   a. Intellectual understanding
- i. Generates a basic list of strategies to avoid risks
- ii. Generates a basic list of appropriate responses should risk factors occur
- iii. Generates a basic list of positive leisure activities
- iv. Adequately sets some realistic short- and long-term goals
- v. Has developed an adequate release/discharge plans (e.g., job, accommodation, etc.)
- vi. Identifies a moderately good support group
- vii. Generates a few warning signs (for himself and for others) that might indicate he is not following RPP
- viii. Adequately able to apply these analyses to other group members appropriately—recognizes whether plans are realistic or not

   b. Emotional acceptance/demonstration
- i. Adequately motivated to follow relapse plan
- ii. In a somewhat meaningful way identifies positive and negative consequences of choices
- iii. With some concern identifies new, effective strategies to address the risk factors he identified previously
- iv. Moderately confident in his ability to use/learn new skills
- v. Making progress in accepting that he controls his own behavior
- vi. Somewhat willing to make sacrifices in order to follow RPP
- vii. Hesitantly provides supportive feedback to others

Level 1

   a. Intellectual understanding
- i. Generates a simple list of strategies to avoid risks
- ii. Generates a simple list of appropriate responses should risk factors occur

    iii. Generates a simple list of positive leisure activities
    iv. With assistance sets some realistic short- and long-term goals
    v. Needs assistance to develop a release/discharge plans (e.g.,
       job, accommodation, etc.)
    vi. Identifies an incomplete support group
    vii. Generates only a few warning signs (for himself and for
       others) that might indicate he is not following RPP
    viii. Has difficulty applying these analyses to other group members
       appropriately—recognizes whether plans are realistic or not
  b. Emotional acceptance/demonstration
    i. Insufficiently motivated to follow relapse plan
    ii. In a limited way identifies positive and negative consequences
      of choices
    iii. With minimal concern identifies new, effective strategies to
      address the risk factors he identified previously
    iv. Insufficiently confident in his ability to use/learn new skills
    v. Making limited progress in accepting that he controls his
      own behavior
    vi. Has difficulty making sacrifices in order to follow RPP
    vii. Has difficulty providing supportive feedback to others

15. Quality of Supports

Level 4

  a. Intellectual understanding
    i. Thoroughly understands why he needs a support group
    ii. Readily understands why his support group must be able to
      challenge him
    iii. Completely understands the need for differences among his
      support group (i.e., not just his family or friends)
    iv. Consistently understands why his support group must be
      readily accessible
  b. Emotional acceptance/demonstration
    i. Independently works to generate a support group
    ii. Has firm contacts from support group members indicating
      they are willing to help him
    iii. Produces significant evidence his family and friends
      understand his offenses
    iv. Expresses a sincere commitment to use his support group

Level 3

a. Intellectual understanding
   i. Appropriately understands why he needs a support group
   ii. Competently understands why his support group must be able to challenge him
   iii. Meaningfully understands the need for differences among his support group (i.e., not just his family or friends)
   iv. Effectively understands why his support group must be readily accessible

b. Emotional acceptance/demonstration
   i. Cooperatively works to generate a support group
   ii. Has sound contacts from support group members indicating they are willing to help him
   iii. Produces appropriate evidence his family and friends understand his offenses
   iv. Expresses a strong commitment to use his support group

Level 2

a. Intellectual understanding
   i. Adequately understands why he needs a support group
   ii. Moderately understands why his support group must be able to challenge him
   iii. Capably understands the need for differences among his support group (i.e., not just his family or friends)
   iv. Adequately understands why his support group must be readily accessible

b. Emotional acceptance/demonstration
   i. Capably works to generate a support group
   ii. Has a few contacts from support group members indicating they are willing to help him
   iii. Produces some evidence his family and friends understand his offenses
   iv. Expresses a somewhat meaningful commitment to use his support group

Level 1

a. Intellectual understanding
   i. Begins to understand why he needs a support group
   ii. Has difficulty understanding why his support group must be able to challenge him

  iii. Has minimal understanding of the need for differences among his support group (i.e., not just his family or friends)

  iv. Has limited understanding why his support group must be readily accessible

 b. Emotional acceptance/demonstration

  i. Has rarely worked to generate a support group

  ii. Has difficulty making contacts from support group members indicating they are willing to help him

  iii. Produces minimal evidence his family and friends understand his offenses

  iv. Rarely expresses a meaningful commitment to use his support group

16. Quality of Release Plans

Level 4

 a. Intellectual understanding

  i. Independently identifies a sensible location for release (i.e., both town and residence)

  ii. Independently identifies potential job plans or educational upgrading

  iii. Fully recognizes the need to avoid a job or a place to live that might give him access to victims

  iv. Readily identifies specific programs he should enter upon release (e.g., sex offender programs, substance abuse programs, other forms of counselling)

  v. Completely recognizes the need to avoid criminal or deviant associates

  vi. Thoroughly recognizes the need for stability

 b. Emotional acceptance/demonstration

  i. Expresses complete and realistic views of the problems he may face

  ii. Fully commits to following his release plan

  iii. Independently makes contacts with possible jobs and residences

  iv. Independently makes contacts with programs in the community

  v. Persistently avoids negative or antisocial relationships in prison

  vi. Refrains from contact with previous criminal or deviant friends

Level 3

a. Intellectual understanding

   i. Competently identifies a sensible location for release (i.e., both town and residence)

   ii. Competently identifies potential job plans or educational upgrading

   iii. Meaningfully recognizes the need to avoid a job or a place to live that might give him access to victims

   iv. Carefully identifies specific programs he should enter upon release (e.g., sex offender programs, substance abuse programs, other forms of counselling)

   v. Effectively recognizes the need to avoid criminal or deviant associates

   vi. Appropriately recognizes the need for stability

b. Emotional acceptance/demonstration

   i. Expresses realistic views of the problems he may face

   ii. Appears committed to following his release plan

   iii. Effectively makes contacts with possible jobs and residences

   iv. Appropriately makes contacts with programs in the community

   v. Effectively avoids negative or antisocial relationships in prison

   vi. Carefully refrains from contact with previous criminal or deviant friends

Level 2

a. Intellectual understanding

   i. Adequately identifies a sensible location for release (i.e., both town and residence)

   ii. With some independence, identifies potential job plans or educational upgrading

   iii. Basically recognizes the need to avoid a job or a place to live that might give him access to victims

   iv. Capably identifies specific programs he should enter upon release (e.g., sex offender programs, substance abuse programs, other forms of counselling)

   v. Able to recognize the need to avoid criminal or deviant associates

   vi. Adequately recognizes the need for stability

b. Emotional acceptance/demonstration

   i. Expresses somewhat realistic views of the problems he may face

   ii. Sporadically appears committed to following his release plan

   iii. Needs some encouragement to make contact with possible jobs and residences

   iv. Beginning to make contacts with programs in the community

   v. Becoming more independent in avoiding negative or antisocial relationships in prison
  vi. Demonstrates more restraint from contact with previous criminal or deviant friends

Level 1

a. Intellectual understanding
   i. With assistance identifies a sensible location for release (i.e., both town and residence)
   ii. With assistance, identifies potential job plans or educational upgrading
   iii. Begins to recognize the need to avoid a job or a place to live that might give him access to victims
   iv. Needs assistance to identify specific programs he should enter upon release (e.g., sex offender programs, substance abuse programs, other forms of counseling)
   v. Inconsistently able to recognize the need to avoid criminal or deviant associates
   vi. Learning to realize the need for stability
b. Emotional acceptance/demonstration
   i. Expresses limited realistic views of the problems he may face
   ii. Inconsistently committed to following his release plan
   iii. Needs encouragement to make contact with possible jobs and residences
   iv. Needs assistance to make contacts with programs in the community
   v. Learning to become more independent in avoiding negative or antisocial relationships in prison
   vi. Learning to refrain from contact with previous criminal or deviant friends

17. Commitment to Maintenance of Change

Level 4

a. Intellectual understanding
   i. Confidently identifies strategies for maintaining change
   ii. Firmly identifies positive benefits of change
   iii. Able to specifically identify negative consequences for himself and others for failing to maintain changes
   iv. Respectfully understands that preoffense lapses may occur
   v. Independently understands the need to be vigilant

     vi. Thoroughly identifies a set of warning signs that will tell himself and others that he is slipping back into preoffense thinking, feelings, and behaving

b. Emotional acceptance/demonstration

     i. Expresses a firm commitment to maintain change

     ii. Speaks positively about the changes he has made in an insightful way

     iii. Expresses sincere distress at the thought of reoffending

     iv. Deals with setbacks thoroughly and learns from them

Level 3

a. Intellectual understanding

     i. Skillfully identifies strategies for maintaining change

     ii. Meaningfully identifies positive benefits of change

     iii. Usually able to identify negative consequences for himself and others for failing to maintain changes

     iv. Generally understands that preoffense lapses may occur

     v. Routinely understands the need to be vigilant

     vi. Aptly identifies a set of warning signs that will tell himself and others that he is slipping back into preoffense thinking, feelings, and behaving

b. Emotional acceptance/demonstration

     i. Expresses a strong commitment to maintain change

     ii. Speaks positively about the changes he has made in a meaningful way

     iii. Expresses strong distress at the thought of reoffending

     iv. Deals with setbacks effectively and learns from them

Level 2

a. Intellectual understanding

     i. Adequately identifies strategies for maintaining change

     ii. Making advances at identifying positive benefits of change

     iii. Sometimes able to identify negative consequences for himself and others for failing to maintain changes

     iv. Learning to better understand that preoffense lapses may occur

     v. Developing a better understanding of the need to be vigilant

     vi. Capably identifies a set of warning signs that will tell himself and others that he is slipping back into preoffense thinking, feelings, and behaving

b. Emotional acceptance/demonstration

     i. Expresses a basic commitment to maintain change

   ii. Sometimes speaks positively about the changes he has made in a meaningful way

  iii. Expresses some distress at the thought of reoffending

  iv. Deals with setbacks adequately and is beginning to learn from them

Level 1

a. Intellectual understanding
    i. Has difficulty identifying strategies for maintaining change
   ii. Makes minimal progress at identifying positive benefits of change
  iii. Rarely able to identify negative consequences for himself and others for failing to maintain changes
  iv. Beginning to understand that preoffense lapses may occur
   v. Developing a basic understanding of the need to be vigilant
  vi. With assistance identifies a set of warning signs that will tell himself and others that he is slipping back into preoffense thinking, feelings, and behaving

b. Emotional acceptance/demonstration
    i. Expresses a minimal commitment to maintain change
   ii. Rarely speaks positively about the changes he has made in a meaningful way
  iii. Expresses limited distress at the thought of reoffending
  iv. With assistance, deals with setbacks adequately and is beginning to learn from them

References

Abel, G. G. (1995). *New technology. The Abel Assessment for Interest in Paraphilias*. Atlanta, GA: Abel Screening Inc.

Abel, G. G., Becker, J. V., & Cunningham-Rathner, J. (1984). Complications, consent and cognitions in sex between children and adults. *International Journal of Law and Psychiatry, 7,* 89–103.

Abel, G. G., Becker, J. V., Mittelman, M. S., Cunningham-Rathner, J., Rouleau, J. L., & Murphy, W. D. (1987). Self-reported sex crimes of nonincarcerated paraphiliacs. *Journal of Interpersonal Violence, 2,* 3–25.

Abel, G. G., Blanchard, E. B., & Becker, J. V. (1978). An integrated treatment program for rapists. In R. Rada (Ed.), *Clinical aspects of the rapist* (pp. 161–214). New York: Grune & Stratton.

Abel, G. G., Gore, D. K., Holland, C. L., Camp, N., Becker, J. V., & Rathner, J. (1989). The measurement of the cognitive distortions of child molesters. *Annual of Sex Research, 2,* 135–152.

Abel, G. G., Huffman, J., Warberg, B., & Holland, C. L. (1998). Visual reaction time and plethysmography as measures of sexual interest in child molesters. *Sexual Abuse: A Journal of Research and Treatment, 10,* 81–95.

Abel, G. G., Lawry, S. S., Karlstrom, E., Osborn, C. A., & Gillespie, C. F. (1994). Screening test for pedophilia. *Criminal Justice and Behavior, 21,* 115–131.

Abel, G. G., Levis, D., & Clancy, J. (1970). Aversion therapy applied to taped sequences of deviant behavior in exhibitionism and other sexual deviations: A preliminary report. *Journal of Behavior Therapy and Experimental Psychiatry, 1,* 58–66.

Abelson, R. P. (1981). Psychological status of the script concept. *American Psychologist, 36,* 715–729.

Abramson, L. Y. (Ed.) (1988). *Social cognition and clinical psychology.* New York: Guilford Press.

Ageton, S. (1983). *Sexual assault among adolescents.* Lexington, MA: Lexington Books.

Ahlmeyer, S., Heil, P., McKee, B., & English, K. (2000). The impact of polygraphy on admissions of victims and offenses in adult sex offenders. *Sexual Abuse: A Journal of Research and Treatment, 12,* 123–128.

Akers, R. L. (1977). *Deviant behavior: A social learning approach* (2nd ed). Belmont, CA: Wadsworth.

Alexander, M. (1999). Sexual offender treatment efficacy revisited. *Sexual Abuse: A Journal of Research and Treatment, 11,* 101–116.

Allan, R. W. (1998). Operant–respondent interactions. In W. O'Donohue (Ed.), *Learning and behavior therapy* (pp. 146–168). Boston: Allyn & Bacon.

American Psychiatric Association. (1980). *Diagnostic and statistical manual of mental disorders* (3rd ed. rev.). Washington, DC: Author.

American Psychiatric Association. (1994). *Diagnostic and statistical manual of mental disorders* (4th ed.). Washington, DC: Author.

American Psychiatric Association. (1996). *Diagnostic and statistical manual of mental disorders* (4th ed.), Sourcebook (Vol. 2). Washington, DC: Author.

American Psychiatric Association. (2000). *Diagnostic and statistical manual of mental disorders* (4th ed. text rev.). Washington, DC: Author.

Anderson, P. A., & Guerrero, L. K. (Eds.) (1998). *Handbook of communication and emotion: Research, theory, applications, and contexts.* San Diego: Academic Press.

Andrews, D. A., & Bonta, J. (1995). *LSI-R: The Level of Supervision Inventory.* Toronto: Multi-Health Systems.

Andrews, D. A., & Bonta, J. (1998). *The psychology of criminal conduct* (2nd ed). Cincinnati, OH: Anderson.

Augoustinos, M., & Walker, I. (1995). *Social cognition: An integrated introduction.* London: Sage Publications.

Ayres, J. J. B. (1998). Fear conditioning and avoidance. In W. O'Donohue (Ed.), *Learning and behavior therapy* (pp. 122–145). Boston: Allyn & Bacon.

Azrin, N. H. (1960). Effects of punishment intensity during variable-interval reinforcement. *Journal of the Experimental Analysis of Behavior, 3,* 123–142.

Azrin, N. H., & Holz, W. C. (1966). Punishment. In W. K. Konig (Ed.), *Operant behavior: Areas of research and application* (pp. 380–447). New York: Appleton-Century-Crofts.

Bagley, C. (1991). The long-term psychological effects of child sexual abuse: A review of some British and Canadian studies of victims and their families. *Annals of Sex Research, 4,* 23–48.

Baker, L. M. (2001). *Learning & behavior: Biological, psychological, and sociological perspectives* (3rd ed). Upper Saddle River, NJ: Prentice Hall.

Bancroft, J. H. J., & Marks, I. (1968). Electric aversion therapy of sexual deviations. *Proceedings of the Royal Society of Medicine, 61*, 796–799.

Bandura, A. (1969). *Social learning theory*. Englewood Cliffs, NJ: Prentice Hall.

Bandura, A. (1977). Self-efficacy: Toward a unifying theory of behavior change. *Psychological Review, 84*, 191–215.

Barbaree, H. E. (1990). Stimulus control of sexual arousal: Its role in sexual assault. In W. L. Marshall, D. R. Laws, & H. E. Barbaree (Eds.), *Handbook of sexual assault: Issues, theories, and treatment of the offender* (pp. 115–142). New York: Plenum Press.

Barbaree, H. E. (1991). Denial and minimization among sex offenders: Assessment and treatment outcome. *Forum on Corrections Research, 3*, 300–333.

Barbaree, H. E. (in press). Psychopathy, treatment behavior, and recidivism: An extended follow-up of Seto and Barbaree (1999). *Journal of Interpersonal Violence.*

Barbaree, H. E., Langton, C., & Peacock, E. (2005). Sexual offender treatment for psychopaths: Is it harmful? In W. L. Marshall, Y. M. Fernandez, L. E. Marshall, & G. A. Serran (Eds.), *Sexual offender treatment: Controversial issues* (pp. 159–171). Chichester, UK: John Wiley & Sons.

Barbaree, H. E., & Marshall, W. L. (1991). The role of male sexual arousal in rape: Six models. *Journal of Consulting and Clinical Psychology, 59*, 621–630.

Barbaree, H. E., & Marshall, W. L. (in press). An introduction to the juvenile sex offender: Terms, concepts and definitions. In H. E. Barbaree & W. L Marshall (Eds.), *The juvenile sex offender* (2nd ed.) New York: Guilford Press.

Barbaree, H. E., Marshall, W. L., & Hudson, S. M. (Eds.). (1993). *The juvenile sex offender*. New York: Guilford Press.

Barbaree, H. E., Marshall, W. L., Yates, E., & Lightfoot, L. O. (1983). Alcohol intoxication and deviant sexual arousal in male social drinkers. *Behaviour Research and Therapy, 21*, 365–373.

Barbaree, H. E., Seto, M. C., Langton, C. M., & Peacock, E. J. (2001, October). *Psychopathy, treatment behavior and sexual offender recidivism: An extended follow-up.* Paper presented at the Annual Research and Treatment Conference of the Association for the Treatment of Sexual Abusers. San Antonio, TX.

Barlow, D. H. (1974). The treatment of sexual deviation: Toward a comprehensive behavioral approach. In K. S. Calhoun, H. E. Adams & K. M. Mitchell (eds.), *Innovative treatment methods in psychopathology* (pp. 121–147). New York: John Wiley & Sons.

Barrett, M., Wilson, R. J., & Long, C. (2003). Measuring motivation to change in sexual offenders from institutional intake to community treatment. *Sexual Abuse: A Journal of Research and Treatment, 15,* 269–283.

Bartholomew, K., & Horowitz, L. (1991). Attachment styles among young adults: A test of a four-category model. *Journal of Personality and Social Psychology, 61,* 226–244.

Bartholomew, K., Perlman, D. (Eds.) (1994). *Attachment processes in adulthood.* London: Jessica Kingsley.

Baumeister, R. F. (1991). *Escaping the self.* New York: Basic Books.

Baumeister, R. F. (Ed.) (1993). *Self-esteem: The puzzle of low self-regard.* New York: Plenum Press.

Baumeister, R. F., Tice, D., & Hutton, D. (1989). Self-presentational motivations and personality differences in self-esteem. *Journal of Personality, 57,* 547–579.

Baumeister, R. F., & Vohs, K. D. (Eds.) (2004). *Handbook of self-regulation: Research, theory, and applications.* New York: Guilford Press.

Beck, A. T. (1999). *Prisoners of hate: The cognitive bases of anger, hostility and violence.* New York: HarperCollins.

Beckett, R., Beech, A., Fisher, D., & Fordham, A. S. (1994). *Community-based treatment of sex offenders: An evaluation of seven treatment programmes.* Home Office Occasional Paper. London: Home Office.

Beckett, R., & Fisher, D. (1994, November). *Assessing victim empathy: A new measure.* Paper presented at the 13th Annual Research and Treatment Conference of the Association for the Treatment of Sexual Abusers. San Francisco.

Beech, A. R., & Fordham, A. S. (1997). Therapeutic climate of sexual offender treatment programs. *Sexual Abuse: A Journal of Research and Treatment, 9,* 219–237.

Beech, A. R., & Hamilton-Giachritsis, C. E. (2005). Relationship between therapeutic climate and treatment outcome in group-based sexual offender treatment programs. *Sexual Abuse: A Journal of Research and Treatment, 17,* 127–140.

Bem, S. L. (1981). Gender schema theory: A cognitive account of sex typing. *Psychological Review, 88,* 354–364.

Berliner, L. (2002). Commentary. *Sexual Abuse: A Journal of Research and Treatment, 14,* 195–197.

Billings, A. B., & Moos, R. H. (1984). Coping, stress, and social resources among adults with unipolar depression. *Journal of Personality and Social Psychology, 46,* 877–891.

Bohart, A. C., & Tolman, K. (1998). The person as active agent in experiential therapy. In L. S. Greenberg, J. C. Watson, & G. Lietaer (Eds.), *Handbook of experiential psychotherapy* (pp. 178–200). New York: Guilford Press.

Bond, I. K., & Evans, D. R. (1967). Avoidance therapy: Its use in two cases of underwear fetishism. *Canadian Medical Association Journal, 96,* 1160–1162.

Booth, R. J., & Pennebaker, J. W. (2000). Emotions and immunity. In M. Lewis & J. M. Haviland-Jones (Eds.), *Handbook of emotions* (2nd ed.) (pp. 558–570). New York: Guilford Press.

Boutin, M. E., & Nelson, J. B. (1998). The role of context in classical conditioning: Some implications for cognitive behavior therapy. In W. O'Donohue (Ed.), *Learning and behavior therapy* (pp. 59–84). Boston: Allyn & Bacon.

Bowlby, J. (1969). *Attachment and loss: Vol. 1. Attachment.* New York: Basic Books.

Bowlby, J. (1973). *Attachment and loss: Vol. 2. Separation: Anxiety and anger.* New York: Basic books.

Bowlby, J. (1980). *Attachment and loss. Vol. 3. Loss: Sadness and depression.* New York: Basic Books.

Bownes, I. T. (1992). Sexual and relationship dysfunction in sexual offenders. *Sexual and Marital Therapy, 8,* 157–165.

Bradford, J. M. W. (2000). The treatment of sexual deviation using a pharmacological approach. *Journal of Sex Research, 3,* 248–257.

Bradford, J. M. W., & Fedoroff, P. (in press). The pharmacological treatment of the juvenile sex offender. In H. E. Barbaree & W. L. Marshall (Eds.), *The juvenile sex offender* (2nd ed.). New York: Guilford Press.

Browne, A., & Finklehor, D. (1986). Impact of child sexual abuse: A review of the research. *Psychological Bulletin, 99,* 16–77.

Buck, R. (1991). Temperament, social skills, and the communication of emotion: A developmental interactionist view. In D. G. Gilbert & J. J. Connolly (Eds.), *Personality, social skills, and psychopathy: An individual differences approach* (pp. 85–105). New York: Plenum Press.

Bumby, K. M. (1994, November). *Cognitive distortions of child molesters and rapists.* Paper presented at the 13th Annual Research and Treatment Conference of the Association for the Treatment of Sexual Abusers. San Francisco.

Bumby, K. M. (1996). Assessing the cognitive distortions of child molesters and rapists: Development and validation of the MOLEST and

RAPE Scales. *Sexual Abuse: A Journal of Research and Treatment,*
    8, 37–54.
Bumby, K. M., & Hansen, D. J. (1997). Intimacy deficits, fear of intimacy,
    and loneliness among sex offenders. *Criminal Justice and Behavior,*
    24, 315–331.
Bumby, K. M., Marshall, W. L., & Langton, C. (1999). A theoretical
    model of the influences of shame and guilt on sexual offending. In
    B. K. Schwartz (Ed.), *The sex offender: Theoretical advances, treating
    special populations and legal developments* (Vol. III, pp. 5.1–5.12).
    Kingston, NJ: Civic Research Institute.
Burgess, A. W., & Holmstrom, L. L. (1974). Rape trauma syndrome.
    American Journal of Psychiatry, 131, 981–986.
Burgess, A. W., & Holmstrom, L. L. (1979). *Rape: Crisis and recovery.*
    Bowie, MD: Brady.
Burt, M. R. (1980). Cultural myths and supports for rape. *Journal of
    Personality and Social Psychology, 38,* 217–230.
Buschman, J. (2003, March). *Victim specific empathy.* Paper presented
    at the Conference Seksualiteit en Delinquentie: Grensverkenningen.
    Nijmegen, the Netherlands.
Buschman, J., & van Beek, D. (2003). A clinical model for the treatment
    of personality disordered sexual offenders: An example of theory
    knitting. *Sexual Abuse: A Journal of Research and Treatment, 15,*
    183–199.
Buss, A. H., & Durkee, A. (1957). An inventory for assessing different
    kinds of hostility. *Journal of Consulting Psychology, 21,* 343–349.
Calkins, S. D. (2004). Early attachment processes and the development of
    self-regulation. In R. F. Baumeister & K. D. Vohs (Eds.), *Handbook
    of self-regulation: Research, theory, and applications* (pp. 324–339).
    New York: Guilford Press.
Carpenter, B. M. (Ed.) (1992). *Personal coping: Theory, research and ap-
    plication.* Westport, CT: Praeger.
Carpentier, M. (1995). Offenders learning to be better parents. *Forum on
    Corrections Research, 7,* 23–24.
Carver, C. S., & Scheier, M. F. (1990). Origins and functions of positive
    and negative affect: A control process view. *Psychological Review,
    97,* 19–35.
Carver, C. S., Scheier, M. F., & Weintraub, J. K. (1989). Assessing coping
    strategies: A theoretically based approach. *Journal of Personality and
    Social Psychology, 56,* 267–283.
Cautela, J. R. (1967). Covert sensitization. *Psychological Record, 20,*
    459–468.

Center for Sex Offender Management. (1999). *Sex offender registration: Policy overview and comprehensive practices*. Silver Spring, MD: Author.

Check, J. V. P. (1984). *The Hostility Toward Women Scale*. Unpublished doctoral dissertation, University of Manitoba, Winnipeg, Canada.

Check, J. V. P., Perlman, D., & Malamuth, N. M. (1985). Loneliness and aggressive behavior. *Journal of Social and Personal Relations, 2*, 243–252.

Clark, L., & Lewis, D. J. (1977). Rape: *The price of coercive sexuality*. Toronto: Canadian Women's Educational Press.

Cliska, D. (1990). *Beyond dieting—psychoeducational interventions for chronically obese women: A non-dieting approach*. New York: Brunner/Mazel.

Colwill, R. M., & Rescorla, R. A. (1986). Associative structures in instrumental learning. In G. K. Bower (Ed.), *The psychology of learning and motivation* (Vol. 20, pp. 54–104). Orlando, FL: Academic Press.

Conte, J. R. (1991). The nature of sexual offenses against children. In C. R. Hollin & K. Howells (Eds.), *Clinical approaches to sex offenders and their victims* (pp. 11–34). Chichester, UK: John Wiley & Sons.

Conte, J. R., & Schuerman, J. R. (1987). The effects of sexual abuse on children: A multidimensional view. *Journal of Interpersonal Violence, 2*, 380–390.

Coopersmith, S. (1967). *The antecedents of self-esteem*. San Francisco: Freeman.

Cortoni, F. A. (1998). *The relationship between attachment styles, coping, the use of sex as a coping strategy, and juvenile sexual history in sexual offenders*. Unpublished doctoral dissertation. Queen's University, Kingston, Ontario, Canada.

Cortoni, F. A., & Marshall, W. L. (2001). Sex as a coping strategy and its relationship to juvenile sexual history and intimacy in sexual offenders. *Sexual Abuse: A Journal of Research and Treatment, 13*, 27–43.

Cosmides, L., & Tooby, J. (2000). Evolutionary psychology and the emotions. In M. Lewis & J. M. Haviland-Jones (Eds.), *Handbook of emotions* (2nd ed.) (pp. 91–115). New York: Guilford Press.

Crowne, D. P., & Marlowe, D. (1960). A new scale of social desirability independent of psychopathology. *Journal of Consulting Psychology, 24*, 349–354.

Darke, J. L. (1990). Sexual aggression: Achieving power through humiliation. In W. L. Marshall, D. R. Laws, & H. E. Barbaree, (Eds.), *Handbook of sexual assault: Issues, theories, and treatment of the offender* (pp. 55–72). New York: Plenum Press.

Davis, M. H. (1983). Measuring individual differences in empathy: Evidence for a multidimensional approach. *Journal of Personality and Social Psychology, 44*, 113–125.

Deci, E. L., & Ryan, R. M. (2000). The "what" and "why" of goal pursuits: Human needs and the self-determination of behavior. *Psychological Inquiry, 11*, 227–268.

Dewhurst, A. M., Moore, R. J., & Alfano, D. P. (1992). Aggression against women by men: Sexual and spousal assault. *Journal of Offender Rehabilitation, 18*, 39–47.

Dhawan, S., & Marshall, W. L. (1996). Sexual abuse histories of sexual offenders. *Sexual Abuse: A Journal of Research and Treatment, 8*, 7–15.

Diener, E., & Lucas, R. E. (2000). Subjective emotional well-being. In M. Lewis & J. M. Haviland-Jones (Eds.), *Handbook of emotions* (2nd ed.) (pp. 325–337). New York: Guilford Press.

Dinsmoor, J. A. (1998). Punishment. In W. O'Donohue (Ed.), *Learning and behavior therapy* (pp. 188–204). Boston: Allyn & Bacon.

DiVasto, P. V., Kaufman, L. R., Jackson, R., Christy, J., Pearson, S., & Burgett, T. (1984). The prevalence of sexually stressful events among females in the general population. *Archives of Sexual Behavior, 13*, 59–67.

Domjan, M. (1998). *The principles of learning and behavior* (4th ed). Pacific Grove, CA: Brooks/Cole Publishing.

Donahoe, J. W. (1998). Positive reinforcement: The selection of behavior. In W. O'Donohue (Ed.), *Learning and behavior therapy* (pp. 169–187). Boston: Allyn & Bacon.

Doren, D. M. (2002). *Evaluating sex offenders: A manual for civil commitments and beyond.* Thousand Oaks, CA: Sage Publications.

Dougher, M. (1995). Behavioral techniques to alter sexual arousal. In B. K. Schwartz & H. R. Cellini (Eds.), *The sex offender: Corrections, treatment and legal practice* (Vol. I, pp. 15.1–15.8). Kingston, NJ: Civic Research Institute.

Dowden, C., Antonowicz, D., & Andrews, D. A. (2003). The effectiveness of relapse prevention with offenders: A meta-analysis. *International Journal of Offender Therapy and Comparative Criminology, 47*, 516–528.

Drake, C. R., & Ward, T. (2003). Treatment models for sex offenders: A move toward a formulation-based approach. In T. Ward, D. R. Laws, & S. M. Hudson (Eds.), *Sexual deviance: Issues and controversies* (pp. 226–243). Thousand Oaks, CA: Sage Publications.

Drapeau, M. (2005). Research on the processes involved in treating sexual offenders. *Sexual Abuse: A Journal of Research and Treatment, 17*, 117–125.

Dunlap, K. (1932). *Habits, their making and unmaking*. New York: Liveright.

Dunn, J., Brown, J., & Beardsall, L. (1991). Family talk about feeling states and children's later understanding of other's emotions. *Developmental Psychology, 27*, 448–455.

D'Zurilla, T. J., & Goldfried, M. R. (1971). Problem solving and behavior modification. *Journal of Abnormal Psychology, 78*, 107–126.

Edwards, N. B. (1972). Case conference: Assertive training in a case of homosexual pedophilia. *Journal of Behavior Therapy and Experimental Psychiatry, 3*, 55–63.

Emmons, R. A. (1999). *The psychology of ultimate concerns*. New York: Guilford Press.

Endler, N. S., & Parker, J. D. A. (1990). Multidimensional assessment of coping: A critical evaluation. *Journal of Personality and Social Psychology, 8*, 844–854.

Endler, N. S., & Parker, J. D. A. (1999). *The coping inventory for stressful situations: manual* (2nd ed.). Toronto: Multi-Health Systems.

Epperson, D. L., Kaul, J. D., & Huot, S. J. (1995, October). *Predicting risk for recidivism for incarcerated sex offenders: Updated development on the Sex Offender Screening Tool (SOST)*. Paper presented at the Annual Research Treatment Conference of the Association for the Treatment of Sexual Abusers. New Orleans, LA.

Evans, D. R. (1968). Masturbatory fantasy and sexual deviation. *Behaviour Research and Therapy, 6*, 17–19.

Falls, W. A. (1998). Extinction: A review of theory and evidence suggesting that memories are not erased with nonreinforcement. In W. O'Donohue (Ed.), *Learning and behavior therapy* (pp. 205–229). Boston: Allyn & Bacon.

Fazel, S., Hope, T., O'Donnell, I., & Jacoby, R. (2002). Psychiatric, demographic and personality characteristics of elderly sex offenders. *Psychological Medicine, 32*, 219–226.

Feelgood, S., Golias, P., Shaw, S., & Bright, D. A. (2000). *Treatment changes in the dynamic risk factors of coping style in sexual offenders: A preliminary analysis*. New South Wales Department of Corrective Services Sex Offender Programmes, Custody-Based Intensive Treatment (CUBIT), Sydney, Australia.

Fehr, B., & Russell, J. A. (1984). Concept of emotion viewed from a prototype perspective. *Journal of Experimental Psychology: General, 113*, 464–486.

Fernandez, Y. M., Anderson, D., & Marshall, W. L. (October, 1997). *The relationship between empathy, cognitive distortions and domain specific self-esteem in sexual offenders*. Paper presented at the 16th

Annual Research and Treatment Conference of the Association for the Treatment of Sexual Abusers. Arlington, VA.

Fernandez, Y. M., Anderson, D., & Marshall, W. L. (1999). The relationship among empathy, cognitive distortions, and self-esteem in sexual offenders. In B. K. Schwartz (Ed.), *The sex offender: Theoretical advances, treating special populations and legal developments* (Vol. III, pp. 4.1– 4.12). Kingston, NJ: Civic Research Institute.

Fernandez, Y. M., & Marshall, W. L. (2003). Victim empathy, social self-esteem and psychopathy in rapists. *Sexual Abuse: A Journal of Research and Treatment, 15*, 11–26.

Fernandez, Y. M., Marshall, W. L., Lightbody, S., & O'Sullivan, C. (1999). The Child Molester Empathy Measure: Description and an examination of its reliability and validity. *Sexual Abuse: A Journal of Research and Treatment, 11*, 17–31.

Fernandez, Y. M., Shingler, J., & Marshall, W. L. (2005). Putting "behavior" back into the cognitive behavioral treatment of sexual offenders. In W. L. Marshall, Y. M. Fernandez, L. E. Marshall, & G. A. Serran (Eds.), *Sexual offender treatment: Controversial issues* (pp. 221–224). Chichester, UK: John Wiley & Sons.

Field, H. (1978). Attitudes toward rape: A comparative analysis of police, rapists, crisis counselors and citizens. *Journal of Personality and Social Psychology, 36*, 156–179.

Finkelhor, D. (1984). *Child sexual abuse: New theory and research*. New York: Free Press.

Finkelhor, D. (1988). The trauma of child sexual abuse. In G. E. Wyatt & G. J. Powell (Eds.), *Lasting effects of child sexual abuse* (pp. 61–82). Beverly Hills, CA: Sage Publications.

Firestone, P., Bradford, J. M. W., Greenberg, D. M., & Larose, M. R. (1998). Homicidal sex offenders: Psychological, phallometric, and diagnostic features. *Journal of the American Academy of Psychiatry & Law, 26*, 537–552.

Firestone, P., & Marshall, W. L. (2003). *Abnormal psychology: Perspectives* (2nd ed.). Toronto: Prentice Hall.

Fischer, L., & Smith, G. M. (1999). Statistical adequacy of the Abel Assessment for interest in paraphilias. *Sexual Abuse: A Journal of Research and Treatment, 11*, 195–205.

Fisher, D., Beech, A. R., & Browne, K. D. (1999). Comparisons of sex offenders to nonsex offenders on selected psychological measures. *International Journal of Offender Therapy and Comparative Criminology, 43*, 473–491.

Fisher, G. (1969). Psychological needs of heterosexual pedophiliacs. *Diseases of the Nervous System, 30*, 419–421.

Fisher, G., & Howell, L. M. (1970). Psychological needs of homosexual pedophiles. *Diseases of the Nervous System, 31*, 623–625.

Fiske, S. T., & Taylor, S. E. (1991). *Social cognition* (2nd ed.). New York: McGraw-Hill.

Flannery, R. B., & Weiman, D. (1989). Social support, life stress, and psychological distress: An empirical assessment. *Journal of Clinical Psychology, 4*, 867–872.

Folkman, S., & Lazarus, R. S. (1986). Stress processes and depressive symptomatology. *Journal of Abnormal Psychology, 95*, 107–113.

Fookes, B. H. (1969). Some experiences in the use of aversion therapy in male homosexuality, exhibitionism and fetishism-transvestism. *British Journal of Psychiatry, 115*, 339–341.

Forgas, J. P., & Vargas, P. R. (2000). The effects of mood on social judgment and reasoning. In M. Lewis & J. M. Haviland-Jones (Eds.), *Handbook of emotions* (2nd ed.) (pp. 350–367). New York: Guilford Press.

Forgas, J. P., Williams, K., & von Hippel, W. (Eds.) (2003). *Social judgments: Implicit and explicit processes.* Philadelphia: Psychology Press.

Forsyth, A. (1993). *A natural history of sex: The ecology and evolution of mating behavior.* Shelburne, VT: Chapters Publishing.

Foucault, M. (1978). *The history of sexuality. Vol 1: An introduction.* New York: Pantheon Books.

Franzoni, S. L., & Shields, S. A. (1984). The Body-Esteem Scale: Multidimensional structure and sex differences in a college population. *Journal of Personality Assessment, 48*, 173–178.

Fredrickson, R. (1992). *Repressed memories: A journey to recovery from sexual abuse.* New York: Simon & Schuster.

Freund, K. (1990). Courtship disorder. In W. L. Marshall, D. R. Laws, & H. E. Barbaree (Eds.), *Handbook of sexual assault: Issues, theories and treatment of the offender* (pp. 195–207). New York: Plenum Press.

Freund, K., & Blanchard, R. (1989). Phallometric diagnosis of pedophilia. *Journal of Consulting and Clinical Psychology, 57*, 1–6.

Furby, L., Weinrott, M. R., & Blackshaw, L. (1989). Sex offender recidivism: A review. *Psychological Bulletin, 105*, 3–30.

Gallagher, C. A., Wilson, D. B., Hirschfield, P., Coggeshall, M. B., & MacKenzie, D. L. (1999). A quantitative review of the effects of sexual offender treatment on sexual offending. *Corrections Management Quarterly, 3*, 19–29.

Gambrill, E. (2002). Assertion training. In M. Hersen & W. Sledge (Eds.), *Encyclopedia of psychotherapy: Vol. 1.* (pp. 117–124). New York: Academic Press.

Garlick, Y., Marshall, W. L., & Thornton, D. (1996). Intimacy deficits and attribution of blame among sexual offenders. *Legal and Criminological Psychology, 1,* 251–258.

Goldfried, M. R. (1982). *Converging themes in psychotherapy: Trends in psychodynamic, humanistic, and behavioral practice.* New York: Springer.

Gomes-Schwartz, B., Horowitz, J., & Sauzier, M. (1985). Severity of emotional distress among sexually abused preschool, school-age and adolescent children. *Hospital and Community Psychiatry, 36,* 503–508.

Goode, E. (1994, September). Battling deviant behavior. *US News and World Report,* 74–75.

Greenberg, L. S., & Pavio, S. (1997). *Working with emotions in psychotherapy.* New York: Guilford Press.

Greenberg, L., Rice, L. N., & Elliott, R. (1993). *Facilitating emotional change: The moment-by-moment process.* New York: Guilford Press.

Griffin, D. W., & Bartholomew, K. (1994). The metaphysics of measurement: The case of adult attachment. In K. Bartholomew & D. Perlman (Eds.), *Advances in personal relationships: Vol. 5. Attachment processes in adulthood* (pp. 17–52). London: Jessica Kingsley.

Guthrie, E. R. (1935). *The psychology of learning.* New York: Harper.

Haaven, J. L., & Coleman, E. M. (2000). Treatment of the developmentally disabled sex offender. In D. R. Laws, S. M. Hudson & T. Ward (Eds.), *Remaking relapse prevention with sex offenders: A sourcebook* (pp. 369–388). Thousand Oaks, CA: Sage Publications.

Haaven, J. L., Little, R., & Petri-Miller, D. (1990). *Treating intellectually disabled sex offenders: Model residential program.* Orwell, VT: Safer Society.

Hair, J. H., Anderson, R. E., Tatham, R. L., & Black, W. C. (1998). *Multivariate data analysis* (5th ed.). Hillside, NJ: Prentice Hall.

Hall, G. (1991). *Perceptual and associative learning.* Oxford, UK: Clarendon Press.

Hall, G. C. N. (1995). Sexual offender recidivism revisited: A meta-analysis of recent treatment studies. *Journal of Consulting and Clinical Psychology, 63,* 802–809.

Hall, G. C. N., & Hirschman, R. (1991). Toward a theory of sexual aggression: A quadripartite model. *Journal of Consulting and Clinical Psychology, 59,* 662–669.

Hanson, R. K. (1997). *The development of a brief actuarial risk scale for sexual recidivism.* Ottawa: Solicitor General of Canada.

Hanson, R. K. (1998a). What do we know about sex offender risk assessment? *Psychology, Public Policy, and Law, 4,* 50–72.

Hanson, R. K. (1998b, September). *Working with sex offenders*. Paper presented at the Conference of the National Organization for the Treatment of Offenders. Glasgow, UK.

Hanson, R. K. (2002). Recidivism and age: Follow-up data on 4,673 sexual offenders. *Journal of Interpersonal Violence, 17*, 1046–1062.

Hanson, R. K., & Bussière, M. T. (1998). Predicting relapse: A meta-analysis of sexual offender recidivism studies. *Journal of Consulting and Clinical Psychology, 66*, 348–362.

Hanson, R. K., Gizzarelli, R., & Scott, H. (1994). The attitudes of incest offenders: Sexual entitlement and acceptance of sex with children. *Criminal Justice and Behavior, 21*, 187–202.

Hanson, R. K., Gordon, A., Harris, A. J. R., Marques, J. K., Murphy, W. D., Quinsey, V. L., & Seto, M. C. (2002). First report of the Collaborative Outcome Data Project on the Effectiveness of Psychological Treatment of Sex Offenders. *Sexual Abuse: A Journal of Research and Treatment, 14*, 169–195.

Hanson, R. K., & Harris, A. J. R. (2000). Where should we intervene? Dynamic predictors of sex offender recidivism. *Criminal Justice and Behavior, 27*, 6–35.

Hanson, R. K., & Morton-Bourgon, K. (2004). *Predictors of sexual recidivism: An updated meta-analysis*. (Cat. No. P53-1/2004-2E-PDF) Ottawa: Public Works and Government Services Canada.

Hanson, R. K., & Scott, H. (1995). Assessing perspective taking among sexual offenders, nonsexual criminals and nonoffenders. *Sexual Abuse: A Journal of Research and Treatment, 7*, 259–277.

Hanson, R. K., & Thornton, D. (1999). *Static-99: Improving actuarial risk assessments for sex offenders*. User Report 99-02. Ottawa: Department of the Solicitor General of Canada.

Hanson, R. K., & Thornton, D. (2000). Improving risk assessments for sex offenders: A comparison of three actuarial scales. *Law and Human Behavior, 24*, 119–136.

Hare, R. D. (1991). *Manual for the Hare Psychopathy Checklist—Revised*. Toronto: Multi-Health Systems.

Hare, R. D. (2003). *Hare Psychopathy Checklist—Revised (PCL-R): 2nd edition technical manual*. Toronto: Multi-Health Systems.

Harris, A. J. R., & Hanson, R. K. (1999). Dynamic predictors of sex offense recidivism—New data from community supervision officers. In B. K. Schwartz (Ed.), *The sex offender: Theoretical advances, treating special populations and legal developments* (Vol. III, pp. 9.1–9.12). Kingston, NJ: Civic Research Institute.

Harris, G. T., Rice, M. E., & Quinsey, V. L. (1993). Violent recidivism of mentally disordered offenders: The development of a statistical prediction instrument. *Criminal Justice and Behavior, 20*, 315–335.

Harris, P. (2000). Understanding emotion. In M. Lewis & J. M. Haviland-Jones (Eds.), *Handbook of emotions* (2nd ed.) (pp. 281–292). New York: Guilford Press.

Hatfield, E., & Rapson, R. L. (1996). *Love & sex: Cross-cultural perspectives*. Boston: Allyn & Bacon.

Hayes, B. J., & Marshall, W. L. (1984). Generalization of treatment effects in training public speakers. *Behaviour Research and Therapy, 22*, 519–533.

Haynes, S. N., & O'Brien, W. H. (1990). Functional analysis in behavior therapy. *Clinical Psychology Review, 10*, 649–668.

Hazan, C., & Shaver, P. (1987). Romantic love conceptualized as an attachment process. *Journal of Personality and Social Psychology, 52*, 511–524.

Heatherton, T. F., & Polivy, J. (1991). Development and validation of a scale for measuring self-esteem. *Journal of Personality and Social Psychology, 60*, 895–910.

Heil, P., Ahlmeyer, S., & Simons, D. (2003). Crossover sexual offenses. *Sexual Abuse: A Journal of Research and Treatment, 15*, 221–236.

Heiman, J. R. (1977). A psychophysiological exploration of sexual arousal patterns in females and males. *Psychophysiology, 14*, 266–274.

Henry, F., & McMahon, P. (2000, May). *What survivors of child sexual abuse told us about the people who abuse them*. Paper presented at the National Sexual Violence Prevention Conference. Dallas, TX.

Herman, J. L. (1990). Sex offenders: A feminist perspective. In W. L. Marshall, D. R. Laws, & H. E. Barbaree (Eds.), *Handbook of sexual assault: Issues, theories, and treatment of the offender* (pp. 177–193). New York: Plenum Press.

Herman, J., & van der Kolk, B. (1987). Traumatic antecedents of borderline personality disorder. In B. van der Kolk (Ed.), *Psychological trauma* (pp. 42–67). Washington, DC: American Psychiatric Press.

Herman, R. L., & Azrin, N. H. (1964). Punishment by noise in an alternative response situation. *Journal of the Experimental Analysis of Behavior, 7*, 185–188.

Hildebrand, M., de Ruiter, C., & de Vogel, V. (2004). Psychopathy and sexual deviance in treated rapists: Association with sexual and nonsexual recidivism. *Sexual Abuse: A Journal of Research and Treatment, 16*, 1–24.

Hirschi, T. (2004). Self-control and crime. In R. F. Baumeister & K. D. Vohs (Eds.), *Handbook of self-regulation: Research, theory, and applications* (pp. 537–552). New York: Guilford Press.

Hirschi, T., & Gottfredson, M. (1983). Age and the explanation of crime. *American Journal of Sociology, 89*, 552–584.

Hollon, S. D., & Garber, J. (1988). Cognitive therapy. In L. Y. Abramson (Ed.), *Social cognition and clinical psychology* (pp. 204–253). New York: Guilford Press.

Hoppe, C. M., & Singer, R. D. (1976). Overcontrolled hostility, empathy, and egocentric balance in violent and non-violent psychiatric offenders. *Psychological Reports, 39,* 1303–1308.

Horowitz, L. M., Rosenberg, S. E., & Bartholomew, K. (1993). Interpersonal problems, attachment styles, and outcome in brief dynamic psychotherapy. *Journal of Consulting and Clinical Psychology, 61,* 549–560.

Howells, K. (1979). Some meanings of children for pedophiles. In M. Cook & G. Wilson (Eds.), *Love and attraction: An international conference* (pp. 519–526). Oxford: Pergamon Press.

Hudson, S. M., Marshall, W. L., Johnston, P., Ward, T., & Jones, R. L. (1995). Kia Marama: New Zealand Justice Department's programme for incarcerated child molesters. *Behaviour Change, 12,* 69–80.

Hudson, S. M., Marshall, W. L., Wales, D. S., McDonald, E., Bakker, L. W., & McLean, A. (1993). Emotional recognition skills of sex offenders. *Annals of Sex Research, 6,* 199–211.

Hudson, S. M., & Ward, T. (1997). Intimacy, loneliness, and attachment style in sex offenders. *Journal of Interpersonal Violence, 12,* 325–339.

Huesmann, L. R. (1988). An information processing model for the development of aggression. *Aggressive Behavior, 14,* 13–24.

Hughes, G. V. (1993). Anger management program outcomes. *Forum on Corrections Research, 5,* 5–9.

Hull, J. G., & Slone, L. B. (2004). Alcohol and self-regulation. In R. F. Baumeister & K. D. Vohs (Eds.), *Handbook of self-regulation: Research, theory, and applications* (pp. 466–491). New York: Guilford Press.

Hunter, J. A., & Mathews, R. (1997). Sexual deviance in females. In D. R. Laws & W. O'Donohue (Eds.), *Sexual deviance: Theory, assessment, and treatment* (pp. 465–480). New York: Guilford Press.

Ingram, R. E. (Ed.) (1986). *Information processing approaches to clinical psychology.* New York: Academic Press.

Ingram, R. E., & Kendall, P. C. (1986). Cognitive clinical psychology: Implications for an information processing perspective. In R. E. Ingram (Ed.), *Information processing approaches to clinical psychology* (pp. 3–21). New York: Academic Press.

Izard, C. E., & Ackerman, B. P. (2000). Motivational, organizational, and regulatory functions of discrete emotions. In M. Lewis & J. M. Haviland-Jones (Eds.), *Handbook of emotions* (2nd ed.) (pp. 253–264). New York: Guilford Press.

Jamieson, S., & Marshall, W. L. (2000). Attachment styles and violence in child molesters. *Journal of Sexual Aggression, 5,* 88–98.

Johnston, P., Hudson, S. M., & Marshall, W. L. (1992). The effects of masturbatory reconditioning with nonfamilial child molesters. *Behaviour Research and Therapy, 30,* 559–561.

Johnson, T. C. (1998). Children who molest. In W. L. Marshall, Y. M. Fernandez, S. M. Hudson & T. Ward (Eds.), *Sourcebook of treatment programs for sexual offenders.* (pp. 337–352). New York: Plenum Press.

Kafka, M. P. (1997). Hypersexual desire in males: An operational definition and clinical implications for men with paraphilias and paraphilia-related disorders. *Archives of Sexual Behavior, 26,* 505–526.

Kafka, M. P., & Hennen, J. (2002). A DSM-IV Axis 1 comorbidity study of males (n = 120) with paraphilias and paraphilia-related disorders. *Sexual Abuse: A Journal of Research and Treatment, 14,* 349–366.

Kaminer, W. (1992). *I'm dysfunctional, you're dysfunctional: The recovery movement and other self-help fashions.* Reading, MA: Addison-Wesley.

Keenan, K. (2000). Emotional dysregulation as a risk factor for child psychopathology. *Clinical Psychology: Science and Practice, 7,* 418–434.

Keenan, T., & Ward, T. (2003). Developmental antecedents of sexual offending. In T. Ward, D. R. Laws, & S. M. Hudson (Eds.), *Sexual deviance: Issues and controversies* (pp. 119–134). Thousand Oaks, CA: Sage Publications.

Kehoe, E. J., & Macrae, M. (1998). Classical conditioning. In W. O'Donohue (Ed.), *Learning and behavior therapy* (pp. 36–58). Boston: Allyn & Bacon.

Keltner, A., Marshall, P. G., & Marshall, W. L. (1981). Measurement and correlation of assertiveness and social fear in a prison population. *Corrective and Social Psychiatry, 27,* 41–47.

Kennedy-Moore, E., & Watson, J. C. (1999). *Expressing emotion: Myths, realities, and therapeutic strategies.* New York: Guilford Press.

Kihlstrom, J. F., & Barnhardt, T. M. (1993). The self-regulation of memory, for better or worse, with and without hypnosis. In D. M. Wegner & J. M. Pennebaker (Eds.), *Handbook of mental control* (pp. 88–125). Englewood Cliffs, NJ: Prentice Hall.

Kilpatrick, J. (1996, November). *From the mouths of victims: What victimization surveys tell us about sexual assault and sex offenders.* Paper presented at the 15th Annual Research and Treatment Conference of the Association for the Treatment of Sexual Abusers. Chicago.

Kirk, S. A., & Kutchins, H. (1994). The myth of the reliability of DSM. *The Journal of Mind and Behavior, 15,* 71–86.

Knopp, F. H., Freeman-Longo, R. E., & Stevenson, W. (1992). *Nationwide survey of juvenile and adult sex-offender treatment programs*. Orwell, VT: Safer Society Press.

Koss, M. P. (1992). The underdetection of rape: Are there differences in the victim's experience? *Psychology of Women Quarterly, 12*, 1–24.

Koss, M. P., & Dinero, T. W. (1989). Predictors of sexual aggression among a national sample of male college students. *Annals of the New York Academy of Sciences, 528*, 133–146.

Koss, M. P., Gidycz, C. A., & Wisniewski. M. (1987). The scope of rape: Incidence and prevalence of sexual aggression and victimization in a national sample of higher education students. *Journal of Consulting and Clinical Psychology, 55*, 162–170.

Koss, M. P., Leonard, K. E., Beezley, D. A., & Oros, C. J. (1985). Nonstranger sexual aggression: A discriminant analysis of the psychological characteristics of undetected offenders. *Sex Roles, 12*, 981–991.

Krafft-Ebing, R. von (1886). *Psychopathia sexualia*. Stuttgart, Germany: Ferdinand Enke.

Kunda, Z. (1999). *Social cognition: Making sense of people*. Cambridge, MA: MIT Press.

Laird, J. D. (1974). Self-attribution of emotion: The effects of expressive behavior on the quality of emotional experience. *Journal of Personality and Social Psychology, 29*, 475–486.

Langevin, R. (1983). *Sexual strands: Understanding and treating sexual anomalies in men*. Hillsdale: NJ: Lawrence Erlbaum Associates.

Langevin, R. (1991). A note on the problem of response set in measuring cognitive distortions. *Annals of Sex Research, 4*, 293–295.

Langevin, R., Wright, M. A., & Handy, L. (1988). Empathy, assertiveness, aggressiveness, and defensiveness among sex offenders. *Annals of Sex Research, 1*, 533–547.

Langton, C. M. (2003). *Contrasting approaches to risk assessment with adult male sexual offenders: An evaluation of recidivism prediction schemes and the utility of supplementary clinical information for enhancing predictive accuracy*. Unpublished doctoral dissertation, University of Toronto, Ontario, Canada.

Langton, C. M., & Marshall, W. L. (2000). The role of cognitive distortions in relapse prevention programs. In D. R. Laws, S. M. Hudson, & T. Ward (Eds.), *Remaking relapse prevention with sex offenders: A sourcebook* (pp. 167–186). Newbury Park, CA: Sage Publications.

Langton, C. M., & Marshall, W. L. (2001). Cognition in rapists: Theoretical patterns by typological breakdown. *Aggression and Violent Behavior: A Review Journal, 6*, 499–518.

Laumann, E. O., Gagnon, J. H., Michael, R. T., & Michaels, S. (1994). *The social organization of sexuality.* Chicago: University of Chicago Press.

Laws, D. R. (1986). *Sexual deviance card sort.* Tampa, FL: Florida Mental Health Institute.

Laws, D. R., Hudson, S. M., & Ward, T. (Eds.) (2000). *Remaking relapse prevention with sex offenders.* Thousand Oaks, CA: Sage Publications.

Laws, D. R., & Marshall, W. L. (1990). A conditioning theory of the etiology and maintenance of deviant sexual preferences and behavior. In W. L. Marshall, D. R. Laws, & H. E. Barbaree (Eds.), *Handbook of sexual assault: Issues, theories, and treatment of the offender* (pp. 209–229). New York: Plenum Press.

Laws, D. R., & Marshall, W. L. (1991). Masturbatory reconditioning with sexual deviates: An evaluative review. *Advances in Behaviour Research and Therapy, 13,* 13–25.

Laws, D. R., & Marshall, W. L. (2003). A brief history of behavioral and cognitive-behavioral approaches to sexual offender treatment: Part 1. Early developments. *Sexual Abuse: A Journal of Research and Treatment, 15,* 75–92.

Laws, D. R., & O'Donohue, W. (Eds.) (1997). *Sexual deviance: Theory, assessment, and treatment.* New York: Guilford Press.

Laws, D. R., & Osborn, C. A. (1983). How to build and operate a behavioral laboratory to evaluate and treat sexual deviance. In J. G. Greer & I. R. Stuart (Eds.), *Sexual aggression: Current perspectives and treatment* (pp. 293–335). New York: Van Nostrand Reinhold.

Laws, D. R., & Serber, M. (1975). Measurement and evaluation of assertive training with sexual offenders. In R. E. Hosford & C. S. Moss (Eds.), *The crumbling walls: Treatment and counseling of prisoners* (pp. 165–172). Champaign, IL: University of Illinois Press.

Laws, D. R., & Ward, T. (2005). When one size doesn't fit all. In W. L. Marshall, Y. M. Fernandez, L. E. Marshall, & G. A. Serran (Eds.), *Sexual offender treatment: Controversial issues* (pp. 241–254). Chichester, UK: John Wiley & Sons.

Lawson, J. S., Marshall, W. L., & McGrath, P. (1979). The Social Self-Esteem Inventory. *Educational and Psychological Measurement, 39,* 803–811.

Lazarus, R. S. (1991). Emotion and adaptation. New York: Oxford University Press.

Lazarus, R. S., & Folkman, S. (1984). *Stress, appraisal and coping.* New York: Guilford Press.

Leary, M. R., & Downs, D. L. (1995). Interpersonal functions of the self-esteem motive: The self-esteem system as a sociometer. In M. Kernis

(Ed.), *Efficacy, agency, and self-esteem* (pp. 123–144). New York: Plenum Press.

Leon, C. (1969). Unusual patterns of crime during La Violencia in Columbia. *American Journal of Psychiatry, 125,* 1564–1575.

Letourneau, E. J. (2002). A comparison of objective measures of sexual arousal and interest: Visual reaction time and penile plethysmography. *Sexual Abuse: A Journal of Research and Treatment, 14,* 207–223.

Letourneau, E. J. (2004). A comment on the first report. *Sexual Abuse: A Journal of Research and Treatment, 16,* 77–81.

Levenson, J. S. (2004). Reliability of sexually violent predator civil commitment criteria. *Law & Human Behavior, 28,* 357–368.

Leventhal, H., & Patrick-Miller, L. (2000). Emotional and physical illness: Causes and indicators of vulnerability. In M. Lewis & J. M. Haviland-Jones (Eds.), *Handbook of emotions* (2nd ed.) (pp. 523–537). New York: Guilford Press.

Lewis, M., & Haviland-Jones, J. M. (Eds.) (2000). *Handbook of emotions* (2nd ed.). New York: Guilford Press.

Licht, H. (1932). *Sexual life in ancient Greece.* London: Routledge & Kegan Paul.

Lightfoot, L. O. (1993). The Offender Substance Abuse Prerelease Program: An empirically-based model of treatment for offenders. In J. S. Baer, G. A. Marlatt, & R. J. M. McMahon (Eds.), *Addictive behaviors across the lifespan: Prevention, treatment and policy.* Newbury Park, CA: Sage Publications.

Lightfoot, L. O., & Barbaree, H. E. (1993). The relationship between substance use and abuse and sexual offending in adolescents. In H. E. Barbaree, W. L. Marshall, & S. M. Hudson (Eds.), *The juvenile sex offender* (pp. 203–224). New York: Guilford Press.

Lindberg, F., & Distad, L. (1985). Post-traumatic stress disorder in women who experienced childhood incest. *Child Abuse and Neglect, 9,* 324–334.

Loftus, E., & Ketchum, K. (1994). *The myth of repressed memory: False memories and accusations of sexual abuse.* New York: St. Martin's Press.

Looman, J. (1999). Mood, conflict, and deviant sexual fantasies. In B. K. Schwartz (Ed.), *The sex offender: Theoretical advances, treating special populations and legal developments* (Vol. III, pp. 3.1–3.11). Kingston, NJ: Civic Research Institute.

Lösel, F., & Schmucker, M. (2005). The effectiveness of treatment for sexual offenders: A comprehensive meta-analysis. *Journal of Experimental Criminology, 1,* 1–29.

Lynn, S. J., & McConkey, K. M. (Eds.) (1998). *Truth in memory*. New York: Guilford Press.

MacVicar, R. (1979). Psychotherapy of sexually abused girls. *Journal of the American Academy of Child Psychiatry, 18*, 342–353.

Malamuth, N. M. (1989). The Attraction to Sexual Aggression Scale: Part two. *Journal of Sex Research, 26*, 324–354.

Malamuth, N. M., & Check, J. V. P. (1983). Sexual arousal to rape depictions: Individual differences. *Journal of Abnormal Psychology, 92*, 55–67.

Maletzky, B. M. (1991). *Treating the sexual offender*. Newbury Park: Sage Publications.

Mann, R. E. (2000). Managing resistance and rebellion in relapse prevention intervention. In D. R. Laws, S. M. Hudson, & T. Ward (Eds.), *Remaking relapse prevention with sex offenders: A sourcebook* (pp. 187–200). Thousand Oaks, CA: Sage Publications.

Mann, R. E., & Beech, A. R. (2003). Cognitive distortion, schemas, and implicit theories. In T. Ward, D. R. Laws, & S. M. Hudson (Eds.), *Sexual deviance: Issues and controversies* (pp. 135–153). Thousand Oaks, CA: Sage Publications.

Mann, R. E., & Hollin, C. R. (2001, November). *Schemas: A model for understanding cognition in sexual offending*. Paper presented at the 20th Annual Research and Treatment Conference of the Association for the Treatment of Sexual Abusers. San Antonio, TX.

Mann, R. E., & Shingler, J. (2005). Schema-driven cognition in sexual offenders: Theory, assessment and treatment. In W. L. Marshall, Y. M. Fernandez, L. E. Marshall, & G. A. Serran (Eds.), *Sexual offender treatment: Controversial issues* (pp. 173–185). Chichester, UK: John Wiley & Sons.

Mann, R. E., Webster, S. D., Schofield, C., & Marshall, W. L. (2004). Approach versus avoidance goals in relapse prevention with sexual offenders. *Sexual Abuse: A Journal of Research and Treatment, 16*, 65–75.

Marlatt, G. A. (1982). Relapse prevention: A self-control program for the treatment of addictive behaviours. In R. B. Stuart (Ed.), *Adherence, compliance, and generalization in behavioral medicine* (pp. 329–378). New York: Brunner/Mazel.

Marques, J. K. (1982, March). *Relapse prevention: A self-control model for the treatment of sex offenders*. Paper presented at the 7th Annual Forensic Mental Health Conference. Asilomar, CA.

Marques, J. K., Day, D. M., Nelson, C., & West, M. A. (1994). Effects of cognitive-behavioral treatment on sex offender recidivism: Preliminary results of a longitudinal study. *Criminal Justice and Behavior, 21*, 28–54.

Marques, J. K., Nelson, C., Alarcon, J.-M., & Day, D. M. (2000). Preventing relapse in sex offenders: What we learned from SOTEP's experimental treatment program. In D. R. Laws, S. M. Hudson, & T. Ward (Eds.), *Remaking relapse prevention with sex offenders: A sourcebook* (pp. 321–340). Thousand Oaks, CA: Sage Publications.

Marques, J. K., Weideranders, M., Day, D. M., Nelson, C., & van Ommeren, A. (2005). Effects of a relapse prevention program on sexual recidivism: Final results from California's Sex Offender Treatment and Evaluation Project (SOTEP). *Sexual Abuse: A Journal of Research and Treatment, 17*, 79–107.

Marshall, L. E., Malcolm, P. B., Marshall, W. L., & Butler, B. (in press). A descriptive and phallometric examination of elderly sexual offenders. *Sexual Abuse: A Journal of Research and Treatment.*

Marshall, L. E., & Marshall, W. L. (2001). Excessive sexual desire disorder among sexual offenders: The development of a research project. *Sexual Addiction & Compulsivity: The Journal of Treatment and Prevention, 8*, 301–307.

Marshall, L. E., & Marshall, W. L. (2002). The role of attachment in sexual offending: An examination of preoccupied-attachment-style offending behavior. In B. Schwartz (Ed.), *The sex offender: Current treatment modalities and systems issues* (Vol. IV, pp. 3.1–3.8). Kingston, NJ: Civic Research Institute.

Marshall, L. E., Marshall, W. L., & Moulden, H. (2000, November). *Sexual addiction, substance abuse, coping, and sexual history in sexual offenders.* Paper presented at the 19th Annual Research and Treatment Conference of the Association for the Treatment of Sexual Abusers. San Diego, CA.

Marshall, L. E., & Moulden, H. (2005). Preparatory programs for sexual offenders. In W. L. Marshall, Y. M. Fernandez, L. E. Marshall, & G. A. Serran (Eds.), *Sexual offender treatment: Controversial issues* (pp. 199–210). Chichester, UK: John Wiley & Sons.

Marshall, L. E., Moulden, H., & Marshall, W. L. (2001, November). *Mood induction with sexual offenders.* Paper presented at the 20th Annual Research and Treatment Conference of the Association for the Treatment of Sexual Abusers. San Antonio, TX.

Marshall, W. L. (1971). A combined treatment method for certain sexual deviations. *Behaviour Research and Therapy, 9*, 292–294.

Marshall, W. L. (1973). The modification of sexual fantasies: A combined treatment approach to the reduction of deviant sexual behavior. *Behaviour Research and Therapy, 11*, 557–564.

Marshall, W. L. (1975). Reducing masturbatory guilt. *Journal of Behavior Therapy and Experimental Psychiatry, 6*, 260–261.

Marshall, W. L. (1979). Satiation therapy: A procedure for reducing deviant sexual arousal. *Journal of Applied Behavioral Analysis, 12,* 10–22.

Marshall, W. L. (1984, March). *Rape as a socio-cultural phenomenon.* The J. P. S. Robertson Annual Lecture, Trent University, Peterborough, Ontario, Canada.

Marshall, W. L. (1985, May). *Social causes of rape.* Visiting Fellows' Public Lecture, University of Western Australia, Perth, Australia.

Marshall, W. L. (1989a). Invited essay: Intimacy, loneliness and sexual offenders. *Behaviour Research and Therapy, 27,* 491–503.

Marshall, W. L. (1989b). Pornography and sex offenders. In D. Zillmann & J. Bryant (Eds.), *Pornography: Recent research, interpretations, and policy considerations* (pp. 185–214). Hillsdale, NJ: Lawrence Erlbaum.

Marshall, W. L. (1992). The social value of treatment for sexual offenders. *Canadian Journal of Human Sexuality, 1,* 109–114.

Marshall, W. L. (1993). The role of attachment, intimacy, and loneliness in the etiology and maintenance of sexual offending. *Sexual and Marital Therapy, 8,* 109–121.

Marshall, W. L. (1994). Treatment effects on denial and minimization in incarcerated sex offenders. *Behaviour Research and Therapy, 32,* 559–564.

Marshall, W. L. (1995). The treatment of sex offenders in a community clinic. In R. R. Ross, D. H. Antonowicz, & G. K. Dhaliwal (Eds.), *Going Straight: Effective delinquency prevention and offender rehabilitation* (pp. 277–305). Ottawa: Air Training & Publications.

Marshall, W. L. (1996). Assessment, treatment, and theorizing about sex offenders: Developments over the past 20 years and future directions. *Criminal Justice and Behavior, 23,* 162–199.

Marshall, W. L. (1997a). Pedophilia: Psychopathology and theory. In D. R. Laws & W. O'Donohue (Eds.), *Handbook of sexual deviance: Theory and application* (pp. 152–174). New York: Guilford Press.

Marshall, W. L. (1997b). The relationship between self-esteem and deviant sexual arousal in nonfamilial child molesters. *Behavior Modification, 12,* 86–96.

Marshall, W. L. (1998, May). *Attachment problems in the etiology of sexual offending.* Invited paper, Royal Netherlands Academy of Arts and Sciences Meeting on Sexual Appetite, Desire, and Motivation, Amsterdam.

Marshall, W. L. (1999). Current status of North American assessment and treatment programs for sexual offenders. *Journal of Interpersonal Violence, 14,* 221–239.

Marshall, W. L. (2001a). Etiologia de la delincuencia sexual. In W. L. Marshall (Ed.), *Agresores sexuales* (pp. 46–83). Barcelona, Spain: Ariel Publishing.

Marshall, W. L. (2001b, February). *Treatment processes and treatment outcome with sexual offenders*. Paper presented at the Australian and New Zealand Criminological Society's 2001 Conference. Melbourne, Australia.

Marshall, W. L. (2002). Historical foundations and current conceptualizations of empathy. In Y. M. Fernandez (Ed.), *In their shoes: Examining the issue of empathy and its place in the treatment of offenders* (pp. 1–15). Oklahoma City, OK: Wood 'N' Barnes Publishing.

Marshall, W. L. (2004a, April). *Therapist processes and treatment procedures with sexual offenders*. Paper presented at the 3rd Biennial Conference of the Australian & New Zealand Association for the Treatment of Sexual Abusers. Auckland, New Zealand.

Marshall, W. L. (2004b). Cognitive–behavioural treatment of child molesters. In R. K. Hanson, F. Pfäfflin, & M. Lütz (Eds.), *Sexual abuse in the Catholic Church: Scientific and legal perspectives* (pp. 97–112). Vatican: Libreria Editrice Vaticana.

Marshall, W. L. (2005a). Diagnostic problems with sexual offenders. In W. L. Marshall, Y. M. Fernandez, L. E. Marshall, & G. A. Serran (Eds.), *Sexual offender treatment: Controversial issues* (pp. 33–43). Chichester, UK: John Wiley & Sons.

Marshall, W. L. (2005b). Therapist style in sexual offender treatment: Influences on indices of change. *Sexual Abuse: A Journal of Research and Treatment, 17*, 109–117.

Marshall, W. L. (2005c). Grenzen der phallometrie. *Recht & Psychiatrie, 23*, 11–23.

Marshall, W. L. (in press-a). Diagnostic issues, multiple paraphilias, and comorbid disorders in sexual offenders: Their incidence and treatment. *Aggression and Violent Behavior: A Review Journal.*

Marshall, W. L. (in press-b). The prevention and treatment of Catholic clergy who sexually abuse: A proposal. *Seminary Journal.*

Marshall, W. L. (in press-c). Olfactory aversion and directed masturbation in the modification of deviant preferences: A case study of a child molester. *Clinical Case Studies.*

Marshall, W. L. (in press-d). Ammonia aversion with an exhibitionist: A case study. *Clinical Case Studies.*

Marshall, W. L. (in press-e). Covert association: A case illustration. *Clinical Case Studies.*

Marshall, W. L., Anderson, D., & Champagne, F. (1997). Self-esteem and its relationship to sexual offending. *Psychology Crime & Law, 3*, 81–106.

Marshall, W. L., Anderson, D., & Fernandez, Y. M. (1999). *Cognitive behavioural treatment of sexual offenders*. Chichester, UK: John Wiley & Sons.

Marshall, W. L., Anderson, D., & Fernandez, Y. M. (2001). *Il trattemento cognitivo-comportamentale degli aggressori sessuali*. Torino, Italy: Centro Scientifico Editore.

Marshall, W. L., & Barbaree, H. E. (1978). The reduction of deviant arousal. *Criminal Justice and Behavior, 5*, 294–303.

Marshall, W. L., & Barbaree, H. E. (1984). A behavioral view of rape. *International Journal of Law and Psychiatry, 7*, 51–77.

Marshall, W. L., & Barbaree, H. E. (1988). The long-term evaluation of a behavioral treatment program for child molesters. *Behaviour Research and Therapy, 26*, 499–511.

Marshall, W. L., & Barbaree, H. E. (1990). An integrated theory of sexual offending. In W. L. Marshall, D. R. Laws, & H. E. Barbaree (Eds.), *Handbook of sexual assault: Issues, theories, and treatment of the offender* (pp. 257–275). New York: Plenum Press.

Marshall, W. L., Barbaree, H. E., & Eccles, A. (1991). Early onset and deviant sexuality in child molesters. *Journal of Interpersonal Violence, 6*, 323–336.

Marshall, W. L., & Barrett, S. (1990). *Criminal neglect: Why sex offenders go free*. Toronto: Doubleday.

Marshall, W. L., Bryce, P., Hudson, S. M., Ward, T., & Moth, B. (1996). The enhancement of intimacy and reduction of loneliness among child molesters. *Legal and Criminological Psychology, 1*, 95–102.

Marshall, W. L., Champagne, F., Brown, C., & Miller, S. (1997), Empathy, intimacy, loneliness, and self-esteem in nonfamilial child molesters. *Journal of Child Sexual Abuse, 6*, 87–97.

Marshall, W. L., Champagne, F., Sturgeon, C., & Bryce, P. (1997). Increasing the self-esteem of child molesters. *Sexual Abuse: A Journal of Research and Treatment, 9*, 321–333.

Marshall, W. L., & Christie, M. M. (1982). The enhancement of social self-esteem. *Canadian Counsellor, 16*, 82–89.

Marshall, W. L., Christie, M. M., Lanthier, R. D., & Cruchley, J. (1982). The nature of the reinforcer in the enhancement of social self-esteem. *Canadian Counsellor, 16*, 90–96.

Marshall, W. L., Cripps, E., Anderson, D., & Cortoni, F. A. (1999). Self-esteem and coping strategies in child molesters. *Journal of Interpersonal Violence, 14*, 955–962.

Marshall, W. L., Earls, C. M., Segal, Z. V., & Darke, J. (1983). A behavioral program for the assessment and treatment of sexual aggressors. In K. Craig and R. McMahon (Eds.), *Advances in clinical behavior therapy* (pp. 148–174). New York: Brunner/Mazel.

Marshall, W. L., & Eccles, A. (1991). Issues in clinical practice with sex offenders. *Journal of Interpersonal Violence, 6,* 68–93.

Marshall, W. L., Eccles, A., & Barbaree, H. E. (1991). Treatment of exhibitionists: A focus on sexual deviance versus cognitive and relationship features. *Behaviour Research and Therapy, 29,* 129–135.

Marshall, W. L., & Fernandez, Y. M. (1998). Cognitive–behavioural approaches to the treatment of the paraphiliacs: Sexual offenders. In V. E. Caballo (Ed.), *International handbook of cognitive and behavioural treatments for psychological disorders* (pp. 281–312). Oxford, UK: Elsevier Science.

Marshall, W. L., & Fernandez, Y. M. (2003). *Phallometric testing with sexual offenders: Theory, research, and practice.* Brandon, VT: Safer Society Press.

Marshall, W. L., Fernandez, Y. M., Serran, G. A., Mulloy, R., Thornton, D., Mann, R. E., & Anderson, D. (2003). Process variables in the treatment of sexual offenders: A review of the relevant literature. *Aggression and Violent Behavior: A Review Journal, 8,* 205–234.

Marshall, W. L., & Hall, G. C. N. (1995). The value of the MMPI in deciding forensic issues in accused sexual offenders. *Sexual Abuse: A Journal of Research and Treatment, 7,* 205–219.

Marshall, W. L., & Hambley, L. S. (1996). Intimacy and loneliness, and their relationship to rape myth acceptance and hostility toward women among rapists. *Journal of Interpersonal Violence, 11,* 586–592.

Marshall, W. L., Hamilton, K., & Fernandez, Y. (2001). Empathy deficits and cognitive distortions in child molesters. *Sexual Abuse: A Journal of Research and Treatment, 13,* 123–131.

Marshall, W. L., Hudson, S. M., & Hodkinson, S. (1993). The importance of attachment bonds in the development of juvenile sex offending. In H. E. Barbaree, W. L Marshall, & S. M. Hudson (Eds.), *The juvenile sex offender* (pp. 164–181). New York: Guilford Press.

Marshall, W. L., Hudson, S. M., Jones, R. L., & Fernandez, Y. M. (1995). Empathy in sex offenders. *Clinical Psychology, Review, 15,* 99–113.

Marshall, W. L., Keltner, A., & Griffiths, E. (1974). *An apparatus for the delivery of foul odors: Clinical applications.* Unpublished manuscript, Queen's University, Kingston, Ontario, Canada.

Marshall, W. L., Kennedy, P., & Yates, P. (2002). Issues concerning the reliability and validity of the diagnosis of sexual sadism applied in prison settings. *Sexual Abuse: A Journal of Research and Treatment, 14,* 310–311.

Marshall, W. L., Kennedy, P., Yates, P., & Serran, G. A. (2002). Diagnosing sexual sadism in sexual offenders: Reliability across diagnosticians. *International Journal of Offender Therapy and Comparative Criminology, 46,* 668–676.

Marshall, W. L., & Langton, C. (2004). Unwanted thoughts and fantasies experienced by sexual offenders: Their nature, persistence, and treatment. In D. A. Clark (Ed.), *Intrusive thoughts in clinical disorders: Theory, research, and treatment* (pp. 199–225). New York: Guilford Press.

Marshall, W. L., & Laws, D. R. (2003). A brief history of behavioral and cognitive behavioral approaches to sexual offender treatment: Part 2. The modern era. *Sexual Abuse: A Journal of Research and Treatment, 15*, 93–120.

Marshall, W. L., & Lippens, K. (1977). The clinical value of boredom: A procedure for reducing inappropriate sexual interests. *Journal of Nervous and Mental Diseases, 165*, 283–287.

Marshall, W. L., & Marshall, L. E. (2000). The origins of sexual offending. *Trauma, Violence, & Abuse: A Review Journal, 1*, 250–263.

Marshall, W. L., Marshall, L. E., Malcolm, P. B., Serran, G. A., & Fernandez, Y. M. *Outcome evaluation of a sexual offenders' treatment program.* Manuscript in preparation.

Marshall, W. L., & McGuire, J. (2003). Effect sizes in treatment of sexual offenders. *International Journal of Offender Therapy and Comparative Criminology, 46*, 653–663.

Marshall, W. L., & McKnight, R. D. (1975). An integrated treatment program for sexual offenders. *Canadian Psychiatric Association Journal, 20*, 133–138.

Marshall, W. L., & Moulden, H. (2001). Hostility toward women and victim empathy in rapists. *Sexual Abuse: A Journal of Research and Treatment, 13*, 249–255.

Marshall, W. L., O'Sullivan, C., & Fernandez, Y. M. (1996). The enhancement of victim empathy among incarcerated child molesters. *Legal and Criminological Psychology, 1*, 95–102.

Marshall, W. L., Payne, K., Barbaree, H. E., & Eccles, A. (1991). Exhibitionists: Sexual preferences for exposing. *Behaviour Research and Therapy, 29*, 37–40.

Marshall, W. L., & Redondo, S. (2002). Control y tratamiento de la aggression sexual. In S. Redondo (Ed.), *Delincuencio sexual y sociedad* (pp. 301–328). Valencia, Spain: Ariel Publishing.

Marshall, W. L., & Segal, Z. V. (1988). Behavior therapy. In C. C. Last & M. Hersen (Eds.), *Handbook of anxiety disorders* (pp. 338–361). New York: Pergamon Press.

Marshall, W. L., & Serran, G. A. (2000). Current issues in the assessment and treatment of sexual offenders. *Clinical Psychology and Psychotherapy, 7*, 85–96.

Marshall, W. L., & Serran, G. A. (2004a). Tratameinto del agresor sexual. In J. Sanmartin (Ed.), *El laberinto de la violencia: Cansas, tipos y efectos* (pp. 309–319). Barcelona, Spain: Ariel.

Marshall, W. L., & Serran, G. A. (2004b). The role of the therapist in offender treatment. *Psychology, Crime and Law, 10,* 309–320.

Marshall, W. L., Serran, G. A., & Cortoni, F. A. (2000). Childhood attachments, sexual abuse, and their relationship to adult coping in child molesters. *Sexual Abuse: A Journal of Research and Treatment, 12,* 17–26.

Marshall, W. L., Serran, G. S., Fernandez, Y. M., Mulloy, R., Mann, R. E., & Thornton, D. (2003). Therapist characteristics in the treatment of sexual offenders: Tentative data on their relationship with indices of behaviour change. *Journal of Sexual Aggression, 9,* 25–30.

Marshall, W. L., Serran, G. A., & Marshall, L. E. (in press). Situational and dispositional factors in child sexual molestation: A psychological perspective. In R. K. Wortley & S. M. Smallbone (Eds.), *Situational perspectives on sexual crimes against children.* New York: Criminal Justice Press.

Marshall, W. L., Serran, G. A., Marshall, L. E., & Fernandez, Y. M. (2005). Recovering memories of the offense in "amnesic" sexual offenders. *Sexual Abuse: A Journal of Research and Treatment, 17,* 31–38.

Marshall, W. L., Serran, G. A., Moulden, H., Mulloy, R., Fernandez, Y. M., Mann, R. E., & Thornton, D. (2002). Therapist features in sexual offender treatment: Their reliable identification and influence on behaviour change. *Clinical Psychology and Psychotherapy, 9,* 395–405.

Marshall, W. L., Thornton, D., Marshall, L. E., Fernandez, Y. M., & Mann, R. E. (2001). Treatment of sexual offenders who are in categorical denial: A pilot project. *Sexual Abuse: A Journal of Research and Treatment, 13,* 205–215.

Marshall, W. L., Ward, T., Mann, R. E., Moulden, H., Fernandez, Y. M., Serran, G. A., & Marshall, L. E. (2005). Working positively with sexual offenders: Maximizing the effectiveness of treatment. *Journal of Interpersonal Violence, 20,* 1–19.

Marshall, W. L., Webster, S., Serran, G. A., Marshall, L. E., & Fernandez, Y. M. (2004). *The Therapist Rating Scale: Interrater reliability.* Unpublished paper, Rockwood Psychological Services, Kingston, Ontario, Canada.

Marshall, W. L., & Williams, S. (1975). A behavioral approach to the modification of rape. *Quarterly Bulletin of the British Association for Behavioural Psychotherapy, 4,* 78.

Marshall, W. L., & Williams, S. (2000). Assessment and treatment of sexual offenders. *Forum on Corrections Research, 12,* 41–44.

Marshall, W. L., & Yates, P. M. (2005). Comment on Mailloux et al.'s (2003) study: "Dosage of treatment of sexual offenders: Are we overprescribing?" *International Journal of Offender Treatment and Comparative Criminology, 49,* 221–224.

Masters, W., & Johnson, V. (1966). *Human sexual response.* Boston: Little, Brown.

Mayer, J. D., & Gaschke, Y. N. (1988). The experience and meta-experience of mood. *Journal of Personality and Social Psychology, 52,* 102–111.

Mayer, J. D., & Salovey, P. (1997). What is emotional intelligence? In P. Salovey & D. Sluyter (Ed.), *Emotional development and emotional intelligence* (pp. 3–34). New York: Basic Books.

McConaghy, M. (1993). *Sexual behavior: Problems and management.* New York: Plenum Press.

McConaghy, N., Zamir, R., & Manicavasagar, V. (1993). Nonsexist sexual experiences survey and scale of attraction to sexual aggression. *Australian and New Zealand Journal of Psychiatry, 27,* 686–693.

McDonald, R. K., & Pithers, W. D. (1989). Self-monitoring to identify high-risk situations. In D. R. Laws (Ed.), *Relapse prevention with sex offenders* (pp. 96–104). New York: Guilford Press.

McFall, R. M. (1990). The enhancement of social skills: An information processing analysis. In W. L. Marshall, D. R. Laws, & H. E. Barbaree (Eds.), *Handbook of sexual assault: Issues, theories, and treatment of the offender* (pp. 311–330). New York: Plenum Press.

McGrath, M., Cann, S., & Konopasky, R. J. (1998). New measures of defensiveness, empathy, and cognitive distortions for sexual offenders against children. *Sexual Abuse: A Journal of Research and Treatment, 10,* 25–36.

McGrath, R. J., Cumming, G. F., & Burchard, B. L. (2003). *Current practices and trends in sexual abuser management: Safer Society 2002 nationwide survey.* Brandon, VT: Safer Society Press.

McKibben, A., Proulx, J., & Lusignan, R. (1994). Relationship between conflict, affect and deviant sexual behavior in rapists and pedophiles. *Behaviour Research and Therapy, 23,* 571–575.

McMullen, R. J. (1987). Youth prostitution: A balance of power. *Journal of Adolescence, 10,* 57–69.

Meloy, R. (1995). Antisocial personality disorder. In G. Gabbard (Ed.), *Treatment of psychiatric disorders* (2nd ed.). Washington, DC: American Psychiatric Press.

Meyer, G. J. (2002). Implications of information—gathering methods for a refined taxonomy of psychopathology. In L. E. Bentler & M. L. Malick (Eds.), *Rethinking the DSM: A psychological perspective* (pp. 69–106). Washington, DC: American Psychological Association.

Miller, R. S., & Lefcourt, H. M. (1982). The assessment of social intimacy. *Journal of Personality Assessment, 46,* 514–518.

Miller, W. R. (1983). Motivational interviewing with problem drinkers. *Behavioural Psychotherapy, 1,* 147–172.

Miller, W. R., & Rollnick, S. (Eds.) (1991). *Motivational interviewing: Preparing people to change addictive behavior.* New York: Guilford Press.

Miller, W. R., & Rollnick, S. (Eds.) (2002). *Motivational interviewing: Preparing people to change addictive behavior* (2nd ed.). New York: Guilford Press.

Mineka, S., & Hamida, S. (1998). Observational and nonconscious learning. In W. O'Donohue (Ed.), *Learning and behavior therapy* (pp. 421–439). Boston: Allyn & Bacon.

Miner, M. H., Day, D. M., & Nafpaktitis, M. K. (1989). Assessment of coping skills: Development of a Situational Competency Test. In D. R. Laws (Ed.), *Relapse prevention with sex offenders* (pp. 127–136). New York: Guilford Press.

Miranda, A. O., & Davis, K. (2002). Sexually abusive children— Etiological and treatment considerations. In B. K. Schwartz (Ed.), *The sex offender: Current treatment modalities and systems issues.* (Vol. IV, pp. 18.1–18.13). Kingston, NJ: Civic Research Institute.

Mitchell, R. E., Cronkite, R. C., & Moos, R. H. (1983). Stress, coping, and depression among married couples. *Journal of Abnormal Psychology, 92,* 443–448.

Moll, A. (1893). *Les perversions de l'instinct genital: Etude sur l'inversion sexuelle basée sur des documents officials.* Paris: G. Carré.

Moos, R. H., & Moos, B. S. (1981). *Family Environment Scale manual.* Palo Alto, CA: Consulting Psychologists Press.

Morgan, R. E., & Riccio, D. C. (1998). Memory retrieval processes. In W. O'Donohue (Ed.), *Learning and behavior therapy* (pp. 464–482). Boston: Allyn & Bacon.

Motiuk, L., & Porporino, F. (1992). *The prevalence, nature, and severity of mental health problems among federal male inmates in Canadian penitentiaries.* Report no. 24. Ottawa: Correctional Services of Canada.

Moulden, H. M., Marshall, L. E., & Marshall, W. L. (2005). A preparatory program for sexual offenders: 2. Achievement of within-treatment goals. In preparation.

Murphy, K. R., & Davidshofer, C. O. (1995). *Psychological testing: Principles and applications* (4th ed.). Upper Saddle River, NJ: Prentice Hall.

Murphy, W. D., & Barbaree, H. E. (1994). *Assessments of sex offenders by measures of erectile response: Psychometric properties and decision making*. Brandon, VT: The Safer Society Press.

Myers, R. (2000). *Identifying schemas in child and adult sex offenders, and violent offenders*. Unpublished master's thesis, University of Leicester, UK.

Neidigh, L. W., & Krop, H. (1992). Cognitive distortions among child sexual offenders. *Journal of Sex Education and Therapy, 18*, 208–215.

Neidigh, L. W., & Tomiko, R. (1991). The coping strategies of child sexual abusers. *Journal of Sex Education and Therapy, 17*, 103–110.

Neisser, U. (Ed.) (1982). *Memory observed: Remembering in natural contexts*. San Francisco: Freeman.

Nelson, C. A. (1995). The ontogeny of human memory: A cognitive neuroscience perspective. *Developmental Psychology, 31*, 723–728.

Nichols, H. R., & Molinder, I. (1984). *Multiphasic Sex Inventory*. Tacoma, WA: Authors.

Oakhill, J., & Garnham, A. (Eds.) (1996). *Mental models in cognitive science*. Hove, UK: Psychology Press.

O'Donohue, W. (Ed.) (1998). *Learning and behavior therapy*. Boston: Allyn & Bacon.

O'Donohue, W. T., Regev, L. G., & Hagstrom, A. (2000). Problems with the DSM-IV diagnosis of pedophilia. *Sexual Abuse: A Journal of Research and Treatment, 12*, 95–105.

Parker, J. D. A., & Endler, N. S. (1996). Coping and defense: A historical overview. In M. Zeidner & N. S. Endler (Eds.), *Handbook of coping: Theory, research, applications* (pp. 3–23). New York: John Wiley & Sons.

Paulhaus, D. L. (1991). Measurement and control of response bias. In J. P. Robinson, P. R. Shaver, & L. S. Wrightman (Eds.), *Measures of personality and social psychological attitudes* (pp. 17–59). New York: Academic Press.

Pearson, H. J., Marshall, W. L., Barbaree, H. E., & Southmayd, S. (1992). Treatment of a compulsive paraphiliac with buspirone. *Annals of Sex Research, 5*, 239–246.

Pennebaker, J. W. (1997). *Opening up: The healing power of expressing emotions* (Rev. ed.). New York: Guilford Press.

Perry, D. G., & Parke, R. D. (1975). Punishment and alternative response training as determinants of response inhibition in children. *Genetic Psychology Monographs, 91*, 257–279.

Person, E. S., Terestman, N., Myers, W. A., Goldberg, E. L., & Salvadori, C. (1989). Gender differences in sexual behaviors and fantasies in a college population. *Journal of Sex and Marital Therapy, 15*, 187–198.

Peters, S. D., Wyatt, G. E., & Finkelhor, D. (1986). Prevalence. In D. Finkelhor (Ed.), *A sourcebook in child sexual abuse* (pp. 15–59). Beverly Hills, CA: Sage Publications.

Pfäfflin, F. (2005). Emotional and intellectual expression during psychotherapy with sexual offenders. *Sexual Abuse: A Journal of Research and Treatment, 17*, 141–151.

Pithers, W. D. (1990). Relapse prevention with sexual aggressors: A method for maintaining therapeutic change and enhancing external supervision. In W. L. Marshall, D. R. Laws, & H. E. Barbaree (Eds.), *Handbook of sexual assault: Issues, theories, and treatment of the offender* (pp. 363–385). New York: Plenum Press.

Pithers, W. D. (1994). Process evaluation of a group therapy component designed to enhance sex offenders' empathy for sexual abuse survivors. *Behaviour Research and Therapy, 32*, 565–570.

Pithers, W. D. (1997). Maintaining treatment integrity with sexual abusers. *Criminal Justice and Behavior, 24*, 34–51.

Pithers, W. D., Beal, L. S., Armstrong, J., & Petty, J. (1989). Identification of risk factors through clinical interviews and analysis of records. In D. R. Laws (Ed.), *Relapse prevention with sex offenders* (pp. 77–87). New York: Guilford Press.

Pithers, W. D., Marques, J. K., Gibat, C. C., & Marlatt, G. A. (1983). Relapse prevention with sexual aggressors: A self-control model of treatment and maintenance of change. In J. G. Greer & I. R. Stuart (Eds.), *The sexual aggressor: Current perspectives on treatment* (pp. 214–239). New York: Van Nostrand Reinhold.

Popper, K. (1963). *Conjecture and refutations: The growth of scientific knowledge.* London: Routledge & Kegan Paul.

Pottharst, K. (1990). *Explorations in adult attachment.* New York: Peter Lang.

Prendergast, W. E. (1991). *Treating sex offenders in correctional institutions and outpatients clinics: A guide to clinical practice.* New York: The Haworth Press.

Prentky, R. A., & Burgess, A. W. (1990). Rehabilitation of child molesters: A cost-benefit analysis. *American Journal of Orthopsychiatry, 60*, 80–117.

Prkachin, K. M., & Prkachin, G. C. (2003). Psychophysiologic disorders. In P. Firestone & W. L. Marshall (Eds.), *Abnormal psychology: Perspectives* (2nd ed.) (pp. 371–396). Toronto: Prentice Hall.

Prochaska, J. O., & DiClemente, C. C. (1994). *The transtheoretical approach: Crossing traditional boundaries of therapy.* Malabar, FL: Krieger Publishing.

Proeve, M. (2003). Responsivity factors in sexual offender treatment. In T. Ward, D. R. Laws & S. M. Hudson (Eds.), *Sexual deviance: Issues and controversies* (pp. 244–261). Thousand Oaks, CA: Sage Publications.

Proeve, M., & Howells, K. (2005). Same and guilt in child molesters. In W. L. Marshall, Y. M. Fernandez, L. E. Marshall, & G. A. Serran (Eds.), *Sexual offender treatment: Controversial issues* (pp. 125–139). Chichester, UK: John Wiley & Sons.

Proulx, J., McKibben, A., & Lusignan, R. (1996). Relationship between affective components and sexual behaviors in sexual aggressors. *Sexual Abuse: A Journal of Research and Treatment, 8,* 279–289.

Quinsey, V. L., & Earls, C. M. (1990). The modification of sexual preferences. In W. L. Marshall, D. R. Laws, & H. E. Barbaree (Eds.), *Handbook of sexual assault: Issues, theories, and treatment of the offender,* (pp. 279–295). New York: Plenum Press.

Quinsey, V. L., Harris, G. T., Rice, M. E., & Cormier, C. A. (1998). *Violent offenders: Appraising and managing risk.* Washington, DC: American Psychological Association.

Quinsey, V. L., Harris, G. T., Rice, M. E., & Lalumière, M. L. (1993). Assessing treatment efficacy in outcome studies of sex offenders. *Journal of Interpersonal Violence, 8,* 512–523.

Quinsey, V. L., Rice, M. E., & Harris, G. T. (1995). Actuarial prediction of sexual recidivism. *Journal of Interpersonal Violence, 10,* 85–105.

Rathus, S. A. (1973). A 30-item schedule for assessing assertive behavior. *Behavior Therapy, 4,* 398–406.

Reid, W. H., Wise, M., & Sutton, B. (1992). The use and reliability of psychiatric diagnosis in forensic settings. *Clinical Forensic Psychiatry, 15,* 529–537.

Reid, W. J., & Gacono, C. (2000). Treatment of antisocial personality, psychopathy, and other characterologic antisocial syndromes. *Behavioral Sciences and the Law, 18,* 647–662.

Rice, M. E., Chaplin, T. E., Harris, G. T., & Coutts, J. (1990). *Empathy for the victim and sexual offender among rapists.* Penetanguishene Mental Health Centre, Research Report No. 7, Ontario, Canada.

Rice, M. E., Chaplin, T. C., Harris, G. T., & Coutts, J. (1994). Empathy for the victim and sexual arousal among rapists and nonrapists. *Journal of Interpersonal Violence, 9,* 435–449.

Rice, M. E., & Harris, G. T. (2003). The size and sign of treatment effects in sex offender therapy. *Annals of the New York Academy of Sciences, 989,* 428–440.

Roemer, L., & Borkovec, T. (1994). Effects about expressing thoughts about emotional material. *Journal of Abnormal Psychology, 103,* 467–474.

Rogers, D., & Masters, R. (1997). The development and evaluation of an emotional control training program for sexual offenders. *Legal and Criminological Psychology, 2*, 51–64.

Root, M. P. P., & Fallon, P. (1988). The incidence of victimization experiences in a bulimic sample. *Journal of Interpersonal Violence, 3*, 161–173,

Rooth, G. (1973). Exhibitionism, sexual violence and paedophilia. *British Journal of Psychiatry, 122*, 705–710.

Rosen, R. C., & Beck, J. G. (1988). *Patterns of sexual arousal: Psychophysiological processes and clinical applications*. New York: Guilford Press.

Rosenberg, M. (1965). *Society and the adolescent self-image*. Princeton, NJ: Princeton University Press.

Ross, R. R. (1995). The Reasoning and Rehabilitation Program for high-risk probationers and prisoners. In R. R. Ross, D. H. Antoniwicz, & G. K. Dhaliwal (Eds.), *Going straight: Effective delinquency prevention & offender rehabilitaion*. Ottawa: Air Training & Publications.

Russek, L. G., & Schwartz, G. E. (1997). Perceptions of parental caring predict health status in midlife: A 35-year follow-up of the Harvard mastery of stress study. *Psychosomatic Medicine, 59*, 144–149.

Russell, D., Peplau, L. A., & Cutrona, C. E. (1980). The Revised UCLA Loneliness Scale. *Journal of Personality and Social Psychology, 39*, 472–480.

Russell, D. E. H. (1984). *Sexual exploitation: Rape, child sexual abuse and workplace harassment*. Thousand Oaks, CA: Sage Publications.

Ryan, G., & Lane, S. (Eds.) (1997). *Juvenile sexual offending: Causes, consequences, and correction*. (2nd ed.) (pp. 267–391). San Francisco: Jossey-Bass.

Safran, J. D., & Segal, Z. V. (1990). *Interpersonal process in cognitive therapy*. New York: Basic Books.

Sapolsky, R. M. (1994). *Why zebras don't get ulcers: A guide to stress, stress-related diseases, and coping*. New York: Freeman.

Sattem, L., Savells, J., & Murray, E. (1984). Sex-role stereotypes and commitment of rape. *Sex Roles, 11*, 849–860.

Sayette, M. A. (2004). Self-regulatory failure and addiction. In R. F. Baumeister & K. D. Vohs (Eds.), *Handbook of self-regulation: Research, theory, and applications* (pp. 447–465). New York: Guilford Press.

Schaap, C., Bennun, I., Schindler, L., & Hoogduin, K. (1993). *The therapeutic relationship in behavioural psychotherapy*. New York: John Wiley & Sons.

Schewe, P. A., & O'Donohue, W. (1993). Sexual abuse prevention with high-risk males: The roles of victim empathy and rape myths. *Violence and Victims, 8,* 339–351.

Schmauk, F. J. (1970). Punishment, arousal, and avoidance learning in sociopaths. *Journal of Abnormal Psychology, 76,* 325–335.

Schmuck, P., & Sheldon, K. M. (Eds.) (2001). *Life goals and well-being.* Toronto: Hogrefe & Huber.

Schwartz, B. K., & Cellini, H. R. (1995). Female sex offenders. In B. K. Schwartz & H. R. Cellini (Eds.), *The sex offender: Corrections, Treatment and legal practice* (Vol. I, pp. 5.1–5.22). Kingston, NJ: Civic Research Institute.

Scott, R. L., & Tetreault, L. A. (1987). Attitudes of rapists and other violent offenders toward women. *Journal of Social Psychology, 127,* 375–380.

Segal, Z. V. (1988). Appraisal of the self-schema construct in cognitive models of depression. *Psychological Bulletin, 103,* 147–162.

Segal, Z. V., & Stermac, L. E. (1984). A measure of rapists' attitudes towards women. *International Journal of Law and Psychiatry, 7,* 219–222.

Seidman, B. T., Marshall, W. L., Hudson, S. M., & Robertson, P. J. (1994). An examination of intimacy and loneliness in sex offenders. *Journal of Interpersonal Violence, 9,* 518–534.

Selzer, M. L. (1971). The Michigan Alcoholism Screening Test (MAST): The quest for a new diagnostic instrument. *American Journal of Psychiatry, 127,* 1653–1658.

Serran, G. A., Fernandez, Y. M., Marshall, W. L., & Mann, R. E. (2003). Process issues in treatment: Application to sexual offender programs. *Professional Psychology: Research and Practice, 34,* 368–374.

Serran, G. A., Firestone, P., Marshall, W. L., & Moulden, H. (2004). Changes in coping following treatment for child molesters. Submitted for *Journal of Interpersonal Violence.*

Serran, G. A., Looman, J., & Dickie, I. (2004, October). *The role of schemas in sexual offending.* Paper presented at the 23rd Annual Research and Treatment Conference of the Association for the Treatment of Sexual Abusers. Albuquerque, NM.

Serran, G. A., & Marshall, L. E. (2005). Coping and mood in sexual offending. In W. L. Marshall, Y. M. Fernandez, L. E. Marshall, & G. A. Serran (Eds.), *Sexual offender treatment: Controversial issues* (pp. 109–126). Chichester, UK: John Wiley & Sons.

Serran, G. A., & Marshall, W. L. (2005). The "Memory Recovery Technique": A strategy to improve recall of offense-related details in men who commit sexual offenses. *Clinical Case Studies, 4,* 3–12.

Servi, K. (1997). *Greek mythology.* Athens: Ekdotike Athenon.

Seto, M. (1992). Victim blame, empathy, and disinhibition of sexual arousal to rape in community males and incarcerated rapists. Unpublished masters thesis, Queen's University, Kingston, Ontario, Canada.

Seto, M. C., & Barbaree, H. E. (1999). Psychopathy, treatment behavior and sex offender recidivism. *Journal of Interpersonal Violence, 14*, 1235–1248.

Shiekh, J. I., Hill, R. D., & Yesavage, J. (1987). Long-term efficacy of cognitive training for age associated memory impairment: A six month follow-up study. *Developmental Neuropsychology, 2*, 413–421.

Silbert, M., & Pines, A. (1991). Sexual child abuse as an antecedent to prostitution. *Child Abuse and Neglect, 5*, 407–411.

Sjöstedt, G., Grann, M., Långström, N., & Fazel, S. (2003, July). *Psychiatric morbidity among sexual offenders*. Paper presented at the International Interdisciplinary Conference of Psychology and Law. Edinburgh, UK.

Skinner, H. A. (1982). The drug abuse screening test. *Addictive Behaviors, 7*, 363–371.

Smallbone, S. W. (2005). Attachment insecurity as a predisposing and precipitating factor for sexual offending by young people. In W. L. Marshall, Y. M. Fernandez, L. E. Marshall, & G. A. Serran (Eds.), *Sexual offender treatment: Controversial issues* (pp. 93–107). Chichester, UK: John Wiley & Sons.

Smallbone, S. W., & Dadds, M. R. (1998). Childhood attachment and adult attachment in incarcerated adult male sex offenders. *Journal of Interpersonal Violence, 13*, 555–573.

Smith, G. S., & Fischer, L. (1999). Assessment of juvenile sexual offenders: Reliability and validity of the Abel Assessment for interest in paraphilia. *Sexual Abuse: A Journal of Research and Treatment, 11*, 207–216.

Sobel, C. P. (2001). *The cognitive sciences: An interdisciplinary approach*. Mountain View, CA: Mayfield Publishing.

Sparks, J., Bailey, W., Marshall, W. L., & Marshall, L. E. (2003, October). *Shame and guilt in sex offenders*. Paper presented at the 22nd Annual Research and Treatment Conference of the Association for the Treatment of Sexual Abusers, St. Louis, MO.

Spencer, A. (1998). *Working with sex offenders in prisons and through release to the community*. London: Jessica Kingsley Publisher.

Sperry, L. (1999). *Cognitive behavior therapy for DSM-IV personality disorders: Highly effective interventions for the most common personality disorders*. Philadelphia: Brunner/Mazel.

Spielberger, C. D. (1988). *State-Trait Anger Expression Inventory (STAXI) professional manual.* Odessa, FL: Psychological Assessment Resources.

Spielberger, C. D., Gorsuch, R. L., & Lushene, R. E. (1970). *Manual for the State-Trait Anxiety Inventory.* Palo Alto, CA: Consulting Psychologists Press.

Sroufe, A. L. (1996). *Emotional development: The organization of emotional life in the early years.* New York: Cambridge University Press.

Starzyk, K. B., & Marshall, W. L. (2003). Childhood, family, and personological risk factors for sexual offending. *Aggression and Violent Behavior: A Review Journal, 8,* 93–105.

Stermac, L. E., Segal, Z. V., & Gillis, R. (1990). Social and cultural factors in sexual assault. In W. L. Marshall, D. R. Laws, & H. E. Barbaree (Eds.), *Handbook of sexual assault: Issues, theories, and treatment of the offender* (pp. 143–158). New York: Plenum Press.

Stevenson, I., & Wolpe, J. (1960). Recovery from sexual deviation through overcoming non-sexual neurotic responses. *American Journal of Psychiatry, 116,* 737–742.

Stewart, D. J. (1972). Effects of social reinforcement on dependency and aggressive responses of psychopathic, neurotic, and subculture delinquents. *Journal of Abnormal Psychology, 79,* 76–83.

Stirpe, T. S., Wilson, R. J., & Long, C. (2001). Goal attainment scaling with sexual offenders: A measure of clinical impact at post-treatment and at community follow-up. *Sexual Abuse: A Journal of Research and Treatment, 13,* 65–77.

Storr, A. (1972). *Human destructiveness.* New York: Morrow.

Tangney, J. P., & Fischer, K. W. (1995). *Self-conscious emotions: Shame, guilt, embarrassment, and pride.* New York: Guilford Press.

Task Force on Juvenile Sexual Offenders and Their Victims. (1996). *Juvenile sexual offenders and their victims.* Tallahassee, FL: Author.

Taylor, G. R. (1954). *Sex in history.* New York: Ballantine.

Terr, L. (1994). *Unchained memories: True stories of traumatic memories, lost and found.* New York: Basic Books.

Thompson, R. A. (1994). Emotion regulation: A theme in search of definition. *Monographs of the Society for Research in Child Development, 59,* 25–52.

Thorndyke, P. W., & Hayes-Roth, B. (1979). The use of schemata in the acquisition and transfer of knowledge. *Cognitive Psychology, 11,* 82–106.

Thornton, D., Beech, A. R., & Marshall, W. L. (2004). Pre-treatment self-esteem and posttreatment sexual recidivism. *International Journal of Offender Therapy and Comparative Criminology, 48,* 587–599.

Thornton, D., & Shingler, J. (2001, November). *Impact of schema level work on sexual offenders' cognitive distortions*. Paper presented at the 20th Annual Research and Treatment Conference of the Association for the Treatment of Sexual Abusers. San Antonio, TX.

Thorpe, G. L., & Olsen, S. L. (1997). *Behavior therapy: Concepts, procedures, and applications*. Boston: Allyn & Bacon.

Tversky, A., & Kahneman, D. (1974). Causal schemata in judgments under uncertainty. In M. Fishbein (Ed.), *Progress in social psychology* (Vol. 1, pp. 49–72). Hillsdale, NJ: Lawrence Erlbaum.

van Dijk, J. A. M., & Mayhew, P. (1992). *Criminal victimization in the industrial world*. The Hague, the Netherlands: Directorate for Crime Prevention.

Vohs, K. D., & Ciarocco, N. J. (2004). Interpersonal functioning requires self-regulation. In R. F. Baumeister & K. D. Vohs (Eds.), *Handbook of self-regulation: Research, theory, and applications* (pp. 392–407). New York: Guilford Press.

Ward, T. (1999). A self-regulation model of the relapse process in sexual offenders. In B. K. Schwartz (Ed.), *The sex offender: Theoretical advances, treating special populations and legal developments* (Vol. III, pp. 6.1–6.8). Kingston, NJ: Civic Research Institute.

Ward, T. (2002). Good lives and the rehabilitation of offenders: Promises and problems. *Aggression and Violent Behavior: A Review Journal, 7*, 513–528.

Ward, T., & Hudson, S. M. (1996). Relapse prevention: A critical analysis. *Sexual Abuse: A Journal of Research and Treatment, 8*, 177–200.

Ward, T., & Hudson, S. M. (1998). The construction and development of theory in the sexual offending area: A meta-theoretical framework. *Sexual Abuse: A Journal of Research and Treatment, 10*, 47–63.

Ward, T., & Hudson, S. M. (2000). A self-regulation model of relapse prevention. In D. R. Laws, S. M. Hudson & T. Ward (Eds.), *Remaking relapse prevention with sex offenders: A sourcebook* (pp. 79–101). Thousand Oaks, CA: Sage Publications.

Ward, T., Hudson, S. M., & Marshall, W. L. (1994). The abstinence violation effect in child molesters. *Behaviour Research and Therapy, 32*, 431–437.

Ward, T., Hudson, S. M., & Marshall, W. L. (1995). Cognitive distortions and affective deficits in sex offenders: A cognitive deconstructionist interpretation. *Sexual Abuse: A Journal of Research and Treatment, 7*, 67–83.

Ward, T., Hudson, S. M., & Marshall, W. L. (1996). Attachment style in sex offenders: A preliminary study. *Journal of Sex Research, 33*, 17–26.

Ward, T., Hudson, S. M., Marshall, W. L., & Siegert, R. J. (1995). Attachment style and intimacy deficits in sex offenders: A theoretical framework. *Sexual Abuse: A Journal of Research and Treatment, 7,* 317–335.

Ward, T., Hudson, S. M., & McCormack, J. (1997). Attachment style, intimacy deficits, and sexual offending. In B. K. Schwartz & H. R. Cellini (Eds.), *The sex offender: New insights, treatment innovations, and legal developments* (Vol. II) (pp. 2.1–2.14). Kingston, NJ: Civic Research Institute.

Ward, T., Hudson, S. M., & Siegert, R. J. (1995). A critical comment on Pithers' relapse prevention model. *Sexual Abuse: A Journal of Research and Treatment, 7,* 167–175.

Ward, T., & Marshall, W. L. (2004). Good lives, aetiology and the rehabilitation of sex offenders: A bridging theory. *Journal of Sexual Aggression, 10,* 153–169.

Ward, T., McCormack, J., & Hudson, S. M. (1997). Sexual offenders' perceptions of their intimate relationships. *Sexual Abuse: A Journal of Research and Treatment, 9,* 57–74.

Ward, T., Nathan, P. Drake, C. R., Lee, J. K. P., & Pathé, M. (2000). The role of formulation based treatments for sexual offenders. *Behavior Change, 17,* 251–264.

Ward, T., & Siegert, R. (2002). Toward a comprehensive theory of child sexual abuse: A theory knitting perspective. *Psychology, Crime, & Law, 9,* 319–351.

Ward, T., & Sorbello, L. (2003). Explaining child sexual abuse: Integration and elaboration. In T. Ward, D. R. Laws, & S. M. Hudson (Eds.), *Sexual deviance: Issues and controversies* (pp. 3–20). Thousand Oaks, CA: Sage Publications.

Ward, T., & Stewart, C. A. (2003a). Good lives and the rehabilitation of sexual offenders. In T. Ward, D. R. Laws, & S. M. Hudson (Eds.), *Sexual deviance: Issues and controversies* (pp. 12–44). Thousand Oaks, CA: Sage Publications.

Ward, T., & Stewart, C. A. (2003b). Criminogenic needs or human needs: A theoretical critique. *Psychology, Crime & Law, 9,* 125–143.

Wasserman, E. A., & Miller, R. R. (1977). What's elementary about associative learning? *Annual Review of Psychology, 48,* 573–607.

Watson, D., & Friend, R. (1969). Measurement of social-evaluative anxiety. *Journal of Consulting and Clinical Psychology, 33,* 448–457.

Watson, J. C., & Greenberg, L. S. (1996). Emotion and cognition in experiential therapy: A dialectical-constructivist position. In H. Rosen & K. T. Kuehlwein (Eds.), *Constructing realities: Meaning-making perspectives for psychotherapists* (pp. 253–274). San Francisco: Jossey-Bass.

Webster, S. D., Bowers, L. E., Mann, R. E., & Marshall, W. L. (2005). Developing empathy in sex offenders: The value of offence re-enactments. *Sexual Abuse: A Journal of Research and Treatment, 17*, 63–77.

Webster, S. D., Mann, R. E., Wakeling, H., Marshall, W. L. (2005). *The justifications of sex with children scale.* Unpublished manuscript. Offender Behaviour Programs Unit, H. M. Prisons, London, UK.

Weiss, R. S. (1982). Attachment in adult life. In C. M. Parkes & I. Stevenson-Hinde (Eds.), *The place of attachment in human behavior* (pp. 171–185). New York: Basic Books.

West, D. J. (1991). The effects of sex offences. In C. R. Hollin & K. Howells (Eds.), *Clinical approaches to sex offenders and their victims.* (pp. 55–73). Chichester, UK: John Wiley & Sons.

Westat (1987). *Study of national incidence and prevalence of child abuse and neglect.* Washington, DC: National Center in Child Abuse and Neglect.

Wiederman, M. W. (2004). Self-control and sexual behavior. In R. F. Baumeister & K. D. Vohs (Eds.), *Handbook of self-regulation: Research, theory, and applications* (pp. 525–536). New York: Guilford Press.

Wilkinson, J. (1988). Context effects in children's event memory. In M. M. Gruneberg, P. E. Morris, & R. N. Sykes (Eds.), *Practical aspects of memory: Current research and issues* (Vol. 1, pp. 107–111). Chichester, UK: John Wiley & Sons.

Wills, T. A. (1981). Downward comparison principles in social psychology. *Psychological Bulletin, 90*, 245–271.

Wilson, B. A. (1987). *Rehabilitation of memory.* New York: Guilford Press.

Wilson, G. D. (1978). *The secrets of sexual fantasy.* London: J. M. Dent.

Wilson, R. J., Abracen, J., Picheca, J. E., Malcolm, P. B., & Prinzo, M. (2003, October). *Pedophilia: An evaluation of diagnostic and risk management methods.* Paper presented at the 22nd Annual Research and Treatment Conference of the Association for the Treatment of Sexual Offenders. St. Louis, MO.

Wilson, R. J., & Picheca, J. E. (in press). Circles of support and accountability: Engaging the community in sexual offender risk management. In B. K. Schwartz (Ed.), *The sex offender: Theoretical advances, treating special populations and legal developments* (Vol. V). Kingston, NJ: Civic Research Institute.

Wilson, R. J., Stewart, L., Stirpe, T. S., Barrett, M., & Cripps, J. E. (2000). Community-based sex offender management: Combining parole supervision and treatment to reduce recidivism. *Canadian Journal of Criminology, 42*, 177–188.

Worling, J. R. (1998). Adolescent sexual offender treatment at the SAFE-T Program. In W. L. Marshall, Y. M. Fernandez, S. M. Hudson, & T. Ward (Eds.), *Sourcebook of treatment programs for sexual offenders*. (pp. 353–365). New York: Plenum Press.

Wright, R. C., & Schneider, S. L. (1997). Deviant sexual fantasies as motivated self-deception. In B. K. Schwartz & H. R. Cellini (Eds.), *The sex offender: New insights, treatment innovations and legal developments* (Vol. II, pp. 8.1–8.14). Kingston, NJ: Civic Research Institute.

Yates, E., Barbaree, H. E., & Marshall, W. L. (1984). Anger and deviant sexual arousal. *Behavior Therapy, 15*, 287–294.

Young, J. E. (1999). *Cognitive therapy for personality disorders: A schema-focused approach*. Sarasota, FL: Professional Resource Press.

Young, J. E., & Brown, G. (2001). *Young Schema Questionnaire: Special edition*. New York: Schema Therapy Institute.

Young, J. E., Klosko, J. S., & Weishaar, M. E. (2003). *Schema therapy: A practitioner's guide*. New York: Guilford Press.

Zeidner, M., & Endler, N. S. (Eds.) (1996). *Handbook of coping: Theory, research, applications*. New York: John Wiley & Sons.

Index